DATE DUE

The Global Ecology

Edited by Edward Moran

The Reference Shelf
Volume 71 • Number 4

The H.W. Wilson Company
New York • Dublin
1999

The Reference Shelf

The books in this series contain reprints of articles, excerpts from books, addresses on current issues, and studies of social trends in the United States and other countries. There are six separately bound numbers in each volume, all of which are usually published in the same calendar year. Numbers one through five are each devoted to a single subject, providing background information and discussion from various points of view and concluding with a subject index and comprehensive bibliography that lists books, pamphlets, and abstracts of additional articles on the subject. The final number of each volume is a collection of recent speeches, and it contains a cumulative speaker index. Books in the series may be purchased individually or on subscription.

Visit H.W. Wilson's Web site: www.hwwilson.com

Library of Congress Cataloging-in-Publication data
The global ecology / edited by Edward Moran.
     p. cm. — (The reference shelf : v. 71, no. 4)
   Includes bibliographical references and index.
   ISBN 0-8242-0965-6 (alk. paper)
   1. Environmental degradation. 2. Pollution. 3. Human ecology.
 I. Moran, Edward. II. Series.
GE140.G55   1999
363.7—dc21   99-39007
                                        CIP

Production Editor: Beth Levy

Printed in the United States of America

Cover: A bulldozer clears land after logging. Photographer: C. Sherburne/Photo-Link. Copyright © Photodisc.

Contents

Preface

As the twentieth century draws to a close, it seems quite appropriate to devote a *Reference Shelf* issue to the theme of "Global Ecology." Issues of global warming, climate change, overpopulation, the ozone layer, species depletion—all impacted by the carbon-based industrial economy of the past two centuries—loom large in the consciousness of billions of human beings, the single species that, for better or worse, has had the deepest impact on Planet Earth and its other living inhabitants. Indeed, for the past two decades or so, the approach of a new millennium has been creating a stir quite apart from the Y2K issue: while some religious millenarians conclude from biblical prophecy that these indeed are the end times, many of their secular counterparts fervently believe that these are the end times for Earth's fragile environment, based on scientific data about mean temperatures, pollution levels, and the disappearance of whole varieties of animals and plants.

A hundred years ago, the editors of such a volume as this might have not even been able to frame "global ecology" as an issue worth discussing, let alone a problem needing solution, so pervasive was the hold of scientific and industrial progress on the Western mind. Just as present-day tourists flock to theme parks, it was not uncommon for late-Victorian Americans on holiday to take excursions to coal mines, steel mills, or factories to gloat over the material affluence being wrought by their vaunted smokestack economy, as pointed out by John Sears in his book *Sacred Places: American Tourist Attractions in the Nineteenth Century.* Americans seem not to have been moved by the dire visions of William Blake, who saw "dark, satanic mills" where Walt Whitman saw "buildings everywhere founded, going up, or finish'd . . . trains of cars swiftly speeding along railroad tracks, drawn by the locomotives"—all created by gung-ho pioneers who marched through the New World exulting "We primeval forests felling." Within a single decade spanning the year 1900 came several inventions that were to change the face of the Planet in the twentieth century: the automobile, the motion picture, radio, the airplane, and the electrification of America's cities and streetcar lines. Within a *single* decade.

In the 1970s, two crises—one political and the other technical, shook many Americans out of their complacency that rapid industrialization could go on forever without serious consequences. An embargo by a cartel of oil-producing nations sent the price of gasoline skyrocketing, with serious impact on all the Western economies, and the Three Mile Island disaster—and the Chernobyl meltdown a decade later—dealt a serious blow to the belief that nuclear fission would be the unblemished savior of industrial capitalism. In the 1970s, I edited "Adventures in Alternate Energy," a monthly department for *Popular Science* magazine that solicited readers' ingenuity for dealing with the energy crisis, in the spirit of the "small is beautiful" and "think globally, act locally" ethos of the time. From coast to coast and even from some ships and sea there came a deluge of manuscripts about ingenious projects that American do-it-yourselfers built to use renewable resources with less negative impact on the environment. Over several years, readers submitted documented evidence of workable solar collectors, wind generators, geothermal heat sinks, electric vehicles, a dizzying array of devices that seemed to herald a new wave of American thinking about the environment. Unfortunately, the promise of those decade was dashed as the world economy became even more dependent on nonrenewable resources, hence the clear and present danger documented in the pages of this *Reference Shelf.*

It would be simplistic to argue that local efforts alone can solve a crisis of global proportions, though local efforts are needed. It would be also simplistic to neglect the complex political nuances of global ecology. Developing nations, for example, argue that "ecology" can even be a form of cultural imperialism by post-industrialized nations whose restrictions on resource depletion are, in effect, denying them the fruits that industrialization might bring to them. It is hoped that the articles presented in these pages will stimulate discussion about equitable use of the earth's resources in the new century and beyond.

Edward Moran

June 1999

I. Framing the Issues

Editor's Introduction

According to the *Barnhart Dictionary of Etymology* (H. W. Wilson, 1988), Henry David Thoreau used the word "ecology" to mean "study of the relation of living things to their environment" in an 1858 letter. Fifteen years later, in 1873, the word appeared in a citation by another writer who spelled it "oecology," as befitting the word's derivation, via the German "Ökologie" from the Greek words that mean "study of the house" (i.e., the Earth as our home, as the matrix of all living things). Although the word "ecology" was used in the literature of biology during the twentieth century, the concept of a truly global ecology—a somewhat redundant term given the Greek etymology—did not sink into Western popular consciousness until the 1970s, spurred on by growing scientific evidence about global warming, the depletion of the ozone layer, and the disappearance of some plant and animal species. During the 1960s, humans had been able to view for the first time photographs of Earth taken from orbiting spacecraft and, in 1969, from the moon. The image of Earth as a blue-green gemstone in the darkness of space—one Planet with no political boundaries—made a deep and visceral impact on global consciousness everywhere. Many of the political activists that had been so prominent in Europe and America during the 1960s took up the green movement during the 1970s and beyond. Some of them, like E. F. Schumacher, have advocated the "small-is-beautiful" mantra; ecofeminists and others have revived earlier concepts of the Earth as Gaia, a living being. The first Earth Day, observed in April of 1970, brought together Americans from coast to coast for exhibits and teach-ins about the fragility of the ecosystem.

The articles in Part I: Framing the Issues offer a philosophical and theoretical framework that is used in contemporary discussions about global ecology. "The Historical Roots of our Ecologic Crisis" by Lynne White, Jr., examines two millennia of thinking about the environment and nature in Western thought and offers insights as to why the radical environmentalism of Francis of Assisi was suppressed in favor of other, more anthropocentric theological traditions that are used as justification for the human species having dominion over the Earth. Jim Motavalli's essay "2000: Planet Earth at the Crossroads" challenges humans to make a choice between "divergent paths leading to unprecedented scarcity and want on the one hand, and a new era of conservation-driven prosperity and plenty on the other." He examines scenarios offered by several futurists, including Allen Hammond, Peter Schwartz, and by several global ecology think tanks. Gordon Straw's "The Great Environmentalists: Cultural Stereotypes and the Environmental Movement" considers the ecological worldview of Native Americans in light of "systems of oppression and exploitation" in the New World since 1492. "Race, Poverty, and the Environment: The Disadvantaged Face Greater Risks," by Paul Mohai and others, remind us that the impact of environmental dysfunction is often felt more severely by economically or culturally disadvantaged groups in the United States and elsewhere, and argues for discussions of a "social ecology" alongside discussions of a purely technological nature. The political, social, and institutional ramifications of the "deep ecology" issue are further amplified in the two articles that follow: "Overview of Social Ecology" and "Comments on the International Social Ecology Network

1

Gathering and the 'Deep Social Ecology' of John Clark" by Murray Bookchin. Finally, John M. Mackenzie's "Empire and the Ecological Apocalypse: the Historiography of the Imperial Environment" critiques the often adversarial relationship between political power and the natural world that characterize the colonial and immediate post-colonial eras of recent human history. Taken together, the articles in this section should offer the reader new insights into why global ecology" belongs in the political and cultural realms as well as in the technological one.

The Historical Roots of Our Ecologic Crisis[1]

A conversation with Aldous Huxley not infrequently put one at the receiving end of an unforgettable monologue. About a year before his lamented death he was discoursing on a favorite topic: Man's unnatural treatment of nature and its sad results. To illustrate his point he told how, during the previous summer, he had returned to a little valley in England where he had spent many happy months as a child. Once it had been composed of delightful grassy glades; now it was becoming overgrown with unsightly brush because the rabbits that formerly kept such growth under control had largely succumbed to a disease, myxomatosis, that was deliberately introduced by the local farmers to reduce the rabbits' destruction of crops. Being something of a Philistine, I could be silent no longer, even in the interests of great rhetoric. I interrupted to point out that the rabbit itself had been brought as a domestic animal to England in 1176, presumably to improve the protein diet of the peasantry.

All forms of life modify their contexts. The most spectacular and benign instance is doubtless the coral polyp. By serving its own ends, it has created a vast undersea world favorable to thousands of other kinds of animals and plants. Ever since man became a numerous species he has affected his environment notably. The hypothesis that his fire-drive method of hunting created the world's great grasslands and helped to exterminate the monster mammals of the Pleistocene from much of the globe is plausible, if not proved. For 6 millennia at least, the banks of the lower Nile have been a human artifact rather than the swampy African jungle which nature, apart from man, would have made it. The Aswan Dam, flooding 5000 square miles, is only the latest stage in a long process. In many regions terracing or irrigation, overgrazing, the cutting of forests by Romans to build ships to fight Carthaginians or by Crusaders to solve the logistics problems of their expeditions, have profoundly changed some ecologies. Observation that the French landscape falls into two basic types, the open fields of the north and the *bocage* of the south and west inspired Marc Bloch to undertake his classic study of medieval agricultural methods. Quite unintentionally, changes in human ways often affect nonhuman nature. It has been noted, for example, that the advent of the automobile eliminated huge flocks of sparrows that once fed on the horse manure littering every street.

---

1. Article by Lynn White, Jr. From *Science* p1203-7 Mar. 10, 1967. Copyright © AAAS. Reprinted by permission of the American Association for the Advancement of Science.

The history of ecologic change is still so rudimentary that we know little about what really happened, or what the results were. The extinction of the European aurochs as late as 1627 would seem to have been a simple case of overenthusiastic hunting. On more intricate matters it often is impossible to find solid information. For a thousand years or more the Frisians and Hollanders have been pushing back the North Sea, and the process is culminating in our time in the reclamation of the Zuider Zee. What, if any, species of animals, birds, fish, shore birds, or plants have died out in the process? In their epic combat with Neptune have the Netherlanders overlooked ecological values in such a way that the quality of human life in the Netherlands has suffered? I cannot discover that the questions have ever been asked, much less answered.

Concern for the problem of ecologic backlash is mounting feverishly.

People, then, have often been a dynamic element in their own environment, but in the present state of historical scholarship we usually do not know exactly when, where, or with what effects man-induced changes came. As we enter the last third of the twentieth century, however, concern for the problem of ecologic backlash is mounting feverishly. Natural science, conceived as the effort to understand the nature of things, had flourished in several eras and among several peoples. Similarly there had been an age-old accumulation of technological skills, sometimes growing rapidly, sometimes slowly. But it was not until about four generations ago that Western Europe and North America arranged a marriage between science and technology, a union of the theoretical and the empirical approaches to our natural environment. The emergence in widespread practice of the Baconian creed that scientific knowledge means technological power over nature can scarcely be dated before about 1850, save in the chemical industries, where it is anticipated in the eighteenth century. Its acceptance as a normal pattern of action may mark the greatest event in human history since the invention of agriculture, and perhaps in nonhuman terrestrial history as well.

Almost at once the new situation forced the crystallization of the novel concept of ecology; indeed, the word *ecology* first appeared in the English language in 1873. Today, less than a century later, the impact of our race upon the environment has so increased in force that it has changed in essence. When the first cannons were fired, in the early fourteenth century, they affected ecology by sending workers scrambling to the forests and mountains for more potash, sulfur, iron ore, and charcoal, with some resulting erosion and deforestation. Hydrogen bombs are of a different order: a war fought with them might alter the genetics of all life on this planet. By 1285 London had a smog problem arising from the burning of soft coal, but our present combustion of fossil fuels threatens to change the chemistry of the globe's atmosphere as a whole, with consequences which we are only beginning to guess. With the population explosion, the carcinoma of planless urbanism, the now geological deposits of sewage and garbage, surely no creature other than man has ever managed to foul its nest in such short order.

There are many calls to action, but specific proposals, however worthy as individual items, seem too partial, palliative, negative: ban the bomb, tear down the billboards, give the Hindus contraceptives and tell them to eat their sacred cows. The simplest solution to any suspect change is, of course, to stop it, or, better yet, to revert to a romanticized past: make those ugly gasoline stations look like Anne Hathaway's cottage or (in the Far West) like ghost-town saloons. The "wilderness area" mentality invariably advocates deep-freezing an ecology, whether San Gimignano or the High Sierra, as it was before the first Kleenex was dropped. But neither atavism nor prettification will cope with the ecologic crisis of our time.

What shall we do? No one yet knows. Unless we think about fundamentals, our specific measures may produce new backlashes more serious than those they are designed to remedy.

As a beginning we should try to clarify our thinking by looking, in some historical depth, at the presuppositions that underlie modern technology and science. Science was traditionally aristocratic, speculative, intellectual in intent; technology was lower-class, empirical, action-oriented. The quite sudden fusion of these two, towards the middle of the nineteenth century, is surely related to the slightly prior and contemporary democratic revolutions which, by reducing social barriers, tended to assert a functional unity of brain and hand. Our ecologic crisis is the product of an emerging, entirely novel, democratic culture. The issue is whether a democratized world can survive its own implications. Presumably we cannot unless we rethink our axioms.

THE WESTERN TRADITIONS OF TECHNOLOGY AND SCIENCE

One thing is so certain that it seems stupid to verbalize it: both modern technology and modern science are distinctively Occidental. Our technology has absorbed elements from all over the world, notably from China; yet everywhere today, whether in Japan or in Nigeria, successful technology is Western. Our science is the heir to all the sciences of the past, especially perhaps to the work of the great Islamic scientists of the Middle Ages, who so often outdid the ancient Greeks in skill and perspicacity: al-Razl in medicine, for example; or ibn-al-Haytham in optics; or Omar Khayyam in mathematics. Indeed, not a few works of such geniuses seem to have vanished in the original Arabic and to survive only in medieval Latin translations that helped to lay the foundations for later Western developments. Today, around the globe, all significant science is Western in style and method, whatever the pigmentation or language of the scientists.

A second pair of facts is less well recognized because they result from quite recent historical scholarship. The leadership of the West, both in technology and in science, is far older than the so-called Scientific Revolution of the seventeenth century or the so-called Industrial Revolution of the eighteenth century. These terms are in fact outmoded and obscure the true nature of what they try to describe—significant stages in two long and separate developments. By A.D. 1000 at the latest—and perhaps, feebly, as much as 200 years earlier—the West began to apply water power to industrial processes other than milling grain. This was followed in the late twelfth century by the harnessing of wind power. From simple beginnings, but with remarkable consistency of style, the West rapidly expanded its skills in the development of power machinery, labor-saving devices, and automation. Those who doubt should contemplate that most monumental achievement in the history of automation: the weight-driven mechanical clock, which appeared in two forms in the early fourteenth century. Not in craftsmanship but in basic technological capacity, the Latin West of the later Middle Ages far outstripped its elaborate, sophisticated, and esthetically magnificent sister cultures, Byzantium and Islam. In 1444 a great Greek ecclesiastic, Bessarion, who had gone to Italy, wrote a letter to a prince in Greece. He is amazed by the superiority of Western ships, arms, textiles, glass. But above all he is astonished by the spectacle of waterwheels sawing timbers and pumping the bellows of blast furnaces. Clearly, he had seen nothing of the sort in the Near East.

By the end of the fifteenth century the technological superiority of Europe was such that its small, mutually hostile nations could spill out over all the rest of the world, conquering, looting, and colonizing. The symbol of this technological superiority is the fact that Portugal, one of the weakest states of the Occident, was able to become, and to remain for a century, mistress of the East Indies. And we must remember that the technology of Vasco da Gama and Albuquerque was built by pure empiricism, drawing remarkably little support or inspiration from science.

In the present-day vernacular understanding, modern science is supposed to have begun in 1543, when both Copernicus and Vesalius published their great works. It is no derogation of their accomplishments, however, to point out that such structures as the *Fabrica* and the *De revolutionibus* do not appear overnight. The distinctive Western tradition of science, in fact, began in the late eleventh century with a massive movement of translation of Arabic and Greek scientific works into Latin. A few notable books—Theophrastus, for example—escaped the West's avid new appetite for science, but within less than 200 years effectively the entire corpus of Greek and Muslim science was available in Latin, and was being eagerly read and criticized in the new European universities. Out of criticism arose new observation, speculation, and increasing distrust of ancient authorities. By the late thirteenth century Europe had seized global scientific leadership from the faltering hands of Islam. It would be as absurd to deny the profound originality of Newton, Galileo, or Copernicus as to deny that of the fourteenth century scholastic scientists like Buridan or Oresme on whose work they built. Before the eleventh century, science scarcely existed in the Latin West, even in Roman times. From the eleventh century onward, the scientific sector of Occidental culture has increased in a steady crescendo.

Since both our technological and our scientific movements got their start, acquired their character, and achieved world dominance in the Middle Ages, it would seem that we cannot understand their nature or their present impact upon ecology without examining fundamental medieval assumptions and developments.

MEDIEVAL VIEW OF MAN AND NATURE

Until recently, agriculture has been the chief occupation even in "advanced" societies; hence, any change in methods of tillage has much importance. Early plows, drawn by two oxen, did not normally turn the sod but merely scratched it. Thus, cross-plowing was needed and fields tended to be squarish. In the fairly light soils and semiarid climates of the Near East and Mediterranean, this worked well. But such a plow was inappropriate to the wet climate and often sticky soils of northern Europe. By the latter part of the seventh century after Christ, however, following obscure beginnings, certain northern peasants were using an entirely new kind of plow, equipped with a vertical knife to cut the line of the furrow, a horizontal share to slice under the sod, and a moldboard to turn it over. The friction of this plow with the soil was so great that it normally required not two but eight oxen. It attacked the land with such violence that cross-plowing was not needed, and fields tended to be shaped in long strips.

In the days of the scratch-plow, fields were distributed generally in units capable of supporting a single family. Subsistence farming was the presupposition. But no peasant owned eight oxen: to use the new and more efficient plow, peasants pooled their oxen to form large plow-teams, originally receiving (it would appear) plowed strips in proportion to their contribution. Thus, distribution of land was based no longer on the needs of a family but, rather, on the capacity of a power machine to till the earth. Man's relation to the soil was profoundly changed. Formerly man had been part of nature; now he was the exploiter of nature. Nowhere else in

We cannot understand their nature or their present impact upon ecology without examining fundamental medieval assumptions and developments.

the world did farmers develop any analogous agricultural implement. Is it coincidence that modern technology, with its ruthlessness toward nature, has so largely been produced by descendants of these peasants of northern Europe?

This same exploitative attitude appears slightly before A.D. 830 in Western illustrated calendars. In older calendars the months were shown as passive personifications. The new Frankish calendars, which set the style for the Middle Ages, are very different: they show men coercing the world around them—plowing, harvesting, chopping trees, butchering pigs. Man and nature are two things, and man is master.

These novelties seem to be in harmony with larger intellectual patterns. What people do about their ecology depends on what they think about themselves in relation to things around them. Human ecology is deeply conditioned by beliefs about our nature and destiny—that is, by religion. To Western eyes this is very evident in, say, India or Ceylon. It is equally true of ourselves and of our medieval ancestors.

The victory of Christianity over paganism was the greatest psychic revolution in the history of our culture. It has become fashionable today to say that, for better or worse, we live in "the post-Christian age." Certainly the forms of our thinking and language have largely ceased to be Christian, but to my eye the substance often remains amazingly akin to that of the past. Our daily habits of action, for example, are dominated by an implicit faith in perpetual progress which was unknown either to Greco-Roman antiquity or to the Orient. It is rooted in, and is indefensible apart from, Judeo-Christian teleology. The fact that Communists share it merely helps to show what can be demonstrated on many other grounds: that Marxism, like Islam, is a Judeo-Christian heresy. We continue today to live, as we have lived for about 1700 years, very largely in a context of Christian axioms.

What did Christianity tell people about their relations with the environment?

While many of the world's mythologies provide stories of creation, Greco-Roman mythology was singularly incoherent in this respect. Like Aristotle, the intellectuals of the ancient West denied that the visible world had had a beginning. Indeed, the idea of a beginning was impossible in the framework of their cyclical notion of time. In sharp contrast, Christianity inherited from Judaism not only a concept of time as nonrepetitive and linear but also a striking story of creation. By gradual stages a loving and all-powerful God had created light and darkness, the heavenly bodies, the earth and all its plants, animals, birds, and fishes. Finally, God had created Adam and, as an afterthought, Eve to keep man from being lonely. Man named all the animals, thus establishing his dominance over them. God planned all of this explicitly for man's benefit and rule: no item in the physical creation had any purpose save to serve man's purposes. And, although man's body is made of clay, he is not simply part of nature: he is made in God's image.

Especially in its Western form, Christianity is the most anthropocentric religion the world has seen. As early as the second century both Tertullian and Saint Irenaeus of Lyons were insisting that when God shaped Adam he was foreshadowing the image of the incarnate Christ, the Second Adam. Man shares, in great measure, God's transcendence of nature. Christianity, in absolute contrast to ancient paganism and Asia's religions (except, perhaps, Zoroastrianism) not only established a dualism of man and nature but also insisted that it is God's will that man exploit nature for his proper ends.

At the level of the common people this worked out in an interesting way. In Antiquity every tree, every spring, every stream, every hill had its own *genius loci*, its guardian spirit. These spirits were accessible to men, but were very unlike men; centaurs, fauns, and mermaids show their ambivalence. Before one cut a tree, mined a mountain, or dammed a brook, it was important to placate the spirit in charge of that particular situation, and keep it placated. By destroying paganism, Christianity made it possible to exploit nature in a mood of indifference to the feelings of natural objects.

It is often said that for animism the Church substituted the cult of saints. True, but the cult of saints is functionally quite different from animism. The saint is not *in* natural objects; he may have special shrines, but his citizenship is in heaven. Moreover, a saint is entirely a man; he can be approached in human terms. In addition to saints, Christianity of course also had angels and demons inherited from Judaism and perhaps, at one remove, from Zoroastrianism. But these were all as mobile as the saints themselves. The spirits *in* natural objects, which formerly had protected nature from man, evaporated. Man's effective monopoly on spirit in this world was confirmed, and the old inhibitions to the exploitation of nature crumbled.

When one speaks in such sweeping terms, a note of caution is in order. Christianity is a complex faith, and its consequences differ in differing contexts. What I have said may well apply to the medieval West where in fact technology made spectacular advances. But the Greek East, a highly civilized realm of equal Christian devotion, seems to have produced no marked technological innovation after the late seventh century, when Greek fire was invented The key to the contrast may perhaps be found in a difference in the tonality of piety and thought which students of comparative theology find between the Greek and the Latin Churches. The Greeks believed that sin was intellectual blindness, and that salvation was found in illumination, orthodoxy—that is, clear thinking. The Latins, on the other hand, felt that sin was moral evil, and that salvation was to be found in right

By destroying paganism, Christianity made it possible to exploit nature in a mood of indifference to the feelings of natural objects.

conduct. Eastern theology has been intellectualist. Western theology has been voluntarist. The Greek saint contemplates; the Western saint acts. The implications of Christianity for the conquest of nature would emerge more easily in the Western atmosphere.

The Christian dogma of creation, which is found in the first clause of all the Creeds, has another meaning for our comprehension of today's ecologic crisis. By revelation, God had given man the Bible, the Book of Scripture. But since God had made nature, nature also must reveal the divine mentality. The religious study of nature for the better understanding of God was known as natural theology. In the early Church, and always in the Greek East, nature was conceived primarily as a symbolic system through which God speaks to men: the ant is a sermon to sluggards; rising flames are the symbol of the soul's aspiration. This view of nature was essentially artistic rather than scientific. While Byzantium preserved and copied great numbers of ancient Greek scientific texts, science as we conceive it could scarcely flourish in such an ambience.

It was not until the late eighteenth century that the hypothesis of God became unnecessary to many scientists.

However, in the Latin West by the early thirteenth century natural theology was following a very different bent. It was ceasing to be the decoding of the physical symbols of God's communication with man and was becoming the effort to understand God's mind by discovering how his creation operates. The rainbow was no longer simply a symbol of hope first sent to Noah after the Deluge: Robert Grosseteste, Friar Roger Bacon, and Theodoric of Freiberg produced startlingly sophisticated work on the optics of the rainbow, but they did it as a venture in religious understanding. From the thirteenth century onward, up to and including Leibnitz and Newton, every major scientist, in effect, explained his motivations in religious terms. Indeed, if Galileo had not been so expert an amateur theologian he would have got into far less trouble: the professionals resented his intrusion. And Newton seems to have regarded himself more as a theologian than as a scientist. It was not until the late eighteenth century that the hypothesis of God became unnecessary to many scientists.

It is often hard for the historian to judge, when men explain why they are doing what they want to do, whether they are offering real reasons or merely culturally acceptable reasons. The consistency with which scientists during the long formative centuries of Western science said that the task and the reward of the scientist was "to think God's thoughts after him" leads one to believe that this was their real motivation. If so, then modern Western science was cast in a matrix of Christian theology. The dynamism of religious devotion, shaped by the Judeo-Christian dogma of creation, gave it impetus.

AN ALTERNATIVE CHRISTIAN VIEW

We would seem to be headed toward conclusions unpalatable to many Christians. Since both science and technology are blessed words in our contemporary vocabulary, some may be happy at the notions, first, that, viewed historically, modern science is an extrapolation of natural theology and, second, that modern technology is at least partly to be explained as an Occidental, voluntarist realization of the Christian dogma of man's transcendence of, and rightful mastery over, nature. But, as we now recognize, somewhat over a century ago science and technology—hitherto quite separate activities—joined to give mankind powers which, to judge by many of the ecologic effects, are out of control. If so, Christianity bears a huge burden of guilt.

I personally doubt that disastrous ecologic backlash can be avoided simply by applying to our problems more science and more technology. Our science and technology have grown out of Christian attitudes toward man's relation to nature which are almost universally held not only by Christians and neo-Christians but also by those who fondly regard themselves as post-Christians. Despite Copernicus, all the cosmos rotates around our little globe. Despite Darwin, we are not, in our hearts, part of the natural process. We are superior to nature, contemptuous of it, willing to use it for our slightest whim. The newly elected Governor of California, like myself a churchman but less troubled than I, spoke for the Christian tradition when he said (as is alleged), "when you've seen one redwood tree, you've seen them all." To a Christian a tree can be no more than a physical fact. The whole concept of the sacred grove is alien to Christianity and to the ethos of the West. For nearly 2 millennia Christian missionaries have been chopping down sacred groves, which are idolatrous because they assume spirit in nature.

What we do about ecology depends on our ideas of the man-nature relationship. More science and more technology are not going to get us out of the present ecologic crisis until we find a new religion, or rethink our old one. The beatniks, who are the basic revolutionaries of our time, show a sound instinct in their affinity for Zen Buddhism, which conceives of the man-nature relationship as very nearly the mirror image of the Christian view. Zen, however, is as deeply conditioned by Asian history as Christianity is by the experience of the West, and I am dubious of its viability among us.

Possibly we should ponder the greatest radical in Christian history since Christ: Saint Francis of Assisi. The prime miracle of Saint Francis is the fact that he did not end at the stake, as many of his left-wing followers did. He was so clearly heretical that a General of the Franciscan Order, Saint Bonaventura, a great and perceptive Christian, tried to suppress the early accounts of Franciscanism. The key to an understanding of Francis is his belief in the virtue of humil-

What we do about ecology depends on our ideas of the man-nature relationship.

ity—not merely for the individual but for man as a species. Francis tried to depose man from his monarchy over creation and set up a democracy of all God's creatures. With him the ant is no longer simply a homily for the lazy, flames a sign of the thrust of the soul toward union with God; now they are Brother Ant and Sister Fire, praising the Creator in their own ways as Brother Man does in his.

Later commentators have said that Francis preached to the birds as a rebuke to men who would not listen. The records do not read so: he urged the little birds to praise God, and in spiritual ecstasy they flapped their wings and chirped rejoicing. Legends of saints, especially the Irish saints, had long told of their dealings with animals but always, I believe, to show their human dominance over creatures. With Francis it is different. The land around Gubbio in the Apennines was being ravaged by a fierce wolf. Saint Francis, says the legend, talked to the wolf and persuaded him of the error of his ways. The wolf repented, died in the odor of sanctity, and was buried in consecrated ground.

What Sir Steven Ruciman calls "the Franciscan doctrine of the animal soul" was quickly stamped out. Quite possibly it was in part inspired, consciously or unconsciously, by the belief in reincarnation held by the Cathar heretics who at that time teemed in Italy and southern France, and who presumably had got it originally from India. It is significant that at just the same moment, about 1200, traces of metempsychosis are found also in western Judaism, in the Provençal *Cabbala*. But Francis held neither to transmigration of souls nor to pantheism. His view of nature and of man rested on a unique sort of pan-psychism of all things animate and inanimate, designed for the glorification of their transcendent Creator, who, in the ultimate gesture of cosmic humility, assumed flesh, lay helpless in a manger, and hung dying on a scaffold.

I am not suggesting that many contemporary Americans who are concerned about our ecologic crisis will be either able or willing to counsel with wolves or exhort birds. However, the present increasing disruption of the global environment is the product of a dynamic technology and science which were originating in the Western medieval world against which Saint Francis was rebelling in so original a way. Their growth cannot be understood historically apart from distinctive attitudes toward nature which are deeply grounded in Christian dogma. The fact that most people do not think of these attitudes as Christian is irrelevant. No new set of basic values has been accepted in our society to displace those of Christianity. Hence we shall continue to have a worsening ecologic crisis until we reject the Christian axiom that nature has no reason for existence save to serve man.

The greatest spiritual revolutionary in Western history, Saint Francis, proposed what he thought was an alternative Christian view of nature and man's relation to it: he tried to substitute the idea of the equality of all creatures, including man, for the idea of man's limitless rule of creation. He failed. Both our present science and our present technology are so tinctured with orthodox Christian arrogance toward nature that no solution for our ecologic crisis can be expected from them alone. Since the roots of our trouble are so largely religious, the remedy must also be essentially religious, whether we call it that or not. We must rethink and refeel our nature and destiny. The profoundly religious, but heretical, sense of the primitive Franciscans for the spiritual autonomy of all parts of nature may point a direction. I propose Francis as a patron saint for ecologists.

2000: Planet Earth at the Crossroads[2]

It is 2010, and the last wild cheetah has finally disappeared from the African savannahs. But is the cheetah really gone? For most people in that not-too-distant era, the fastest animal on Earth is as alive as it ever was. There are still plenty of cheetahs in zoos, where most people see them, and they will live eternally in millions of digital images, many of which can be downloaded from the Net in less than a second. Computer graphics can bring stunningly real "cheetahs" to life in advertisements and magazine articles, even have them interact with the characters in feature films.

Looking forward, will there be a world saturated with ever-richer visual imagery, while nature itself is pushed inexorably back by a rising tide of population, pollution and developmental pressure? Transfixed by television and manipulated by corporate "greenwashing" to think that nothing is amiss, will we even know what we have lost?

Transfixed by television and manipulated by corporate "green-washing" to think that nothing is amiss, will we even know what we have lost?

In 1999, as we approach the next millennium, the world stands at a crossroads, with divergent paths leading to unprecedented scarcity and want on the one hand, and a new era of conservation-driven prosperity and plenty on the other. Never before have environmental factors—beyond simple supply-and-demand economics, and beyond partisan politics—played such a critical role in determining the future health and happiness of mankind.

Even though most developed countries are producing children at below replacement level, the world's population (led by a birth explosion in Africa) is still expected to reach six billion by this summer, and grow rapidly in the new century. The United Nations projects that 9.4 billion people will be sharing the planet by 2050, a number that will profoundly strain the world's natural resources.

Meeting the needs of this burgeoning population would be difficult in the best of circumstances, but the world is also facing a series of unexpected environmental threats, including global warming and air pollution, food scarcity, deforestation, declining landfill space, pervasive toxins, biodiversity disappearance, biotechnology abuses, the loss of arable land, a dwindling supply of fresh water, the rise of infectious diseases, spiraling consumption rates, and challenges to fossil fuel supplies. Each of these problems represents a worldwide crisis, and each is at a turning point. Fortunately, a growing body of environmental knowledge, including both age-old

2. Article by Jim Motavalli. Reprinted with permission from *E/The Environmental Magazine*, Subscription Department: P.O. Box 2047, Marion, OH 43306; Telephone: (815) 734-1242. Subscriptions are $20 per year.

and ultra-modern approaches, gives us options for averting these crises.

In his book, *Which World? Scenarios for the 21st Century*, Allen Hammond offers three widely varying projections for the near future. In the first, "Market World," a triumphant global capitalism uses the hidden hand of markets to bring forth technological innovations. By privatizing, deregulating and joining together in vast new economic alliances, a worldwide economic boom eliminates all but pockets of poverty. Through great improvements in agricultural technology, food production is skyrocketing, and want has largely been eliminated through efficient international distribution systems. Population has been controlled, human longevity prolonged, and pollution all but eliminated as a financially wasteful misuse of a resource. Advanced technology has created a kind of "global village," with information flowing instantly to even the most remote location. Philanthropy creates a cultural and educational renaissance.

There are obvious flaws in this scenario—the global economy has not, so far, shown that much interest in eliminating pollution—but it does carry several unmistakable current trends to a logical, if perhaps overly optimistic, conclusion. The theory is heartily endorsed by futurist Peter Schwartz, chairman of the Global Business Network, who sees a "Long Boom" driven by free markets and high technology extending until at least 2020. Schwartz thinks that the death of the internal-combustion engine, also by 2020, will help control pollution. "There's been a sea change, from profound skepticism about fuel cell and hybrid cars, to a real commitment," he says.

Population has been controlled, human longevity prolonged, and pollution all but eliminated as a financially wasteful misuse of a resource.

Another distinct optimist about the restorative powers of the market is futurist John Petersen, founder of The Arlington Institute and a frequent consultant to the military. "In the long term, the trends are clearly positive," he says. "We have a generation of kids growing up around the planet who are much more sensitive to the environment, and see it in systems terms. They see people as part of the whole system we live in, not as outside that system."

Petersen thinks we have a wonderful opportunity to help nations like China, currently bent on embracing the material world long denied to them, "leap across the industrial age as we have traditionally defined it. They don't have to make the mistakes we made." He sees the Chinese building fuel cell cars and natural gas power plants, connecting their rural communities with cellular telephones rather than outdated wires.

New technology will make it happen, Petersen says. Voice-recognition software will reduce language barriers. Holographic "virtual meetings" will cut down on the need for commuting and traffic tie-ups. Even the poorest villagers will have $10 handheld communication devices capable of real-time interaction with video and audio imagery from the Internet. By 2025, he predicts, super-computers on single chips will have 50 times the computing power that the largest mainframes had three years ago. And these chips will cost only a penny to manufacture.

Fortress World

In Hammond's second scenario, a global market system hasn't led to a second renaissance, but instead to a bitterly conflicted "Fortress World" of haves and have-nots. Environmental factors play a big part, as growing populations in Latin America, Africa and India deplete productive farmland. Health conditions worldwide also deteriorate, a product of an increasingly polluted water supply and skies made smoggy by rapidly growing fleets of cars and trucks. Forests disappear, making firewood scarce, and fisheries collapse because of overfishing. Global warming causes widespread flooding, species extinctions, dislocation and crop damage.

Desperate conditions in the Third World lead to a rise in terrorism and international organized crime, causing the still-affluent developed countries to tighten immigration and patrol their borders. As Africa collapses completely, and chronic instability spreads, international markets stagnate. This scenario focuses on an acceleration of current environmentally-destructive trends, and the tendency of international markets to consider the developing world as so much "roadkill on the global investment highway." This gloomy theory, decidedly Malthusian, is certainly a realistic possibility, and the seeds of it could be seen in the current worldwide economic crisis.

Ecotopia

The third scenario, "Transformed World," is almost eco-utopian in its assumptions that sustainable ideas—now tiny seedlings planted around the world—will thrive and grow. It envisions that corporate policy takes a green path, that public opinion crystallizes around a shared sense of environmental commitment, that international treaties stabilize energy use (and eliminate the internal-combustion automobile), and that recycling eliminates waste. The rainforests are saved, global climate preserved, and biodiversity loss halted. Cities are reborn as hives of sustainable living, mass transit flourishes, and public participation in government—aided by new communications technologies—reaches new highs.

The "Transformed World" can be seen in organizations like the Switzerland-based World Business Council for Sustainable Development, which argues that market forces must become more conscious of environmental issues or risk running out of raw materials. And such thinking is reflected through the findings of the three-year Harvard Project on Religion and Ecology, which concluded that the world's reli-

gions need to be more involved in solving the global environ
mental crisis.

International commitment to significant change can be
seen in such agreements as The Montreal Protocol, which
seems to be successfully controlling ozone-depleting chemicals; the Kyoto Accords reducing emission of greenhouse
gases; and the near-unanimous adoption of a treaty, pushed
by 700 citizens' groups around the world, to ban land mines.
To be sure, there are many forces for dramatic global transformation at work today, but can they act fast enough to prevent an environmentally-led catastrophe?

"It's a tough call," says Nancy Jack Todd, vice president of
Ocean Arks International, which works to spread sustainable
ideas around the world. "The fortress scenario may very well
occur. But when I heard about Gaviotas, a sustainable community built in the heart of Colombia, one of the world's
most politically turbulent countries, I began to see that anything was possible. I guess I'm an intellectual pessimist but a
glandular optimist, sad of mind, glad of heart." Todd's combination of hope and doubt are shared by philosopher John
Leslie, who in his provocatively titled *The End of the World:
The Science and Ethics of Human Extinction*, gives the people
only a 70 percent chance of surviving the next five centuries.

*We're already
seeing that even
minute changes
can have serious
consequences.*

The Planet in Peril

The many environmental factors that will shape the future
are worth examining in some detail, since they're likely to
profoundly affect the political and economic choices made
by world leaders. Some of these factors, like global warming
and population-induced challenges to food production, could
lead to a dramatically altered world order in the 21st century.

Global warming. According to Dr. James Hansen, director
of the NASA Goddard Institute for Space Studies, "The greatest threat to the long-term health of our planet, as the danger
of nuclear war declines, is probably global climate change.
For most climate scientists, it's no longer a question of
whether global warming will occur, but when." The Intergovernmental Panel on Climate Change (IPCC), made up of
2,500 scientists, predicts that we will see a doubling of prein-
dustrial levels of carbon dioxide in the atmosphere by 2050,
raising global temperatures from one to 3.5 degrees Celsius
by 2100.

Some commentators ridicule the effects of such seemingly
small temperature shifts, and even proclaim them beneficial.
But we're already seeing that even minute changes can have
serious consequences. In the Antarctic, warming temperatures have affected the supply of tiny, shrimp-like krill, subsequently causing a 40 percent population drop among the
Adelie penguins that feed on them. By 2050, a Dutch study
predicts, 24 percent of the world's parks and protected areas
could see major vegetation changes because of warming.
Already, Alpine plants that thrive on cold weather are being

found only at higher and higher elevations. Butterflies have also relocated because of changing climate, the University of California reports. And according to U.S. Geological Survey scientist Dr. Bruce Molnia, glaciers in Alaska, British Columbia and the Yukon are retreating and thinning significantly following major regional temperature shifts.

Will these trends accelerate and produce catastrophic environmental damage in the near future? A three-foot rise in sea levels, which could occur by 2100, would put 80 percent of the Marshall Islands under water, displace 70 million in Bangladesh, and inundate coastal areas in Japan, China and the U.S.

Early warning signs like this have so far not been heeded. The human race now produces 30 billion tons of carbon dioxide annually, two-thirds of it by burning fossil fuels at a rate four times that of 1950. One consequence could be severe water shortages. According to the IPCC, the frequency of severe droughts that now occur only five percent of the time in the U.S. could rise to 50 percent by 2050. Another consequence is food shortages. An Environmental Protection Agency study recently found that, at a time when global food demand is likely to soar, actual international production of wheat, rice and other grains is likely to drop 7.6 percent by 2060.

Much depends, obviously, on how seriously the world's nations take the Kyoto Accords, which would, if implemented, at least stabilize worldwide production of greenhouse gases. In the U.S., prospects for ratification of the accords are somewhat dim, and it has not yet been scheduled for a vote in the Senate. But there are some encouraging trends to watch in the next decade, including growing corporate recognition of the problem and the rapid technological advance of alternative-fueled automobiles.

Food and water for a needy world. Around the world, erosion is increasingly pushing marginal farmland out of productive use. The former Soviet Union had 300 million acres of harvested grain in 1977; by 1994, that amount had shrunk to 230 million acres. Every year, even as it adds 360,000 people, the Indonesian island of Java loses 50,000 acres of productive land, enough to feed annual population increases. Around the world, 15 million acres of what was once useful land becomes desert every year.

The global grain supply has basically remained stagnant since 1990, while the world's population has increased by 420 million people. The problem is compounded by increasing grain-intensive meat production and consumption, particularly in Asia. Lester Brown of The Worldwatch Institute, whose report on likely grain shortages in China caused an international furor in 1996, says, "What's happening in China teaches us that, despite rising affluence, our likely world population of 10 billion people won't be able to live as high on the food chain as the average American. There simply won't be enough food."

Unfortunately, food from the sea is not available to serve as a buffer against crop scarcity. The United Nations reported in 1995 that "about 70 percent of the world's marine fish stocks are heavily exploited, overexploited, depleted or slowly recovering." Nine of the world's 17 major fishing grounds are in serious decline, with four "fished out." By 2000, the report said, fish demand could exceed supply by 30 million tons. Already, popular food stocks like swordfish, tuna, orange roughy, halibut and salmon are in serious decline. Looking ahead, these problems don't have to spell doom for the world's fish supplies. A report in *Science* magazine indicates that most of the depleted commercial species could repopulate by 2025 if left alone.

If the world's fishing nations can agree on moratoriums for specific species, reduce bycatch (unwanted "take" that's thrown overboard, usually dead) and end some of the worst excesses of factory fishing—a feat that has so far proved elusive—healthy fish stocks can be maintained in the 21st century. "The sea is in serious trouble and we need to take action now," warns Elliot Norse of the Marine Conservation Biology Institute in Redmond, Washington.

The limits of both agricultural and fisheries production have been reached as food demand rapidly increases, due to the addition of 80 million people each year. But optimists like Dennis Avery of the Hudson Institute's Center for Global Food Issues believe that alarmist scenarios like Brown's are unfounded because advances in farm productivity will be more than a match for population increases. "There is no real threat of famine," says Avery, who believes that new fertilizers will continue to increase crop yields.

Meanwhile, in developing countries, more than one-third of people lack access to clean water. Even in the U.S., an estimated one-fifth of citizens drink untreated or untested water. Across the globe, countries are now beginning to openly compete with each other for access to fresh water supplies and such conflicts are figuring prominently in international politics. Water-scarce areas of the American West are looking for relief from increasingly reluctant, wetter neighbors to the north and east. Fresh water supplies are also threatened by agricultural irrigation (which consumes two-thirds of American freshwater), dam construction, run-off from pesticide use and fertilizers, and livestock production.

Water is central to our lives—it accounts for approximately 60 percent of human body weight. Yet, paradoxically, water is still one of the most poorly managed—and severely threatened—resources on Earth.

Deforestation, habitat and biodiversity loss. While threats to forest cover in the U.S. and Europe draw the most vocal

Water is central to our lives—it accounts for approximately 60 percent of human body weight. Yet, paradoxically, water is still one of the most poorly managed—and severely threatened—resources on Earth.

opposition, the long-term trend is for accelerating deforestation in the tropical parts of the world. Between 1960 and 1990, a fifth of all tropical rainforest was lost, and Asia lost a full third of its original cover. Africa is losing its rainforest at a similar rate.

The human race exploits about 7,000 species for food, but 1.4 million species have been identified, and as many as 40 million may exist in nature. As the National Academy of Sciences speculates in One Earth, One Future, "Scientists and the public worry that, with deforestation and the loss of natural habitat, many of these species will be gone before they are even known to exist."

Why does the loss of biodiversity matter? Because we're losing species whose benefits to humankind are unknown. An estimated 75,000 plants have edible parts, and many thousands of others have medicinal benefits, like the rosy periwinkle of Madagascar, which is the basis of an effective Hodgkin's disease treatment. The birth control pill has its origins in the Mexican yam.

Thomas Lovejoy of the Smithsonian Institute sees preserving biodiversity as a critical issue in the next decades. "Much as this century has been dominated by the physics and information revolutions, the next and those to follow will be the centuries of biology," he writes. "To reap the benefits, and for a healthy and productive society, we will need biodiversity." Although many of the people questioned in a recent New York Times straw poll didn't know what biodiversity was, that lack of awareness is changing, particularly through such high-profile efforts as the new Hall of Biodiversity at the American Museum of Natural History.

Biotechnology. With great rapidity, global conglomerates are forming giant life-science companies with interests in food production, biotechnology, medicine and health, agrichemicals and pharmaceuticals. While there's nothing new about human tampering to create hybrid plants and animals, the experimentation has always respected species boundaries. But international biotech companies are planning to introduce thousands of new genetically-engineered life forms into the environment in the next century. These range from animals that never existed in nature, like the sheep/goat hybrid "geep," to cloned animals and herbicide-tolerant and pest-resistant plants.

It's not just plants and animals that are being tampered with. Scientists are actually competing to complete the mapping of the 100,000 genes in the human "genome," a breakthrough that when coupled with advances in genetic screening, somatic gene therapy and the manipulation of human eggs, sperm and cells, could lead to a 21st century eugenics movement.

Dr. Robert Gallo, a pioneer in linking AIDS to the human retrovirus HIV, warns that tampering with the basic human genetic code as proposed in some gene therapy experiments, could produce disastrous consequences. "It is a matter for debate whether we have the intelligence, let alone the wisdom, to institute measures that will affect future generations," he writes.

The waste problem. The U.S. may have only five percent of the world's population, but it generates a massive 19 percent of its wastes. Despite nearly 30 years of active recycling, 96 percent of American plastic still goes into landfills. Two-thirds of our waste paper still gets thrown away—and Mexico actually recycles more glass per capita than the U.S. does.

But the future of recycling, both in the U.S. and around the world, is far from bleak. Most Americans (73 percent in a recent Gallup poll) support home-based recycling, and most states are trying to reach a 25 percent municipal recycling rate. What's more, industries are realizing that waste pays. In the 1990s, 45 recycled paper mills opened, and $10 billion in new investment was committed. Newspapers across the country are switching to recycled newsprint. Another recycling success story is steel—overall, 68 percent of it is recycled, including 17 billion steel cans in 1995. The recycling of PET soda bottles took a dip in recent years, but supporters like Evelyn Haught of the Institute of Scrap Recycling say the market is growing. "When people see how well recycling works over the course of time, the demand will increase," she says.

The rise of infectious diseases. Many futurists, looking ahead to the millennium, predicted that serious infectious diseases would have been eliminated by the year 2000, largely because of major advances in medical care, sanitary practices and public awareness. Yet infectious diseases still kill more people than car accidents, cancer or war—17.3 million in 1995 alone, and the numbers are increasing. Many of the factors in this rising specter are environmental: from deforestation to contaminated water, global warming and the shift of populations from rural locations to cities.

Modern human mobility has given wings to pathogens that were previously hidden safely in remote rainforests. The HIV, Ebola and Hanta viruses are examples of diseases that are believed to have traveled around the world from their origins in Africa. The spread of these diseases is notoriously hard to track. "Mad cow" disease, for instance, has such a long incubation period that it may be many years before its existence in the U.S. can be confirmed or denied.

The public health implications of all major disruptions to the natural order—from dams to clearcuts—need to be integrated into all future planning, environmentalists say. "Where there is disharmony in the world, death follows," according to Navajo medicine men.

Spiraling consumption rates. Americans are earning more, working more and consuming more, but enjoying it less.

"Where there is disharmony in the world, death follows," according to Navajo medicine men.

And, faced with that problem, they're increasingly willing to cut back. According to a Merck Family Fund poll, 28 percent of Americans have "voluntarily made changes in their lives that resulted in making less money." The poll found that 82 percent agree with the statement that, "Most of us buy and consume far more than we need; it's wasteful."

Despite growing awareness that it's impossible to shop your way to happiness, the U.S. still has the highest consumption rate in the world. The average American is fueled by 300 shopping bags full of raw materials every week, a rate that would require the resources of three planets if it were spread to the rest of the world.

The runaway success of books like Vicki Robin and Joe Dominguez's *Your Money Or Your Life* (it has sold 450,000 copies since 1992) has given birth to a nascent "voluntary simplicity" movement, dedicated to living well on less.

Meeting the Kyoto goals will not be easy, and the auto industry is in no way ready to do its part.

The most recent development was the 1997 founding of the Maryland-based Center for a New American Dream, which brings together some of the most prominent figures in the voluntary simplicity movement. "Signs of hope are emerging," the Center says. "There are groups promoting healthy communities, green product design, new tax policies, appropriate technology, sustainability education, simple living study circles and voluntary initiatives in the private sector."

Transportation. In one year, the average gas-powered car produces five tons of carbon dioxide (CO_2) which, as it slowly builds up in the atmosphere, causes global warming. Every gallon of gasoline burned up in an auto engine sends 20 pounds of CO_2, containing five pounds of pure carbon, into the atmosphere. It's like tossing a five-pound bag of charcoal briquettes out my window every 20 miles or so," writes John Ryan in his book *Over Our Heads: A Local Look at Global Climate.* He adds that cars and trucks produce by far the biggest share of fossil-fuel emissions (47 percent by one measure).

The international agreement on global warming signed by 150 countries in Kyoto, Japan late in 1997 makes the effort to cut down on automobile exhaust even more urgent. As the world's largest producer of CO_2 emissions, the U.S. was asked to reduce the greenhouse gases it emits to seven percent below 1990 levels by 2012.

Meeting the Kyoto goals will not be easy, and the auto industry is in no way ready to do its part. A start would be a tightening of what's known as Corporate Average Fuel Economy (CAFE), the federal standard for cars and trucks. The auto industry has fought tenaciously against any attempt to tighten CAFE, and has succeeded in shielding its beloved sport-utility vehicles from the tougher regulations. The result is that actual fuel economy has declined since 1988.

But some attitudes are changing. Toyota was the first auto company to announce, in the spring of 1998, that it was joining with other large manufacturers in an alliance to fight global warming, not the scientists who are warning the world about it. Toyota's support, if not its cash, will go to the Pew Center on Global Climate Change.

And then there's the question of oil scarcity, a concept sure to evoke merriment in motorists who've become used to spending less for gas than for bottled water. But as Scientific American observed in a recent special report, "The End of Cheap Oil" may be at hand. Demand, the magazine says, could soon start to exceed supply, a problem exacerbated by the concentration of most remaining large reserves in a few Middle Eastern countries. What's more, some experts say, the size of many countries' oil reserves has been systematically exaggerated for political and economic reasons.

Will mass transit keep pace with the growth of the "green car"? While developments like the Los Angeles subway and Chattanooga's free electric shuttle bus service are good signs, and "people movers" received substantial funding in the recently adopted Transportation Equity Act for the 21st Century (TEA-21), highways received the bulk of the money. The new roads make it possible for the nation's suburbs to continue their outward sprawl, making effective mass transit difficult. The federally-funded light rail systems and pedestrian walkways in Portland, Oregon, and the bike racks on Seattle's buses, are models that some of the more enlightened "eco-cities" are beginning to adopt.

Pervasive toxins. As we head towards a population of seven billion by the year 2010, human influence has reached the most remote corners of the globe. The natural ecology of 70 percent of the Earth's habitable spaces is significantly disturbed. As Greenpeace has noted, at least some degree of chemical contamination is common to nearly all of mankind. "All the evidence points to a substantial global problem affecting human health," says the group. "These problems are likely to increase in scale and scope. Consumption of metals and the products made from them is linked to, and fueled by, increase in population and rising gross national products."

One of the most pervasive chemical poisons is lead, estimated to have put 130 to 200 million people around the world at risk (as gauged from blood lead levels). As a whole, toxic exposure to heavy metals is probably affecting one billion people. According to Dr. Christopher Williams, a scientist at London University, pollutants like lead are already affecting the intelligence of one in 10 British children, and as much as 90 percent of children in some African countries.

Some 63,000 chemicals are in use around the world today, and as many as 1,000 synthetics enter the market every year. Many, if not most, of these chemicals have been inadequately studied, and some are potent carcinogens. Among the substances likely to produce growing health risks in the

21st century are: organochlorine pesticides and PCBs; chlori-
nated dioxins; and the so-called "endocrine disrupters,"
which interfere with human and animal reproductive health.
The latter trend can be seen in the declining sperm counts
noted in European males for the last 50 years.

The world obviously faces daunting challenges. You'd have
to be crazy to be an optimist, but what other choice do we
have?

CONTACTS:

Global Business Network
900 Suite X Hollis Street
Emeryville, CA 94608
Tel. (510) 547-6822
URL: http://www.gbn-net.com/

World Resources Institute
1709 New York Avenue NW
Washington, DC 20006
Tel: (202) 638-6300
URL: http://www.wri.org

Worldwatch Institute
1776 Massachusetts Avenue NW
Washington, DC 20036
Tel: (202) 452-1999
URL: http://www.worldwatch.org

The Great Environmentalists: Cultural Stereotypes and the Environmental Movement[3]

One of my childhood heroes was "Ironeyes" Cody. You may not remember the name, but you most likely remember the face of this man, if you owned a television around the first Earth Day in 1970. His face is unforgettable to me: the wrinkles around the eyes that denote wisdom, the shocking black hair in braids, a look of sadness and near-disgust, and a single tear, creeping for a lifetime, from his eye. "Ironeyes" Cody was the Native American on horseback in the pro-environment commercial which immortalized him in the early 1970's. He was my hero because he seemed to share my concern for what was happening to the earth due to the ignorance or malevolence of others. Besides, he was the first Native person in a commercial that I can think of that was not portrayed as a grunting savage.

Nowadays, I still have a great deal of respect for "Ironeyes" Cody, but I could not say that he still is a hero of mine. I say that, because I see his role in that famous commercial a little bit differently now. Since that commercial, I have heard the phrase, "the Indian's love of nature" more times than I would care to count. Native American peoples have become stereotyped as the "great environmentalists" of this country. It is true that Native peoples have a different relationship with the earth than do the immigrants to this land; the earth is their mother, not property to be exploited. But that is not what I am hearing from non-Indians. In my capacity as director for Native American ministries of the ELCA I hear from congregations that want to learn more about Native spirituality and "their great love of nature". I hear from church leaders that the church needs the involvement of more Native people because we Native American people can teach the church about "our great love of nature." Environmental groups want Native people involved to "exemplify" the movement's "great love of nature." Native American peoples find odious assumptions and examples of stereotypical thinking, both implicit and explicit, contained in these statements. Most objectionable is the underlying assumptions about Native American contributions to the environmental movement, when Native American people are not really being asked their opinions about the current crisis. In many ways Native Americans are merely serving as mascots to the environmental movement. There are three illustrations which I feel best demonstrate this point: 1) the myth of the generic

Environmental groups want Native people involved to "exemplify" the movement's "great love of nature."

---

3. Article by Gordon Straw from Web of Creation < www.webofcreation.org > . Copyright © Web of Creation. Reprinted with permission.

Indian, 2) the myth of "a once noble people," and 3) the absence of Native Americans in leadership in the environmental movement.

One of the prevailing myths about Native Americans in this country I call the myth of the generic Indian. This myth portrays all Native Americans as if they belonged to one huge, monolithic tribe. This view assumes that all tribes have the same traditions, customs, language, lifestyle and government. This is far from the truth. In fact, Native Americans represent less than one percent of the U.S. population, but represent half of its language diversity. Fifty percent of the languages spoken in the United States are Native languages. There are hundreds of tribes with differing traditions, governments, and strategies for the future. It is absolutely naive to think that all Native Americans could be represented by one image of what non-Natives think they are.

A second false assumption is that Native American peoples and their cultures are frozen in the past, specifically in the nineteenth century. The "Ironeyes" Cody commercial does this: a Native person riding on horseback, in the woods, in breechcloth and feathers, and keeping his distance from a teeming highway. Most people subconsciously, and many blatantly, assume that Indians no longer exist and that their cultures are dead. It is true that the 1800's John Wayne Indians no longer exist; they never did. The movie *Dances With Wolves* has a lot to commend it, but even it leaves this assumption inviolate. I would say this is changing with the advent of Indian gaming and casinos, and more non-Indians being exposed to contemporary Native American peoples and culture. Even so, the view persists. Donald Trump, a casino owner himself, went before the House Natural Resources Subcommittee on Indian Affairs and testified that his competitors, the Mashantucket Pequot, "don't look like Indians to me." This myth is dangerous because it places Native peoples outside the consciousness of everyday life in this country. A striking example of this came out of the analysis of the 1980 census. It was determined, with the data of the 1980 census, that for every species of plant or animal on the endangered species list, there are five Native languages (thus, cultures) that are in danger of extinction. It seems to be easier to whip up support for the spotted owl or the snail darter, than living cultures of living people. It is one thing for a German American to lose her or his language and culture in this country; it only takes a trip to Germany to remedy it. But if the languages of Native Americans are lost in this country, they are lost forever. This is one of the real consequences of such a stereotypical view.

Finally, with respect to the sensitivities of well-meaning people, particularly in the environmental movement, if indeed Native Americans have a lot to teach this dominant society about care of the earth, and if they could be so help-

It is absolutely naive to think that all Native Americans could be represented by one image of what non-Natives think they are.

ful to the environmental movement, why are there no Native Americans in leadership in the environmental movement? My apologies to those few who probably are doing just that, but the question remains valid. Why are there so few people of color in the environmental movement? This is more than an issue of representation or tokenism; it is a challenge to bring people of differing world views and viewpoints to work together on a crisis that affects us all.

A few years ago, I was visiting on the Hoopa Indian Reservation in northern California. I was sitting in the kitchen of one of the members of the tribe, who was attending several meetings with some of the environmental groups in the area planning strategies around a local environmental issue. She was asked by her tribe to bring their view to the group, which was slightly at variance to the other's. She expressed a great deal of frustration, because the leaders of the environmental groups refused to listen to her. It appeared they wanted her to remain part of the group, because it was good for publicity, not because of her values as a Native person. They had their grand scheme all set up and they were not going to let her or her tribe's position on the issue get in the way of their strategy to achieve environmental justice.

If the environmental movement is serious about its stated commitments to being concerned for all peoples, the movement will need to be more open to divergent opinions, more willing to settle these differences in honest dialogue. One place to start is for the environmental organizations to become more familiar with the current issues and struggles of tribes and tribal people, not only the ones that fall into their agenda. Environmental groups must recognize and affirm tribal sovereignty, the inherent right for tribes to govern themselves and their people. One of the corollaries of this is that environmental groups cannot continue to choose individual Native Americans and portray their opinions as normative for all Native Americans. Native Americans too, must get past their own stereotypes of environmental groups, conjured up through past experience. Tribes will most likely not "buy into" everything on the environmental movements agenda; neither will the reverse be true. What is essential, however, is to find out what can be done together and respect each other as equals even when there is disagreement.

I do acknowledge that Native Americans are not the only peoples to suffer under stereotypes in this country or within the environmental movement. I cannot adequately treat the other examples of stereotypes due to space limitations. Suffice it to say that any stereotype will hurt the larger agenda, because it will prevent people from treating each other with respect. Not all Hispanics, for instance, are migrant workers; not all Asians are high-tech moguls or gurus, meditating under a tree; not all African Americans are inner-city dwell-

Native Americans are not the only peoples to suffer under stereotypes in this country or within the environmental movement.

ers and more interested in dealing drugs than in saving our environment; not all White environmentalists are vegetarians or animal rights activists.

The real irony of cultural stereotypes in the environmental movement is that the environmental crisis and racism come from the same root: injustice and the abuse of power. In 1992, I spent a great deal of my time talking to groups about the 1992 Columbus Quincentenary. The significance of this quincentenary is not in the person Columbus; it is in the systems of oppression and exploitation that were set in place and which have been operating for the past 500 years in the Americas. It is no surprise to any Native person that a country that chased them onto reservations is the same country that is dealing with environmental degradation and injustice, with racism and sexism, and an increasing gulf between rich and poor.

Acknowledging this history can also be our hope for the future. If we continue to ignore or sweep this history of oppression and exploitation under the rug, we will be doomed to repeat it. We can choose to acknowledge this history and learn from it. We can choose to be part of the new vision for the next 500 years. We can choose to be part of a history that emphasizes mutual understanding and respect, encourages diversity and healing, and which cares for the earth as much as the individual citizens of the earth. Let us join together and choose life for the whole earth.

Race, Poverty, and the Environment: The Disadvantaged Face Greater Risks[4]

Americans have tended to assume that pollution is a problem faced equally by everyone. But awareness and concern about inequities in the distribution of environmental hazards have been steadily increasing. The first event to focus national attention on environmental injustice occurred in 1982 when officials decided to locate a PCB landfill in predominantly black Warren County, North Carolina. Protests very similar to those of the civil rights movement of the 1960s erupted. They led to an investigation the following year by the General Accounting Office (GAO) of the socio-economic and racial composition of communities surrounding the four major hazardous waste landfills in the south. The GAO report found that three of the four sites were located in predominantly black communities.

The Warren County incident and the GAO report led the United Church of Christ's Commission for Racial Justice, a participant in the Warren County protests, to sponsor a nationwide study in 1987. The study used systematic and statistically analyzable data to determine whether the distribution of commercial hazardous waste facilities in minority communities fit the pattern found in the south. It did. Specifically, the proportion of minorities in communities which have a commercial hazardous waste facility is about double that in communities without such facilities. Where two or more such facilities are located, the proportion of minorities is more than triple.

The striking findings of the United Church of Christ study led us to investigate whether other studies existed and to determine whether the evidence from these studies, taken together, demonstrated a consistent pattern of environmental inequity based on socio-economic and racial factors. We also conducted a study of our own to examine the distribution of commercial hazardous waste facilities in the Detroit metropolitan area.

We found 15 studies that, like the United Church of Christ study, provide objective and systematic information about the social distribution of environmental hazards. A number of interesting and important facts emerged.

First, information about environmental inequities has been available for some time. Rather than being a recent discov-

---

4. Article by Paul Mohai and Bunyan Bryant from the Web of Creation < www.webofcreation.org > . Copyright © Web of Creation.

ery, documentation of environmental injustices stretched back two decades. In fact, information about inequities in the distribution of environmental hazards was first published in 1971 in the annual report of the Council on Environmental Quality! There were nine other such studies published in the 1970s. Clearly, it has taken some time for public awareness to catch up to the issues of environmental injustice.

Second, in nearly every case, the distribution of pollution has been found to be inequitable by income. And, with only one exception, it has been inequitable by race. Where the distribution of pollution has been analyzed by both income and race, and where it is possible to weigh the relative importance of each, in five out of eight cases race has been more strongly related than has income.

In our own Detroit area study, we found that minority residents in the metropolitan area are four times more likely than white residents to live within one mile of a commercial hazardous waste facility. We also found that race was a better predictor of residents' proximity to such facilities than income.

Currently, there are no public policies in place which require monitoring equity in the distribution of environmental quality.

Ultimately, knowing whether race or class has a more important effect on the distribution of environmental hazards may be less relevant than understanding how the conditions that lead to it can be addressed and remedied. Currently, there are no public policies in place which require monitoring equity in the distribution of environmental quality. Hence, policymakers have little knowledge about the equity consequences of programs designed to control pollution in this country. Are some groups receiving fewer environmental and health benefits than others from existing programs? Have the risks to some actually increased? If the social, economic, and political disadvantages faced by the poor and minorities are unlikely to be compensated any time soon, then proactive government policies will be needed to address the issue of environmental inequity. The distribution of environmental hazards will need to be monitored, existing policies and programs adjusted, and new programs designed to ensure that all groups share equitably in the efforts to control pollution.

A quarter of a century ago, the Kerner Commission warned, "To continue present policies is to make permanent the division of our country into two societies: one largely Negro and poor, located in the central cities, the other predominantly white and affluent, located in the suburbs and in outlying areas." Our study and those of others indicate that current environmental policies have contributed to the division. To know that environmental inequities exist and to continue to do nothing about them will perpetuate separate societies and will deprive the poor, blacks, and other minorities of equitable environmental protection.

Overview of Social Ecology[5]

Hardly anyone today needs to be told that the biosphere of this planet is endangered, and that its ability to support life, including human life, can no longer be taken for granted. Yet as recently as thirty-five years ago, the concept of ecology was little known outside the biological sciences. In the late 1950s and early 1960s, when social theorist Murray Bookchin first began to develop the ideas that became social ecology, few people were aware that an environmental crisis was looming. In the decades since, in numerous books and articles and through a wide range of political activities, Bookchin has articulated social ecology into a distinctive set of ideas for radical social transformation.

Since those years, too, the ecological crisis has only worsened. In the next century global warming alone is expected to wreak havoc with the earth's climate, causing rising sea levels, catastrophic weather extremes, epidemics of infectious diseases, and diminished arable land and hence agricultural capacity. It is reported that, at a U.S. cabinet meeting in September 1997, Robert Rubin, the U.S. Treasury secretary, exclaimed to Vice President Al Gore: "This damn global warming issue could send the economy into a death spiral!" Rubin was almost certainly not reading Murray Bookchin at the time, and unlike Bookchin, he was speaking as a leading representative of the capitalist system, but in this phrase Rubin expressed an idea that Bookchin had been advancing since the early 1950s. The present market society is structured around the brutally competitive imperative of "grow or die," in which enterprises are driven by the pressures of the marketplace to seek profit for capital expansion at the expense of all other considerations; otherwise they will be vanquished by their equally driven competitors. This imperative stands radically at odds with the capacity of the planet to sustain complex forms of life. It must necessarily lead capitalist societies to plunder the planet, to turn back the evolutionary clock to a time when only simpler organisms could exist.

Unfortunately, many other approaches to ecological issues do not recognize that the ecological crisis is most immediately a product of capitalism. As a result, they tend to wrongly hold other phenomena to blame. Perhaps the most widespread and popularly accepted explanation for the ecological crisis is overpopulation—too many people using up too many of the earth's limited resources. The corollary is that only by somehow reducing the rate at which human beings reproduce can humanity arrive at an ecological bal-

Unfortunately, many other approaches to ecological issues do not recognize that the ecological crisis is most immediately a product of capitalism.

---

5. Article by Janet Biehl from the Social Ecology Web site < http://homepages.together.net/ ~ jbiehl/overview.htm > .Copyright © Social Ecology. Reprinted with permission.

ance. Other writers assert that the ecological crisis ultimately
has religious origins: that the patriarchal Judeo-Christian
religion commanded humans to "be fruitful and multiply"
and to dominate other creatures, thereby leading to today's
crisis. Still others blame science and technology for ecological damage, observing that if toxic chemicals and nuclear
power had never been invented, the earth would today be a
better place to live.

Such views often completely ignore the *social* causes of the
crisis. Overpopulation does not cause ecological disloca-
tions; rather, the way people organize their societies is to
blame, regardless of population size. Similarly, science and
technology are not to blame—the problem is the uses to
which society–especially capitalist society–puts science and
technology. (Exceptions are nuclear power and pesticides,
which are anti-ecological in themselves.) Finally, religious
outlooks are far less to blame than the social relations that
underpin them: The biblical injunction that gave command
of the living world to Adam and Noah, for example, was
above all an expression of a social dispensation. All these
explanations ignore the "grow or die" imperative of modern
capitalism: trade for profit, industrial expansion, and the
identification of progress with corporate self-interest. In
short, these explanations focus on the symptoms rather than
on the pathology itself, and the efforts of those who advance
them, however well-meaning they are, will inevitably be limited to goals whose attainment is less than curative.

In contrast to viewpoints that offer strictly biological, religious, or technological explanations, social ecology emphasizes that the ecological crisis has its origins in social
relations—in the way in which human beings have been
organized into various economic and political institutions
over the course of history. In this account, the very idea of
dominating the natural world (first nature) initially emerged
with the social domination of human by human, that is, into
hierarchies and exploitative classes. As the anthropological
and historical records show, such domination—according to
age, then gender, ethnicity, and race, as well as distinct economic classes—preceded and gave rise to the idea of dominating the biosphere. Social ecology adds that the mastery of
some human social groups by others in early societies made
it possible for people even to conceive of mastering the natural world in the interests of social and finally class elites.

Social ecology is therefore opposed to all forms of hierarchy and domination, as well as to class exploitation and
oppression. Even as we struggle to save the biosphere, it
argues, we must strive to eliminate domination, be it in matters of race, gender, sexual identity, and class exploitation.
But today the most immediate cause of the ecological crisis
is the set of social relations known as capitalism. And the
nation-state is essential to the system, constituting the appa-

Social ecology is therefore opposed to all forms of hierarchy and domination, as well as to class exploitation and oppression.

ratus by which capitalist societies maintain social control through a monopoly of the use of force—and at the same time mollify social unease to a tolerable level by providing certain minimal social services.

The effort in some quarters of the ecology movement to prioritize a pantheistic, often mystical "eco-spirituality" over social analysis raises serious questions about their ability to come to grips with reality. At a time when a blind social mechanism, the market, is turning soil into sand, covering fertile land with concrete, poisoning air and water, and producing sweeping climatic and atmospheric changes, we cannot ignore the impact that hierarchical and class society has on the natural world. Economic growth, gender oppressions, and ethnic domination—not to speak of corporate, state, and bureaucratic interests—are much more capable of shaping the future of the natural world than are privatistic forms of spiritual self-regeneration. Forms of domination must be confronted by collective action and by major social movements that challenge the social sources of the ecological crisis, not simply by personalistic forms of consumption and investment. The present highly cooptative society is only too eager to foster personalism and add ecological verbiage to its advertising and customer-relations efforts.

An Ecological Humanism

Some ecological outlooks blame human beings generically for the ecological crisis, as if the species itself was tainted with some irreversible defect. By contrast, social ecology, as an expressly ecological humanism, sees human beings as the most differentiated and complex life-forms on the planet, without which neither consciousness nor freedom would exist. Potentially, at least, human beings are the only possible source of an ethics on this planet, especially an ethics that calls for the preservation of the biosphere.

This vast drama of nonhuman nature is in every respect stunning and wondrous. Its evolution is marked by increasing subjectivity and flexibility and by increasing differentiation that makes organisms more adaptable to new environmental challenges and opportunities and, in the case of rational humans, to so alter their environment as to best meet the needs of all living beings. Social ecology conceives nonhuman nature as its own evolution rather than as a frozen pictorial vista, which has profound implications—ethical as well as biological—for ecological politics and philosophy. Human beings embody, at least potentially, the ability to go beyond mere environmental adaptation to creative innovation; this potentiality in no way removes them from their place in the natural world but rather makes them conscious agents within the broad stream of evolution.

. . .

The idea of dominating nature is not inherent in the human species. Rather, it has its primary source in the domination of human by human and in the structuring of the natural world into a hierarchical chain of being. Such an idea can be overcome only through the creation of a society that is free of those class and hierarchical structures that make for rule and obedience in all aspects of social life. That this new dispensation would involve changes in attitudes and values should go without saying. But these attitudes and values must be given substance through objective institutions (the structures by which humans concretely interact with each other) and through the realities of everyday life from child rearing to work and play. Until human beings cease to live in societies that are structured around hierarchies as well as economic classes, we shall never be free of domination, however much we try to dispel it with rituals, incantations, ecotheologies, and the adoption of seemingly "natural" lifeways.

Humanity's vast capacity to alter first nature is itself a product of natural evolution—not of a deity or the embodiment of a cosmic Spirit.

Humanity's vast capacity to alter first nature is itself a product of natural evolution—not of a deity or the embodiment of a cosmic Spirit. From an evolutionary viewpoint, humanity has been constituted to intervene actively, consciously, and purposively into first nature with unparalleled effectiveness and to alter it on a planetary scale. To denigrate this capacity is to deny the thrust of natural evolution itself toward organic complexity and subjectivity—the potentiality of first nature to actualize itself in self-conscious intellectuality. There is a natural tendency toward greater complexity and subjectivity in first nature, arising from the very interactivity of matter, indeed a nisus toward self-consciousness, as well as the play of natural selection in evolutionary development. Humanity's natural capacity to consciously intervene into and act upon first nature has given rise to a "second nature," a cultural, political, and social "nature" that today, like it or not, has virtually absorbed first nature.

Second nature is, in fact, an unfinished, indeed inadequate, development of evolution as a whole.

Hierarchy, class, private property, the state, and the like are evidence—and by no means, purely accidental evidence—of the unfulfilled potentialities of nature to actualize itself as a nature that is self-consciously creative, both in reflection and in practice. Humanity as it now exists is not nature rendered self-conscious. The future of the biosphere depends overwhelmingly on whether second nature can be transcended in a new system of social and organic complementarity, or "free nature"—a nature that would diminish, wherever possible, the pain and suffering that exist in both first and second nature. Free nature, in effect, would be a conscious and ethical nature, embodied in an ecological society.

Dialectical Naturalism

The ecology movement understandably distrusts conventional (instrumental) reason, yet too often ecological thinkers turn to arbitrary and anti-intellectual tendencies toward the sentimental and theistic, even to the antirational and mystical. The philosophy of dialectical naturalism, which underpins social ecology, offers a distinct alternative to both of these choices. By adding a developmental perspective to ecological thinking, it discerns evolutionary phenomena fluidly and plastically, yet it does not divest evolution of rational interpretation. A dialectic that has been "ecologized," or given a naturalistic core, and a truly developmental understanding of reality could provide the basis for a living ecological ethics.

Dialectical naturalism is also integrally wedded to the objective world, grasping reality as an existentially unfolding continuum. At the same time it forms an objective framework for making ethical judgments. Based on the objectivity of rational potentialities—of the existing but implicit reality of freedom and self-consciousness—dialectical naturalism tries to educe the phases of development, both existentially and speculatively, that yield the actuality or realization of a free, ecological society. This gives rise to an ethics is not merely a matter of personal taste and values, it is factually anchored in the world itself as an objective standard of possible and logical self-realization. Whether a society is "good" or "bad," moral or immoral, for example, can thus be *objectively* determined by whether it has fulfilled its potentialities for rationality and ethics. Potentialities that are themselves actualizations of a dialectical continuum present the very real challenge of ethical self-fulfillment—not simply in the privacy of the mind but in the reality of the processual world. Herein lies the only meaningful basis for a truly ethical socialism, one that is more than a body of subjective "preferences" that rest on opinion and taste.

. . .

Social ecology seeks to fundamentally transform society to abolish the nation-state and capitalism.

Anarchism, Marxism, and Revolutionary History

Social ecology seeks to fundamentally transform society to abolish the nation-state and capitalism. As such it is integrally embedded in the tradition of the left, especially the revolutionary libertarian left.

Many aspects of Marx's writings are immensely relevant to a libertarian communist social analysis and theory of revolutionary change. Most fundamentally, Marx's basic project of formulating a coherent socialism integrates philosophy, history, economics, and politics. Social ecology especially affirms this project at a time when fragmentation is so all-pervasive, when postmodernism compels us, in the name of relativism and pluralism, to deal only with episodes and events, rather than formulate generalizations. Although Marx's claim that socialism can be a "science" is untenable, his demand for a coherent socialism is refreshing, and his demand for coherence is as living today as it was a century ago.

. . .

Libertarian Municipalism

Social ecology calls for a decentralized, libertarian politics based on the tradition of direct democracy, known as libertarian municipalism. It proposes a face-to-face democracy that can potentially create an institutional counterpower to the nation-state and capitalism, and thereby lead to the creation of an ecological society.

To this end, libertarian municipalists seek to resuscitate a largely lost local political realm and expand it into a widespread local direct democracy. They aim to institutionalize this direct democracy in citizens' assemblies—in neighborhood and town meetings—where citizens of a given municipality may meet, deliberate, and make decisions on matters of common public concern. They seek to build that democracy into a strong force, by which citizens may manage society as a whole, in a rational, ecological, libertarian society.

. . .

Social Revolution

As capitalism creates deeper and deeper inroads into social and political life, we cannot stand back and watch the process happen with resignation or prayers for spiritual regeneration. Many of the appalling changes that society is undergoing at the century's end are not fated to take place but may well be aborted. Together as we create a clearly definable movement to transform society, we can curtail such regressions. Nor can the nation-state and the capitalist system survive indefinitely. Not only is this system widening the divisions between rich and poor around the world into a yawning chasm, but it is also on a collision course with the natural world.

If the "death spiral" of the capitalist economy does develop, however, its social outcome will by no means necessarily be a rational, ecological, libertarian society. States may well attempt to become even more authoritarian in order to repress social unrest. If the crisis is to result in human emancipation, the liberatory alternative will have to already be in place at least to a considerable extent. Increasingly, our choice seems clear: Either people will establish a democratic, cooperative, ecological society, or the ecological and natural underpinnings of society will collapse. The recovery of politics and citizenship is thus not only a precondition for a free society; it may very well be a precondition for our survival as a species. In effect, the ecological question demands a fundamental reconstruction of society, along lines that are cooperative rather than competitive, democratic rather than authoritarian, communal rather than individualistic—above all by eliminating the capitalist system that is wreaking havoc on the biosphere.

. . .

Comments on the International Social Ecology Network Gathering and the "Deep Social Ecology" of John Clark[6]

Between August 14 and 19, 1995, an international social ecology network gathering met near Dunoon, Scotland, to discuss the topic 'Democracy and Ecology. Its agenda featured, among other presentations, a one-hour summary of a long essay by John Clark titled "The Politics of Social Ecology: Beyond the Limits of the City."

My age and growing disabilities prevented me from attending the gathering, which caused me some concern since Clark has broken with social ecology and become, as he impishly denominated himself in *The Trumpeter,* an organ of the deep ecology "movement," a "deep social ecologist, or social deep ecologist" (Clark, *Trumpeter,* p. 104). For quite some time, in fact, Clark's writings in the deep ecology and anarchist press had already been fundamentally at odds with social ecology and were blurring major differences between the two tendencies, at a time when it is of essential importance to distinguish them clearly. The views he had been advancing were essentially mystical and, from a social ecological and social anarchistic perspective, reactionary.

I strongly objected in two personal conversations with Michael Small, the gathering's convener, that highlighting Clark as a major speaker was legitimating him as a social ecologist—when he had been in the process of shedding social ecology for quite some time. Not only did I feel that Clark's tendency to grossly confuse—and even mislead—people who regard themselves as social ecologists would likely create problems at the gathering; I was also deeply concerned that the gathering would not remain the "educational experience" or "interchange of views" among social ecologists that it was intended to be, but attempt to function instead as a founding congress for a social ecology network.

Further, I voiced to Small my strong fears that any "statement" that might emerge from such a gathering would almost certainly compromise the basic principles of social ecology. Small, in turn, assured me emphatically that "we would know how to deal with Clark" (or words to that effect) and that the gathering would remain strictly educational in nature. To express my own views on social ecology as unequivocally as possible, I sent on to the gathering sev-

---

6. Article by Murray Bookchin from Anarchist Archives web site Sept. 20, 1995. Copyright © Murray Bookchin. Reprinted with permission of the author.

eral "Theses on Social Ecology in a Period of Reaction" that I had written.

As it turned out, some of my deepest concerns about this gathering appear to have been confirmed. It does appear to have tried to function as something of a founding congress, by producing a one-page draft statement of "Principles of the International Social Ecology Network." To my astonishment, I learned that when the committee was formed to draft the statement, Clark was nominated to participate—and that he did participate in its preparation. The confused, indeed bizarrely hybridized nature of the draft statement that resulted from the committee's work appears to be due in large measure to the wrangling that Takis Fotopoulos, editor of *Society and Nature*, who also sat on the committee, was obliged to engage in with Clark. Fotopoulos, who is explicitly committed to libertarian municipalism, had to defend the document's meager political contents against Clark's insistent efforts to denature it in favor of spiritualistic formulations.

We are facing a real crisis in this truly counter-revolutionary time—not only in society's relationship with the natural world but in human consciousness itself.

Having piggybacked his Taoist version of ecology atop social ecology for many years, John Clark's more recent writings often involve an unsavory denaturing of concepts filched from social ecology and from serious social anarchist movements of the past. (I shudder to think what older Spanish anarchist comrades whom I came to know like Gaston Leval and Jose Peirats would have made of his misuse of the phrase "affinity group.") Now, as he shifts his ideological identification from "social ecologist" to "social deep ecologist," he can in all probability look forward to a new career among deep ecologists as a revered apostate, riding on the current wave of antihumanism and mysticism that threatens to render the ecology movement socially irrelevant. Indeed, he has already plunged with vigor into his new career by writing appreciatively of the works of Father Thomas Berry, Arne Naess, et al. in the deep ecology press, while his own "surregionalist" writings have been republished with appreciation in the lifestyle anarchist periodical *The Fifth Estate*.

. . .

We are facing a real crisis in this truly counterrevolutionary time—not only in society's relationship with the natural world but in human consciousness itself. By designating himself as a "social deep ecologist or a deep social ecologist," Clark has obfuscated earnest attempts to demarcate the differences between a deadening mystical, often religious, politically inert, and potentially reactionary tendency in the ecology movement, and one that is trying to emphasize the need for fundamental social change and fight uncompromisingly the "present state of political culture."

II

As to the essay that Clark summarized and apparently distributed at the Scotland gathering, it reveals how far he has drifted from social ecology, and more importantly, it reflects the kind of irresponsible thinking that increasingly marks the present period. This document, titled "The Politics of Social Ecology: Beyond the Limits of the City," bears the following caveat: "Note: This is a draft. Please do not copy or quote it. Comments are welcome"

Bluntly speaking, I regard this caveat as scandalous. Clark is not simply circulating his paper to a few friends and colleagues for comment, which is what one usually does with essays so marked, before their publication. Instead, he seems to have distributed this twenty-six-page single-spaced propaganda tract against libertarian municipalism to a gathering of several score people from different parts of the world. Having distributed the essay and summarized its contents in his presentation, Clark apparently permitted the participants to take his "restricted" criticism of libertarian municipalism back home to their respective countries, where they would be likely to circulate it further.

In short, despite his injunction against quoting from the essay, Clark clearly brought his attack on libertarian municipalism into the public sphere and used it to try to obstruct an attempt by social ecologists to build a movement on terms with which he disagrees. And what those terms are, Clark has recently made clear in his house organ, the *Delta Greens Quarterly*: "We need a spiritual revolution more than a political platform, and a regenerated community more than a political movement."

> *"We need a spiritual revolution more than a political platform, and a regenerated community more than a political movement."*

. . .

III

The central component of Clark's dispute with me is his objection to libertarian municipalism, a view that I have long argued constitutes the politics of social ecology, notably a revolutionary effort in which freedom is given institutional form in public assemblies that become decision-making bodies. It depends upon libertarian leftists running candidates at the local municipal level, calling for the division of municipalities into wards, where popular assemblies can be created that bring people into full and direct participation in political life. Having democratized themselves, municipalities would confederate into a dual power to oppose the nation-state and ultimately dispense with it and with the economic forces that underpin statism as such. Libertarian municipalism is thus both a historical goal and a concordant means to achieve the revolutionary "Commune of communes."

Libertarian or confederal municipalism is above all a *politics* that seeks to create a vital democratic public sphere. In my *Urbanization Without Cities* as well as other works, I have made careful but crucial distinctions between three societal realms: the social, the political, and the state. What people do in their homes, what friendships they form, the communal lifestyles they practice, the way they make their living, their sexual behavior, the cultural artifacts they consume, and the rapture and ecstasy they experience on mountaintops—all these personal as well as materially necessary activities belong to what I call the *social* sphere of life. Families, friends, and communal living arrangements are part of the social realm. Apart from matters of human rights, it is the business of no one to sit in judgment of what consenting adults freely engage in sexually, or of the hobbies they prefer, or the kinds of friends they adopt, or the mystical practices they may choose to perform.

However much all aspects of life interact with one another, none of these *social* aspects of human life properly belong to the *public* sphere, which I explicitly identify with *politics* in the Hellenic sense of the term. In creating a new politics based on social ecology, we are concerned with what people do in this *public or political sphere,* not with what people do in their bedrooms, living rooms, or basements.

. . .

VII

Given Clark's Taoist proclivities, we should not be surprised to find that he rejects intervention into the natural world and attempts to "manage" the "world's future," even to "'forge' a self," as "Promethean." In general, Asian mystics and deep ecology quietists denounce the figure of Prometheus because they oppose virtually all human intervention into first nature as "anthropocentric," except to satisfy people's "vital needs" (such as for computers, perhaps).

I must confess that being called a Promethean causes no chills to run up my spine, especially in a time when a pious quietism has become so widespread. Prometheus's greatest malfeasance against the Olympian deities was his sympathy for humanity, to whom he gave fire and the arts that they needed for a decent life, not any proclivity to "dominate Nature," whatever such a formulation would have meant to the Greeks, who passionately denounced *hubris.* Nor can we forget that the great democratic tragedian Aeschylus singled out Prometheus as a heroic figure for his defiance of the deities as well as for his humanism.

The sins of the Prometheans, common wisdom has it today, include the imposition of technology upon the natural world, and behind the anti-Promethean thinking lies a very privileged disdain for human intervention as such into the natural world, especially for technology—a prejudice that I explore in my forthcoming book *Re-enchanting Humanity.* Yet whether we like it or not, the human species was organized by biological evolution—not by a technophilic plot—to mediate its relationship with the nonhuman world technologically. That is to say, human beings are biologically unique organisms precisely in that they have the nervous system and anatomy to intervene into first nature and "manage" their future—to *innovate*, not merely to *adapt* to a pre-given environment, as nearly all other life-forms do. Humans are the only life-form—largely as a result of evolution—that has a rational sense of futurity and that can think out goals on an unprecedentedly high level of generality and expressiveness.

The current antitechnological impulse is not without its own hypocrisies. Gary Snyder, the best-known poet of deep ecology, celebrated his own acquisition of a personal computer for a full page in *The Whole Earth Review*, while the *Fifth Estate* anarchist crowd, militantly critical of technology and the "industrial system" generally, recently purchased a computer to produce their periodical, proclaiming it was a necessity but nonetheless adding, "we hate it," as though great revolutions had never been stirred up by hand presses. This kind of sham about technology goes on quite frequently, as though the key technological issue of our time were not whether technology is used rationally and ecologically but whether technology as such is intrinsically bad or good.

Clark's anti-Prometheanism points to a growing tendency in liberal circles these days to demand of all of us a demeanor that is passive-receptive, quietistic, and ultimately submissive. Quite recently, the Oklahoma City bombing and the violent American landscape generally have been attributed in whole or in part to the "cult of violence" in American history—as exemplified by, say, Patrick Henry's famous declaration, "Give me liberty or give me death" on the eve of the American Revolution, and by the embattled verses in the "Battle Hymn of the Republic." ("He hath trampled out the vintage . . . his terrible swift sword.") Apparently fighting—even dying!—for a righteous cause is now frowned upon in polite circles as violent (*Boston Globe*, p. 1). By the same reasoning, we should dispense with great, fervent revolutionary hymns like "The Marseillaise," "The Internationale," "A Las Barricadas" and replace them with the insipid saccharine fare of *Mary Poppins*. What a sterile and gray world it would be if we did! What feebleness would prevail over robustness and combativeness in a worthy cause! Here Clark can claim his palm. I, for one, want to deal neither with him nor his supporters, who are graying the world in the name of greening it.

VIII

. . .
I should point out that the Left Green Network, which Howard Hawkins and I initiated in the late 1980s to counter the largely reformist and often mystical U.S. Greens, initially tried to radicalize the Green movement, such as it was, and deflect many of its members from collaborating with the Democratic Party. The centerpiece of the Network's original program was libertarian municipalism, which entailed an uncompromising fight for a direct democracy and a frontal

Apparently fighting—even dying!—for a righteous cause is now frowned upon in polite circles as violent.

attack on the existing social order. Subsequently, Hawkins, the author of the draft program that Janet and I criticized, attempted to curry popularity among a variety of reformists, syndicalists, socialists, and social democrats by increasingly denaturing the original tenets of the Left Greens until he not only called for "democratizing the United Nations" but began to support Third Party bids for statewide and national offices. His draft program's absurd demand for a 95 percent cut in Pentagon expenditures implicitly legitimated the very existence of the Pentagon and was part of a politically opportunistic tendency that had to be opposed resolutely.

Before Hawkins began to warp it, the Left Green program had been frankly revolutionary and tried to point out that liberal economistic demands *viewed as ends in themselves* merely supply a humane patina for capitalism, just as a nonsense demand for reducing the Pentagon's budget or claptrap about "democratizing the United Nations" legitimates the Pentagon and the United Nations alike. Nor did Janet and I think it the job of Left Greens, as a revolutionary tendency, to legitimate the wage system (read: capitalism) by raising commonplace economistic demands, including more pay, shorter hours, and a modicum of "workers' control," as Hawkins's program called for. All of these seemingly "Left" Green demands had been raised by reformists who were and still are denaturing what remains of the Left everywhere in the United States. Coming from Hawkins, in particular, they threatened dissolve a left-wing program into a basically liberal one. Hence the thrust of our criticism. We wanted the Left Green Network to clearly stand for basic social change, not advance a cacophony of demands that intermingled radical appeals with liberal views.

In his defense of reformism, Clark observes that over a century ago, the Chicago "anarchists who fought for the forty-hour work week did not give up their goal of the abolition of capitalism." There is a point to be made here about the relationship of reforms to revolution, which Clark separates as two separate efforts rather than seeing them as dialectically intertwined. For the Chicago anarchists, the eight-hour day was not a mere "reform" for rendering the "what is" more palatable; nor was the fight for it separate from the goal of insurrection. On the contrary, the eight-hour demand was designed to reinforce what was virtually an armed conflict that pitted an increasingly militant proletariat against an intractable bourgeoisie. The Chicago anarchists hoped that the eight-hour day struggle would generate a revolutionary struggle—not the achievement of an economistic trade union demand, still less a food coop or a "countercultural" commune.

In the Left Green Network, it was Janet's and my hope to create what is most notably *absent* and very *needed* today: a revolutionary Left, not another hodgepodge of reformist (largely personalistic) "improvements." Particularly in the transitional program I advanced for the Left Greens, we always placed our seemingly "reformist" demands in the context of *basic social change* and formulated them in terms of institutional developments that would pit popular assemblies against the state and the capitalist economy. Admirable as charity may be, we were not interested, despite all the goodwill in the world, in enhancing the probity of the United Way or Catholic Charities any more than we were eager to enhance the reputation of the United Nations. Cast within this transitional perspective, even the demand for a *municipally* controlled food coop has a very different meaning— and, let me emphasize, a stridently *political one*—from a food coop that is engaged primarily in merchandising "good food." Removed from a libertarian municipalist context and political movement focused on achieving revolutionary municipalist goals as a *dual power* against corporations and the state, food coops are little more than benign enterprises that capitalism and the state can easily tolerate with no fear of challenge.

. . .

XVI

Important as the development of agriculture, technology, and village life was in moving toward this moment in human emancipation, the emergence of the city was of the greatest importance in freeing people from mere ethnic ties of solidarity, in bringing reason and secularity, however rudimentarily, into human affairs. For it was only by this evolution that segments of humanity could replace the tyranny of mindless custom with a definable and rationally conditioned *nomos*, in which the idea of justice could begin to replace tribalistic "blood vengeance"—until later, when it was replaced by the idea of freedom. I speak of the *emergence* of the city, because although the development of the city has yet to be completed, its moments in History constitute a discernible dialectic that opened an emancipatory realm within which "strangers" and the "folk" *could* be reconstituted as *citizens*, notably, secular and fully rational beings who approximate, in varying degrees, humanity's *potentiality* to become free, rational, fully individuated, and rounded.

Moreover, the city has been the originating and authentic sphere of *politics* in the Hellenic democratic sense of the term, and of civilization—not, as I have emphasized again and again, the state. Which is not to say that city-states have not existed. But democracy, conceived as a face-to-face realm of policy-making, entails a commitment to the Enlightenment belief that all "ordinary" human beings are potentially *competent* to collectively manage their political affairs—a crucial concept in the thinking, all its limitations aside, of the Athenian democratic tradition, and more radically, of those Parisian sections of 1793 that gave an equal voice to women

as well as all men. At such high points of political development, in which subsequent advances often self-consciously
built on and expanded more limited earlier ones, the city
became more than a unique arena for human life and politics, and municipalism—*civicism*—which the French revolutionaries later identified with "patriotism"—became more
than an expression of love of country. Even when Jacobin
demagogues gave it chauvinistic connotations, "patriotism"
in 1793 meant that the "national patrimony" was not the
"property of the King of France" (whose title the Revolution,
in its early stages, changed to the "King of the French").
France, in effect, now belonged to *all* the people.

Over the long run, the city was conceived as the sociocul-
tural *destiny* of humanity, a place where, by late Roman
times, there were no "strangers" or ethnic "folk," and by the
French Revolution, no custom or demonic irrationalities, but
rather *citoyens* who lived in a *free* terrain, organized themselves into discursive assemblies, and advanced canons of
secularity and *fraternité,* or more broadly, solidarity and
philia, hopefully guided by reason.

Moreover, the French revolutionary tradition was strongly
confederalist until the dictatorial Jacobin Republic came into
being—wiping out the Parisian sections as well as the ideal
of a *fête de la fédération.* One must read Jules Michelet's
account of the Great Revolution to learn the extent to which
civicism was identified with municipal liberty and *fraternité*
with local confederations, indeed a "republic" of confederations, between 1790 and 1793. One must explore the endeav-
ors of Jean Varlet and the Evêché militants of May 30-31,
1793, to understand how close the Revolution came in the
insurrection of June 2 to constructing the cherished confederal "Commune of communes" that lingered in the historical
memory of the Parisian *fédérés,* as they designated themselves, in 1871.

Hence, let me stress that a libertarian municipalist politics
is not a mere "strategy" for human emancipation; it is a rig-
orous and ethical concordance, as I have already noted, of
means and ends (of instrumentalities, so to speak) with historic goals—which implies a concept of History as more than
mere chronicles or a scattered archipelago of self-enclosed
"social imaginaries." The *civitas,* humanly scaled and democratically structured, is the potential home of a universal
humanitas that far transcends the parochial blood tie of the
tribe, the geo-zoological notion of the "earthling," and the
anthropomorphic and juvenile "circle of all Beings" (from
ants to pussycats) promoted by Father Berry and his aco-
lytes. It is the *immediate* sphere of public life—not the most
"intimate," to use Clark's crassly subjectivized word—
which, to be sure, does not preclude but indeed should foster intimacy in the form of solidarity and complementarity.

The *civitas*, humanly scaled and democratically structured, is the initiating arena of rational reflection, discursive decision-making, and secularity in human affairs. It speaks to us from across the centuries in Pericles's magnificent funeral oration and in the earthy, amazingly familiar, and eminently secular satires of Aristophanes, whose works demolish Castoriadis's emphasis on the *"mysterium"* and "closure" of the Athenian *polis* to the modern mind. No one who reads the *chronicles* of Western humanity can ignore the rational dialectic that underlies the accumulation of mere events and that reveals an unfolding of the human potentiality for universality, rationality, secularity, and freedom in an eductive relationship that alone should be called *History*. This History, to the extent that it has culminations at given moments of development, on which later civilizations built, is anchored in the evolution of a secular public sphere, in *politics*, in the emergence of the rational city—the city that is rational institutionally, creatively, and communally. Nor can imagination be excluded from History, but it is an imagination that must be elucidated by reason. For nothing can be more dangerous to a society, indeed to the world today, than the kind of unbridled imagination, unguided by reason, that so easily lent itself to Nuremberg rallies, fascist demonstrations, Stalinist idolatry, and death camps.

XVII

Clark crudely effaces this vast movement toward citification and the emergence of the citizen by decontextualizing the city of its historical development. Indeed, he writes off the lessons—the failings and achievements of municipal history by advising his readers that they "must avoid idealizing [!] past forms such as the *polis*, medieval free cities, or revolutionary sections and [Parisian] communes," lest they miss "their flaws, limitations, and especially, their ideological aspects"—as if our exploration of them (which Clark outrageously transmutes into "idealizations") ignored their limitations. This man can only conceive of libertarian municipalism (coarsely enough, as "municipal socialism"!) as a "strategy," weighing its chances of success against its possible failings, and recklessly shifting his critical positions from outright elitism to the "possible" failure of full popular participation in assembly meetings. The importance of distinguishing policy-making from administration, so crucial in understanding power relationships in free municipalities (a point regarding which Marx so significantly erred in *The Civil War in France*), is eclipsed by philistine concerns about the dangers of charismatic leaders and "factionalism"—as though factionalism, which terrified the oligarchical American constitutionalists of 1787, were a danger even to a republican polity!

This distinction must be emphasized because Clark radically collapses the *political* domain—the most *immediate*

The civitas, *humanly scaled and democratically structured, is the initiating arena of rational reflection, discursive decision-making, and secularity in human affairs.*

public sphere that renders a face-to-face democracy possible—into the *social* sphere. Thus, we are told that it is "not clear . . . why the municipality should be considered quite so fundamental" if municipalism "*rejects* the view of some anarchists and many utopians that the most *intimate personal sphere,* whether identified with the affinity group [!], the familial group or the communal *living* group is most fundamental *socially* and *politically*" (emphasis added). In this rambling conflation of the most "immediate" with the most "intimate," of the "political" with the "personal," and of the "familial" and communal "living group" with the "political," Clark reduces the public sphere—the arena of the political or the self-management of the *polis*—to the bedroom, living room, and kitchen, or, if you like, to the café and park, in short, to the personal. One could dwell at considerable length on this overly subjectivistic, narcissistic, indeed Yuppie vision of social life. If "some anarchists and many utopians" ignore the historic development of humanity out of the parochial kin-oriented domestic life that prevailed in tribal society, toward the confederation of free cities, so much the worse for current anarchism—which indeed has largely failed to distinguish politics of *any* kind from statism, not to speak of "utopianism," whatever that may be today. Indeed, nothing has been more paralyzing to anarchism (an ecumenical word that encompasses vastly contradictory ideologies) than the proclivity of many young anarchists today to relegate public activity to throwing a brick at a plate-glass window or painting numbingly moronic "revolutionary" and largely personalistic slogans on walls.

One could dwell at considerable length on this overly subjectivistic, narcissistic, indeed Yuppie vision of social life.

Nor can we ignore Clark's wild swings from "mediations" that justify elitist administrative councils, to "vast networks" of affinity groups, communes, and coops; his criticism of a presumably apocalyptic revolution on one page and his plea for an "imaginary break" with existing conditions that will encompass "the impossible" on the next; his philosophical idealism that assigns to imagination a sovereignty over human affairs, that contrasts to his flip-flop concern for material class interests—not to speak of his mechanical grids and endless "possibilities" that might frustrate almost *any* political activity, including the activities of his own "network," with its very imaginary forms of interaction.

This methodology, if such it can be called, is not evidence of intellectual roundedness, especially if all of his complaints against libertarian municipalism can be used more effectively against his own alternatives, but a crude etherealization of "democracy." It coincides completely with the lifestyle anarchism of Hakim Bey, who despises every attempt to change society apart from personalistic, bluntly "chaotic," explosions of personal self-indulgence. In Clark's "surregionalist" world, democracy exists primarily insofar as we "imagine" it and presumably personally "practice" it in every sphere of life. It is notable that Clark's journey "beyond the limits of the city" makes no mention of capitalism but patently accepts a market economy, presumably of small partnerships and enterprises.

But what is fundamentally at issue in going "beyond Clark" is the ideological fluff from which his intuitions arise. The cultural and social barbarism that is closing around this period is above all marked by ideologies of regression: a retreat into an often mythic prelapsarian past; a narcissistic egocentricity in which the political disappears into the personal; and an "imaginary" that dissolves the various phases of a historical development into a black hole of "Oneness" or "interconnectedness," so that all the moments of a development are flattened out. Underpinning this ideological flattening is a Heideggerian *Gelassenheit*, a passive-receptive, indeed quietistic, "letting things be," that is dressed up in countervailing Taoist "contraries"—each of which cancels out its opposite to leave practical reason with a blank sheet upon which *anything* can be scrawled, however hierarchical or oppressive. The Taoist ruler, who Clark adduces, who does not rule, who does nothing yet accomplishes more than anyone else, is a contradiction in terms, a mutual cancellation of the very concepts of "ruler" and "sage"—or, more likely, a tyrant who shrewdly manipulates his or her subject while pretending to be self-effacing and removed from the object of his or her tyranny.

The Chinese ruling classes played at this game for ages. What Marx's fetishism of commodities is for capitalism, this Heideggerian *Gelassenheit* is for present-day ideology, particularly for deep ecology and all its "social ecological" off-spring. Thus, we do not *change* the world; we "dwell" in it. We do not *reason* out a course of action; we "intuit" it, or better, "imagine" it. We do not pursue a rational eduction of the moments that make up an evolution; instead, we relapse into a magical reverie, often in the name of an aesthetic vanguardism that surrenders reality to fancy or imagination.

Hence the explosion these days of mystical ecologies, primitivism, technophobia, anticivilizationalism, irrationalism, and cheap fads from devil worship to angelology. Put the prefix *bio-* before a word, and you are come up with the most inane, often asocial body of "ideas" possible, such as bioregionalism, which overrides the very fundamental cultural differences that demarcate one community or group of communities from another by virtue of a common watershed, lake, or mountain range.

We can now begin to see the face of a barbarism that is culturally devolutionary, of "new social movements" that are irrelevant to the problems of human experience at best and quietistic, submissive, and self-effacing at worst. If we require "a spiritual revolution more [!] than a political platform, and a regenerated community more [!] than a political

We do not change the world; we "dwell" in it. We do not reason out a course of action; we "intuit" it, or better, "imagine" it.

movement"; indeed, if democracy is an "imaginary" and that the process of legislating is everywhere, in everything we do; if we must build a vast network of affinity groups, communes, and other largely personalist entities; if we must "dwell" in Taoist quietism—not only on Father Berry's "Earth," but within the bosom of the present society—then indeed, we need no "political movement." A vast network of ashrams will do—and no bourgeois would have cause to fear this development.

　. . .

Empire and the Ecological Apocalypse: The Historiography of the Imperial Environment[7]

The environmental history of the British and other European empires has been one of the great growth areas of contemporary historical scholarship. Historians of science, medicine and natural history, geographers and natural scientists have all contributed to this burgeoning field, creating in effect a completely new subdiscipline. More recently, cultural historians have also become active in the field. Nevertheless, notable American practitioners like Donald Worster and Alfred Crosby have re-emphasized both the alleged American origins and continued domination of environmental history. This injection of nationalism is ironic, since Worster has argued that environmental history constitutes the major replacement for historians' concentration on the history of the nation-state in the late nineteenth and early twentieth centuries. In any case, as with all nationalist interpretations, there has been a rapid and spirited response. American pre-eminence has been contested by Richard Grove, both in *Green Imperialism* and in a recent paper. At first sight this may seem a relatively sterile debate, but it has had the useful effect of uncovering the multidisciplinary sources of modern historical concerns.

Worster and Crosby have stressed the moral roots of environmental studies in the development of the (American) green movement of the early 1970s. They can equally be distinguished in the moral climate of decolonization and European concerns about the imperial interaction with the wider world. This notable strand of environmental history is now sufficiently broad for it to be possible to distinguish at least four historiographical tendencies within it, and new approaches are continually being uncovered, not least by the contributions to this volume. These four can be briefly characterized as the apocalyptic, the neo-Whiggish, the longer perspective, and the fully integrated cultural schools. They are not, of course, mutually exclusive and other defining modes can be overlaid upon them; for example, it is possible to distinguish Eurocentric, peripheralist, neo-centric, and ethnic perspectives. Moreover, some at least of these developments can be seen to mirror the intellectual and practical odyssey of imperial rule itself, from arrogant self-confidence to apprehensive questioning and doubt.

---

7. Article by John M. MacKenzie from the book *Ecology and Empire: Environmental History* (1998). Copyright © 1998 Edinburgh Press Ltd. Reprinted with permission.

Empire, power and the apocalypse

Before examining the apocalyptic school of imperial environmental history, it is necessary to turn to imperialists' estimation of themselves, for, as frequently happens in the discipline of history, modern analyses often stand past ideologies on their heads, at least in identifying the gulf between objectives and results. It used to be thought that, if western European empires had anything positive to offer the rest of the world, it was surely their capacity to act as the bearers of the scientific, medical and engineering cargo upon which they ultimately based their claims of superiority. If, in the words of Michael Adas, "machines" were "the measure of men," then Europeans clearly perceived themselves as giants. The kind of self-confidence offered by this sense of technical power comes through in David Livingstone's conviction in the positively redemptive powers of steam engines—even if they seldom worked for him as he hoped in Rudyard Kipling's fascination with machines and the potential of the engineer to dominate and harness nature, and in the countless examples of contemporary wonder at the development of marine engineering, machine tooling, the submarine cable and the railways. Daniel Headrick has built a career out of arguing for their importance in his books *The Tools of Empire*, *The Tentacles of Progress*, and *The Hidden Weapon*.

If, in the words of Michael Adas, "machines" were "the measure of men," then Europeans clearly perceived themselves as giants.

One of the objections to Headrick is that he takes Europeans too much at their own estimation. Certainly, their overweening environmental confidence, founded on such technical progress, can be found in any number of sources throughout the nineteenth and twentieth centuries. The Scots missionary Robert Moffat perceived environmental control as the distinctive characteristic of the Christian, contrasted with the heathen African's alleged helplessness. An engraving of his mission in his book *Missionary Labours and Scenes in Southern Africa*, published in 1842, reveals ordered hedges, paths, plantings and buildings contrasting with the wildness beyond. Such polarities appeared in the illustrations to countless works on settlers and their power. Livingstone's vision of great cotton fields down the Zambezi, populated by the poor of the central belt of Scotland, was surely influenced by the dramatic changes that he himself had observed in the agriculture of the Scottish Lowlands, in enclosure, draining, selective breeding, new approaches to hydrology and the rest.

For Sir Charles Eliot, Commissioner of the East Africa Protectorate at the turn of the nineteenth and twentieth centuries, the problem with Africa was precisely that its environment required to be controlled and transformed. The past of the continent was "uneventful and gloomy" because of the lack of contact with the outside world as a result of

the natural obstacles, deserts, marshes or jungles which sep-
arated the coast from the interior. He went on:

> Nations and races derive their characteristics
> largely from their surroundings, but on the other
> hand, man reclaims, disciplines and trains nature.
> The surface of Europe, Asia and north America has
> been submitted to this influence and discipline, but it
> has still to be applied to large parts of South America
> and Africa. Marshes must be drained, forests skill-
> fully thinned, rivers be taught to run in ordered
> course and not to afflict the land with drought or
> flood at their caprice; a way must be made across
> deserts and jungles, war must be waged against
> fevers and other diseases whose physical causes are
> now mostly known.

It is a fascinating statement. Having slid smartly from environmental determinism to ecological control, he applies the
language of discipline and training to nature in the same way
in which it was invariably used of indigenous peoples. Natural forces, like people, were to be acculturated to the modern
world. Ronald Ross's final exposure of the causes of malaria
had clearly convinced him that the caprice of the microbe
could be ordered like that of the flood. In a final peroration,
he asserted that "this contest with the powers of Nature
seems a nobler and more profitable struggle than the international quarrels which waste the brain and blood of Europe
and Asia." Sir Charles Calwell's characterization of small
colonial wars as "campaigns against nature" becomes a battle with the environment itself instead of with other humans.

This pride in environmental control was expressed in
countless other ways. It can be found in the rolling periods of
the purple prose of Viceroy Curzon's speeches at the opening
of Indian bridges; in the two enormous recumbent lion stat-
ues that the British installed to guard the ends of the great
Ganges Canal, imperial hydrological despotism expressed
through the king of beasts; or in the creation everywhere of
zoos, menageries and botanic gardens by imperial governors
in their gubernatorial residences, a classic and symbolic taming of nature in the very backyards of the rulers of empire. It
can also be found in the tremendous puffing of the resources
of Africa by early explorers and commissioners like Sir Harry
Johnston and Sir Arthur Hardinge. This propaganda continued throughout the era of imperial rule. It was still being projected in the rapturous descriptions of such imperial
environmental designs as the groundnut scheme in Tanganyika in 1947—"solid ground for hope, hundreds of miles of
jungle cleared by science and the bulldozer with a real promise of a better life for African and European" —or in the
movement of people and animals consequent upon the
building of the Kariba Dam and the formation of the vast
lake in the 1950's a project which came to symbolize and

even justify the very unit of the Central African Federation. Sir Harry Johnston portrayed the shift from assurance to anxiety in his own career and writings. He regarded himself as a natural history collector, zoologist and artist before he was an explorer and administrator. He wrote ecstatically of the economic potential of Africa and its natural attributes, creating botanic gardens and small zoos wherever he established a government house. However, he also expressed mounting alarm at degradation and decline. Like so many natural history enthusiasts and hunters of the period, he was particularly anxious about the decline of animal numbers. When he had visited Tunisia in the late 1870s, he had found it still full of big game. When he returned as Consul-General in Tunis in 1897, the game had already disappeared. He joined the Society for the Preservation of the Wild Fauna of the Empire when it was founded in 1903 and was active in its demands for stricter controls upon African hunting. Even more interestingly, he has an almost throw-away line about Tanganyika in his autobiography, published in 1923. When he had visited the Nyasa-Tanganyika plateau in what is now south-western Tanzania in 1890, he had seen excellent crops, a profusion of wild flowers and an abundance of game: "The Tanganyika in those days was a paradise; later it was to be ravaged by wars, depopulated by sleeping sickness and afflicted in many other ways." In the rivalries of the partition, Johnston was a notable Germano-phobe and there can be little doubt that he was implicitly ascribing this degradation to German rule.

This is indeed a characteristic of the apprehensive imperialist: the agency for ecological decline was invariably placed elsewhere. This was true of the disappearance of African game and the decline of forests and increased desertification. British foresters in India (probably more than the Germans, whom the British employed) worried constantly about the damage caused by indigenous forest dwellers. When E. P. Stebbing visited West Africa in the 1930s, he attributed the alarming denudation of tree and bush cover to the damaging effects of African pastoralism and shifting cultivation. Indeed, swidden agriculture and the use of fire were excoriated everywhere by imperial rulers and their technical advisers. In the interwar years, irrigation engineers in India could not fail to observe that the grand canal schemes of the British were going wrong, but they were all too ready to place the blame upon poor maintenance and misuse by the agriculturalists whom they were supposed to benefit. These observations form a ready bridge to the apocalyptic school of imperial environmental history.

The apocalypse

Elizabeth Whitcombe's pioneering work on the canal systems of British India, published as early as 1972, illustrates this beautifully. She demonstrated that British engineers and agronomists set about the amazing canal developments of the twentieth century with an environmental zeal that can only be described as religious. The British set about rebuilding and massively extending the canal systems of the Yamuna (Jumna), Ganges and Indus Rivers in north India and the Cauvery and Godavery in the south. They had a complex of motivations: extended settlement would increase the land revenue, the fiscal basis of their power; they would yet again find a means of fitting themselves into the Mogul legacy; by overcoming intermittent precipitation and groundwater shortages they would illustrate command of the environment. The results were, however, very different from those intended. Since both the system and its execution were misconceived, it produced not economic regeneration, but extensive and damaging waterlogging, as well as high levels of salination akin to those found in ancient Middle Eastern irrigation systems which had similarly gone wrong.

More recently, Whitcombe has written of the medical consequences in the resultant expansion in the incidence of malaria.

Whitcombe's work has a magisterial coolness about it, belying the heat, dust and hydrological rush of its subject. Perhaps the prime early and hotter example of the historiography of the imperial apocalypse is to be found in the publications of Alfred Crosby. If, for Whitcombe, the grand environmental projects had gone wrong, Crosby saw Europeans as initiating a successful biological conquest of the globe. In both his *Columbian Exchange* of 1972 and his more ambitious *Ecological Imperialism* of 1986, he painted a picture of organisms of all sorts being marshalled, consciously and unconsciously, for just such a campaign. Mammals, birds, freshwater fish, insects, pathogens, trees, plants and weeds set about the creation of neo-Europes, exotic environments comprehensively overlaid with the extensive biota of the new conquerors. These events were promoted by economics, aesthetics, sport, nostalgia, or simply absent-mindedness and inefficiency. Yet his vision was not entirely global, for Crosby paid little attention to Africa and he also argued that the well-established historic peasant cultures of Asia had been able to resist these processes, a contention that some modern Indian scholars deny. What is more, Crosby suggested, highly dubiously, the surprising thing was that so little came back. In his determination to see biological imperialism as a one-way process, illustrated by the imperialist urges of the dandelion, he seemed to know little of the expansion of the eucalypt and Australian wattle, the depredations of the rhododendron, Japanese knotweed or Himalayan balsam, the territorial hunger of the grey squirrel, the mink or the New Zealand flatworm.

Meanwhile Lucile Brockway had already provided a conspiratorial twist for this biological expansion by seeing conti-

These events were promoted by economics, aesthetics, sport, nostalgia, or simply absent-mindedness and inefficiency.

nental and intercontinental plant transfers as part of a global plot masterminded by scientific controllers at Kew Gardens. Moreover, as many other environmental and economic historians have pointed out, rather more convincingly, such plants, in their frequent transformations from foraged to cultivated product, spread plantations through out the world. And such plantations created maximum social and environmental damage through being land-extensive and soil- and labor-intensive. Vast tracts of pre-colonial nature were overwhelmed as sugar, coffee, tea, indigo, the opium poppy, cinchona, jute, sisal, tobacco and rubber marched across the landscape. These plants were the shock troops of economic and natural historical warfare.

Studies in East and Central Africa powerfully developed this sense of imperial catastrophe. Helge Kjekshus, in his *Ecology Control and Economic Development in East African History*, strongly contrasted images of a period of plenty in pre-colonial times with the shattering effect of a series of environmental and medical disasters attendant upon the arrival of Europeans in the 1890s. Some of these, like rinderpest, afflicting both cattle and game, smallpox and jigger fleas, menaces to human health, were introduced directly, albeit inadvertently, by European agency. Others, like the prevalence of drought and the spreading of locust swarms, happened to coincide with the appearance of Europeans, leading contemporary Africans to draw appropriately hostile conclusions. Others again, like the spread of nagana and East Coast fever among cattle and sleeping sickness among humans, were the results of misconceived colonial policies. In rather more sophisticated studies spanning parts of Zambia, Malawi and Mozambique, Leroy Vail has argued that a "major ecological catastrophe" resulted from the combined impact of expanding capitalism and colonial administration in the region. If some evidence of pre-colonial problems can be identified, then imperial rule seized a system that was already under stress and pushed it over the edge.

To heighten this sense of an imperial apocalypse, historians and others have felt it necessary to offer a contrasting image of a pre-colonial past that was in harmony or balance with nature. Kjekshus has been criticized for creating just such a vision of "Merrie Africa"—and, indeed, parallel images of "Merrie Australia" and "Merrie India" can be found in the literature. William Lines's *Taming the Great South Land* of 1991 is a record of rapine and plunder, of the piling of environmental disaster upon natural catastrophe since the arrival of Europeans in Australasia. Whereas, according to Lines, Aboriginal occupation had only touched the environment lightly and did "not greatly disturb relationships within the community of plants and animals," Europeans brought destruction in their wake. Such a view is hardly sustainable, as had been suggested by Bolton several years earlier. In *This Fissured Land* (also of 1991), Madhar Gadgil and Ramachandra Guha create a theory of modes of resource use to illustrate the greater harmony between humans and nature in the pre-imperial period in India. In this and other works by Guha, Indian hunters, pastoralists and cultivators are all seen as promoting sustainable yield policies as well as establishing mutually beneficial ecological niches. Europeans disrupted and destroyed these fine balances, not least in their exaggerated and exclusivist forest policies.

Such visions of global apocalypse have been assiduously fed through into populist green histories. Clive Ponting's *Green History of the World* presents a strikingly doom-laden picture. In his reading, it is not only a case of "Apocalypse Now," but also of "Apocalypse Then." Influenced by Marshall Sahlins's *Stone Age Economics*, Ponting, like some other popular writers, fingers the Neolithic revolution as the start of human ecological madness. Since then, successive civilizations have been doomed to destruction through self-inflicted environmental degradation. This dramatic counter-progressivism views world history as one long free fall, with imperialism as its global accelerator. The entire past is colored with fear of the future.

Neo-Whiggism

It is perhaps inevitable that the post-modernist age should have rediscovered a powerful progressive antidote to this "apocalyptism." This tendency privileges European sensibilities in producing environmentalist ideas from the seventeenth, eighteenth or nineteenth centuries. It can be dubbed neo-Whiggish, because it does indeed chart progress through the development of the bourgeois intellect. The model is perfectly symbolized by the word "roots," which tends to appear frequently in its titles. It fits into long-standing Eurocentric and Anglocentric traditions, which have been developed particularly in the last sixty years or so. It can be found in the work of the sociologist Norbert Elias, *The Civilizing Process* of 1939, which charted the development of manners in late eighteenth- and early nineteenth-century Europe, or again in the words of Harold Perkin, who suggested that: "between 1780 and 1850 the English ceased to be one of the most aggressive, brutal, rowdy, outspoken, riotous, cruel and bloodthirsty nations in the world and became one of the most inhibited, polite, orderly, tenderminded, prudish and hypocritical." Famously, Keith Thomas carried this notion into the English—and his work is highly Anglocentric—relationship with nature. The science of the Enlightenment, as well as of the Romantic and post-Enlightenment periods, produced a "revolution in perceptions" which created "new sensitivities that have gained in intensity ever since." David Allen and Harriet Ritvo, both of them in well-contextualized works that give due attention to both class and power,

It is perhaps inevitable that the post-modernist age should have rediscovered a powerful progressive antidote to this "apocalyptism."

tended to shift these growing sensitivities from the beginning towards the end of the nineteenth century.

While James Serpell has identified the moral contradictions in the human approach to domestic and wild animals, the philosopher Mary Midgley has also analyzed nineteenth-century hunting works in terms of heightened sensibilities. She has even argued, wholly unconvincingly in my view, that the Highland butcher of a Nimrod, Roualeyn Gordon Cumming, clad in his kilt and Badenoch brogues, demonstrated "a true belief in the consciousness, complexity and independence of the victim." In suggesting that apparent cruelty towards elephants is not necessarily analogous to callousness towards people, Midgley demonstrates an inadequate understanding of the vast range of imperial hunting literature and of imperial campaigns, in which hunting imagery was applied to humans right down to the time of Mau Mau in Kenya in the 1950s.

In some respects, though decidedly not in others, Richard Grove writes within this tradition, though his imperial focus and his command of primary material is greater than that of all his predecessors. In his defiantly titled *Green Imperialism*, he has been involved in identifying the roots of environmental ideas as lying much further back in history than has ever occurred to the American practitioners, blinkered as they are by the nationalist obsession with George Perkins Marsh, John Muir and Henry David Thoreau. Through his study of ecological ideas relating to oceanic islands, the development of desiccation theory and anxieties about deforestation and species extinction, Grove has convincingly demonstrated not only the antiquity of such environmental thinking, but also its international and peripheral character. For him, the key ideas come not from the European metropolis, but from the periphery, and are relayed through international scientific networks, particularly those of the French and the Scots. By an attractively neat analytical sleight of hand, he has linked such ideas to radical politics in the late eighteenth century.

He has also provided a significant ethnic context to the development of such ideas, not only through the capacity of colonial ecologists to draw on indigenous knowledge, but also through the particular interests and expertise of the Scots. The botanist doctors of the Indian Medical Service, largely trained in Scottish universities, were the intellectual propagators of such ideas within India, the Cape and elsewhere in the British Empire. Although Grove's work has considerable strengths (not least in its remarkable globalization) and offers strikingly new interpretations, it often privileges ideas over policy, almost suggesting that the former lead ineluctably to the latter. In any case, he gives hostage to fortune by ending *Green Imperialism* in 1860, just as the exploitative force of imperial rule moves up several gears with the working through of the "second industrial revolution" of the period. It should be said, however, that other publications of Grove have noted the economic shifts and the constraints and barriers to environmental ideas in the political, social and cultural contexts of late nineteenth-century imperialism.

The longer-perspective school

As fresh historiographical schools continue to emerge, it is no longer possible to see this third strand as the final element in that satisfying rule of three that has so often been a central feature of philosophy, culture and the arts. It decidedly cannot be privileged within a challenge, response and resolution paradigm. Nevertheless, the fundamental problem with both "apocalyptism" and "neo-Whiggism" is that, in their different ways, they ascribe too much power to empire. The British Empire, vast and apparently despotic as it seemed, was in reality a ramshackle conglomerate, very far from the all-seeing, all-powerful monolith envisaged by Edward Said and his followers among the discourse theorists. It was decentralized and highly heterogeneous, bearing within it many different types of rule as well as social, economic and racial systems. What is more, its influence was felt in distinct parts of the globe over very different time-spans.

Perhaps it is significant that this third school has been developed largely, though not exclusively, in the case of Africa, where the imperial period has been characterized (in one book title at least) as *The Colonial Moment in Africa*. As the post-colonial era lengthens, perspectives and time-scales have tended to open up. Much new work, particularly in Africa, has reduced the tendency to see the imperial experience as both profoundly transformatory and uniquely destructive. A great deal of this new work has been concerned with fragile ecologies, with forest and marginal zones, with regions of transhumant pastoralism, with faunal extinctions and survivals, with issues involving relationships between peoples and power, demographic and climatic change and the incidence of famine.

Much of this research has tended to see the changes wrought by imperial power as but one phase in much longer cycles of environmental ups and downs not unlike those of the "dismal science" of economics. Indeed, indigenous knowledge in many regions of Asia, Africa and Australasia reveals that many peoples have their own awareness of some form of the biblical cycle of feast and famine. At the same time, climatic history has been catching up with its sophisticated use in the natural sciences, and historians and archaeologists are increasingly coming to grips with pluvials and inter-pluvials, little ice ages, volcanic and El Niño-induced transformations. Linguists, historians and anthropologists have revealed words for "dearth," like that powerfully expressive word of the Shona of Zimbabwe, *shangwa*.

At any rate, the repeated incidences of dearth must have produced both human and zoological demographic swings.

Moreover, pre-colonial peoples had more power to transform their environments, mainly through fire, than imperial rulers or modern scholars have ever allowed. This is true, as we now know, of Australia, India and Africa. In comparatively recent times, there were almost certainly pre-colonial species extinctions caused by overhunting and at times, profligate killing. Examples of the latter have been found in North America and Australia. The arrival of new migrant peoples, like the Bantu-speakers in Africa or dominant elites in India, had the capacity to transform the human relationship with botanical and zoological contexts as much as, or, in some cases, more than, colonial rulers, not least because they had a longer time to do so. Hunters and gatherers were perhaps, well aware of this: there is a celebrated bush-man cave-painting not far from Harare in Zimbabwe which, very movingly, depicts an immigrant Bantu-speaker cutting down a tree with an axe, an action which must have been technically and environmentally inconceivable to the painter.

At any rate, the repeated incidences of dearth must have produced both human and zoological demographic swings. In the African case, Europeans almost certainly arrived during one a long series of environmental downturns, which both indigenous contemporaries and modern protagonists of the apocalyptic view attributed to their agency. Thus, we have to understand the mutual effects and complex oscillations of both the natural cycle and human-induced change. We now know more of the historical depth of famine in, for example, both Ethiopia and India, knowledge which in both cases go back to the sixteenth century and earlier. We know that deforestation is far from being just a modern phenomenon; nor is the tight control of forests, their resources and who may live within them. Recent research has indicated the scale of environmental degradation in Indian forests under the Moguls, as well as the manner in which successor states to the Mogul Empire may have developed forest policies which became a model for the British at a later date. There has been a good deal of speculation about the extent to which ecological problems had effects not only on a medieval state like Zimbabwe, but also on eighteenth- and nineteenth-century African polities in Zululand, Angola and Malawi.

Other scholars have pointed to the complex diversity of the imperial impact. McCracken, for example, has suggested that capitalism, in the shape of commercial tobacco growing in Malawi, interacted with environments rather than dominated them, producing a mix of deleterious and favorable outcome. In any case, environmental enlightenment is not the sole prerogative of any one side in the imperial relationship. At times, indigenous peoples succeeded in frustrating attempts at botanical and forestry protection—examples have been found in both West and East Africa. Moreover, the imperial monolith has increasingly fragmented. Experts and administrators sometimes tried desperately to settle nomadic pastoralists, not always successfully; elsewhere, pastoralists were culturally valued more highly than the supposedly softer, stationary peasantry. Some colonial authorities in Africa sought to destroy game to try to beat back the incidence of the tsetse fly, which used game as a host; others created vast national parks to encourage the regeneration of game stocks. The policy pursued largely depended on whether the territory contained white settlers with cattle to be protected. As always, expert opinion was highly attuned to the political contexts that it served.

Towards the end of imperial rule, there were at least the beginnings of a better understanding of the interrelationship between forest peoples and their environment and between pastoralists, their herds and game. The nationalist historiography has often influenced historians of natural history to concentrate on instances of resistance to European policies, when submission and collaboration may have been just as prominent a part of indigenous responses. In many cases, post-colonial states have been more susceptible to sectional interests than imperial rulers. No modern state likes people to move around, and many post-colonial states have been even more concerned to settle pastoral nomads than their colonial predecessors. Hunters and gatherers invariably come in for a raw deal, as recent examples in Africa and elsewhere demonstrate repeatedly. What is more, such states have often proved more responsive to powerful international conservation lobbies which do not always take indigenous needs into account. Just as the longer perspective school can dip deeper into the past, so, too, can it come closer to the present.

The fully integrated cultural school

This tendency in environmental history is a distinctively modern one, insofar as it often deals with constructions of nature as much as the supposed realities. It also attempts to set environmental issues into their full economic, political and cultural contexts. In the process, however, it has often tended to re-nationalize environmental history. In the past, the great strength of environmental history has been its capacity to transcend national, regional or even continental boundaries. This has certainly been the case with the work of Crosby, Grove and others. In *The Empire of Nature*, I very self-consciously wrote about both Africa and India in an attempt to demonstrate aspects of the common scientific, cultural and legal cultures that obtained throughout the British Empire. In that work, I also set out to place imperial hunting into both indigenous and metropolitan cultural contexts. I argued that conservationist policies had to be understood not in terms of the development of sensitivities, but as ideas that were only possible once the economic need for the

This tendency in environmental history is a distinctively modern one, insofar as it often deals with constructions of nature as much as the supposed realities.

exploitation of animals had begun to pass away. They also had to be analyzed—together with the legislation that they spawned— within their racial, scientific and settler environments. As alarm about the decline of animals increased in the 1890s and early years of this century, European hunters produced an apocalyptic vision which often produced equally apocalyptic solutions: the creation of vast reserves and national parks, the movement of peoples, widespread culling of both domestic and wild animals, particularly so-called "vermin," and the imposition of hunting bans that were highly culturally determined. Ultimately, many of these policies were as disastrous, to the interests of both humans and animals, as the problems they were designed to overcome. This was particularly the case with the spread of tsetse fly and the incidence of nagana and sleeping sickness.

This kind of cultural approach has been developed in much more sophisticated ways in recent times. *The Kruger National Park* by Jane Carruthers has an importance far beyond its relatively brief length or apparently specialist focus. Her subtitle, "A Social and Political History," could perhaps be expressed more accurately as a cultural and racial history. She studies the development of that vast park not only in terms of the lives of Africans, Europeans and animals interacting with each other through hunting, subsistence, war and leisure, but also in the context of Afrikaner nationalism. Although Afrikaners often paid no more than lip-service to conservationist measures, they soon recognized the significance of the Kruger Park not only for their wilderness myths, but also for their search for international acceptability, particularly once the full nationalist racial programme had been inaugurated after 1948. The nakedness of apartheid was clothed in the fig-leaf of the conservationist Kruger.

Tom Griffiths's superbly suggestive *Hunters and Collectors: The Antiquarian Imagination in Australia*, approaches constructions of the environment through successive interpretations of the human past. He analyzes the controversies about so-called wildernesses and the preservation of ecologies complete with their palimpsests of human endeavour superimposed or interleaved within them. This rich blend includes issues of tourism, the often contradictory phases of ecological management and preservation of the built environment, as well as private and museum collecting and their related exhibitions. Hunting and collecting took place within a landscape that was repeatedly being re-evaluated by settlers, even as their relationship with Aborigines, geological and human timescales, and their own ancestors was progressively transformed.

Geoff Park's *Ñga Urzora* ("the groves of life" in the Maori language) brings together a personal and romantic experience of landscape with a sustained analysis of the Maori and

Pakeha (white) approaches to exploitation, degradation and sustainability in the fertile coastal plains of both North and South Islands of New Zealand. It also explores the responses of art and photography to these lands, where survival, economics and spirituality profoundly intermingle. There is, perhaps, a tendency towards a pre-colonial "Merrie New Zealand" here, and the repeated interposition of the author's own personal responses is reminiscent of Simon Schama's *Landscape and Memory*. Schama, however, renders his study of the nationalist constructions of landscape within Europe almost unreadable through his labyrinthine, post-modernist and obtrusively personal approach.

The partial re-nationalization of environmental history by Carruthers, Griffiths, Park and Schama is not necessarily a bad thing. Constructions of nature inevitably have a national or racial component. Additionally, these approaches represent the multilayered richness of the field and also offer all kinds of comparative methodologies useful elsewhere. They should help to promote, rather than hinder, the globalizing of environmental history. Indeed, Mahesh Rangarajan has recently asserted that the distinctive and extensive character of environmental studies in South Asia calls for a two-way process of global understanding and mutual fertilization.

Other examples of the "longer perspective" and "culturally integrated" schools appear within this volume. Moreover, new neo-centric and peripheralist analyses can also be identified here. As the human past in Australia, as well as the antiquity of all its life-forms, is pushed further back, geographical as well as chronological perspectives can shift strikingly. A new prospectus repeatedly asserts itself, one which must develop indigenous conceptualizations of the environment, together with ethno-botany, ethno-entomology and natural history, and the capacity of Europeans to learn from these. The manipulation of the environment in the processes of resistance and collaboration must also be on the agenda, together with distinctive religious, philosophical and intellectual inputs. Since the histories of science and medicine have ceased to be the rather specialist and esoteric fields that they once were, there is also a need to develop the very productive work in these fields along with all the other cultural and ecological work in progress. It is abundantly apparent that four schools of environmental history represent no more than an opening bid.

II. Technical Considerations

Editor's Introduction

Given that ecology is as much a philosophical or cultural worldview as a set of statements about the physical universe, it is well to be reminded of the half-jocular comment that "Science is the prevailing superstition of our modern age." Pre-Enlightenment cultures had their own systems of thought, belief, and epistemology that made sense within their world-views, regardless of how "primitive" we might think them to be. Still, we do inhabit a technical world: a world in which the truth-value of propositions belongs to the realm of reasoning in which evidence and experimentation are primary. Even the most romantic of ecologists will cite scientific data in support of a particular view about how the material universe behaves or should be managed. For that reason, it is impossible to neglect technical information that has accumulated over many decades and centuries: information that helps us understand the crisis of global ecology.

This section offers several articles from the scientific community about some of the technical dimensions of the crisis in the environment and threats to the global ecosystem. James F. Kasting, in "The Carbon Cycle, Climate, and the Long-Term Effects of Fossil Fuel Burning," presents data to support a hypothesis now accepted by many scientists around the world: that the carbon-based fuel economy (coal, petroleum, and their derivatives) since the Industrial Revolution in Europe and North America since the eighteenth century has had an adverse effect on the planet's health by affecting the concentration of so-called "greenhouse gases" like carbon dioxide. For many years, carbon has been a marker for life itself. Generations of schoolchildren were taught that living things were defined by the presence or absence of carbon compounds in their structure. This is an oversimplification, of course; still, the term "carbon-based" has been used increasingly in recent years to describe an ecology (and an economy) built upon the extraction and burning of such fossil fuels as coal or petroleum. It was coal that fueled the early industrial revolution, just as it is petroleum that fueled the latter one, which continues through the end of the twentieth century. Above and beyond his role as an "objective" observer of data and phenomena, Kasting believes that his role as a scientist includes offering warnings about the future consequences of such an industrial society. "Although caution is warranted in matters that involve economic choices," he writes, "I am among those who feel that the United States in particular has already procrastinated longer than is prudent and conscionable on this issue. While many of the details of global warming have yet to be sorted out, we know enough about the general nature of the problem to justify certain actions."

Dissenting views to this prevailing orthodoxy are offered by Richard S. Lindzen of the Massachusetts Institute of Technology, whose "Global Warming: The Origin and Nature of the Alleged Scientific Consensus" believes there "no substantive basis" to believe there is a global-warming crisis, and by Julian Simon in his essay "A Dying Planet: How the Media Have Scared the Public," who argues that rumors about the death of the planet by overpopulation have been exaggerated. Lindzen writes that "as a scientist, I can find no substantive basis for the warming scenarios being popularly described. Moreover, according to many studies I have read by economists, agronomists, and hydrologists, there would be little difficulty adapting to such warming if it were to occur." Writing not as a physical scientist, but as a professor of business administration, Julian Simon rails against the "doomsday scenarios" being advanced by the media and by religious leaders up to the Pope himself. He criticizes the fact that "even grammar-school tests and children's books fill young minds with unsupported assertions that mankind is a destroyer rather than a creator of the environment."

Since the 1970s, concern about the growing "hole" in the ozone layer, especially over Antarctica, has become one of the most talked-about pieces of evidence that Earth's ecosystem is being damaged by industrial pollution. Some scientists, though, claim that this may be part of a natural cycle, and that not enough long-term statistical evidence is available to determine whether ozone depletion is indeed an unusual phenomenon. Frank R. DeGrujil, in "Impacts of a Projected Depletion of the Ozone Layer," presents a historical overview of human understanding of the ozone layer over the centuries, and focuses especially on the debate that has engaged scientists and the lay public for the past thirty years: namely, that industrial activity and the use of chlorofluorocarbons, as in aerosol spray cans and refrigerants, has an adverse impact on the ozone layer. He also discusses the impact of ozone depletion on living systems, citing studies about melanoma in humans and disturbances to marine and plant life. Finally, Anthony C. Janetos, in his "Do We Still Need Nature? The Importance of Biological Diversity" warns humans against forgetting their own survival as a species ultimately depends on the viability of other species and of the complex network that has come to be known as the global ecosystem. "In the long run," he concludes, "we must be concerned about maintaining the capability of the biological world to adapt, through adjustment and evolution, to changes in the physical environment . . . and a commitment to preserve [biodiversity] so that our children and their children will continue to realize the benefits of a biologically rich Earth."

The Carbon Cycle, Climate, and the Long-term Effects of Fossil Fuel Burning[1]

Much has been said—and written—about the probable effects of human activities on the Earth's climate. Without question, the concentrations of carbon dioxide and the other greenhouse gases that act to keep the planet warm—and therefore habitable—are increasing very rapidly, and governments around the world are rightfully concerned about what we need do about it. A wealth of information has been gathered on different aspects of the problem, and since 1990 the Intergovernmental Panel on Climate Change (IPCC) has published a continuing series of reports that represent an unprecedented international consensus of scientific and economic thinking.

Two general conclusions have been reached by most researchers who have looked carefully at the subject. The first is that the mean surface temperature of the Earth will most likely rise by 1–2° C (2–4° F) over the next fifty to one hundred years, if we continue to burn oil and coal and other fossil fuels at ever-increasing rates. The other is that the effects of what we have already burned are not unequivocally apparent in global temperature records.

While there have been pauses and year-to-year fluctuations, the mean surface temperature has systematically risen over the past century, and particularly in the last two or three decades. But while many scientists suspect that greenhouse gases of *anthropogenic* origin (that is, arising from human activities) are responsible for at least a part of this 100-year rise, the change (about 0.6° C) is as yet within the limits of what might occur naturally. Many policymakers and other informed citizens have therefore taken an attitude of wait-and-see: that is, while global warming could indeed emerge as a serious problem, they believe that the scientific evidence is not yet strong enough to call for immediate action.

Although caution is warranted in matters that involve economic choices, I am among those who feel that the United States in particular has already procrastinated longer than is prudent and conscionable on this issue. While many of the details of global warming have yet to be sorted out, we know enough about the general nature of the problem to justify certain actions. In particular, we can predict with some confidence that over the next several hundred years, the continued, unrestricted use of fossil fuels will dramatically alter the

---

1. Article by James F. Kasting from *Consequences* vol. 4, no. 1. Reprinted with permission.

Earth's climate, in ways that will impact nearly every living thing.

Surprisingly, this more distant prediction is in some sense more robust than are projections made for the next fifty or one hundred years: that is, we are more certain about what will happen over the long term than over a shorter one. The reason is that short-term predictions fall within the range of natural climate variability and are subject to uncertainties in the rates at which excess carbon dioxide (CO_2) will be removed by plants and by the oceans. In contrast, predicted long-term climate changes are large compared to the natural variations of the last 1000 years or so, and are not so dependent on the rate of absorption: the long-term uptake of CO_2 by the land and oceans is determined more by the ultimate capacities of these storage reservoirs than by the rates at which they are filled.

The long-term climatic effects of the other greenhouse gases differ from those of CO_2.

If significant global warming is a certainty in the long term—as most scientists now believe—then we may be justified in taking action now to slow the process, and to ultimately diminish the potentially harmful effects. In particular, we need to invest in the development of alternative energy sources and to discourage the construction of new coal-and oil-fired power plants that for the next forty to fifty years will release even more CO_2 into the air. As I shall endeavor to demonstrate, taking these actions now would be not only environmentally responsible but also, in the long run, economically beneficial.

The Different Greenhouse Gases

We need to remember that concerns about impending global warming are not based on CO_2 alone: there is an entire suite of greenhouse gases that have been increasing in modern times as a result of human activities. The most important of the others are methane (CH_4), nitrous oxide (N_2O), and various chlorofluorocarbons (CFCs). Studies at the NASA Goddard Institute for Space Studies in New York have shown that over the past few decades the combined warming effect of these other greenhouse gases should have been comparable to that from CO_2.

But while each of them acts to warm the surface of the Earth, the long-term climatic effects of the other greenhouse gases differ from those of CO_2. Methane, for example, has an *atmospheric lifetime* of only about twelve years: thus, most of the CH_4 that our activities add to the air this year, in 1998, will be gone by 2010. By comparison, newly added CO_2 will remain from decades to thousands of years. As a result, about 65 percent of the carbon dioxide that human activities have generated since the start of the Industrial Revolution—in the early 1700s—is in the air we breathe today, as is some that arose from the campfires of Attila the Hun, more than a thousand years before.

Another difference is that the principal anthropogenic sources of methane—bacterial fermentation in rice paddies and in the intestines of cattle—are related to food production and, hence, are roughly proportional to the number of people on the planet. Because CH_4 has such a short atmospheric lifetime, the amount that is in the air is a good indicator of how much is being added at the time. Should global population double over the next half century, the concentration of CH_4 could also double, but it is not likely to rise by much more than that. This would add, at most, a few tenths of a degree to the mean temperature of the Earth. As discussed below, future CO_2 increases could, in contrast, warm the climate by 10° C or more.

Nitrous oxide and chlorofluorocarbons are in some ways more like CO_2 in that once released they remain in the atmosphere for a century or more. The production of N_2O, however, is only indirectly dependent on human activities. Its principal source is a natural one the bacterial removal of nitrogen from soils—and as population swells in coming years the amount in the air should increase only slowly.

The outlook for many CFCs is even more promising. Today, the most abundant of these man-made compounds, freon-11 and freon-12, are by international agreement being phased out of production altogether because of their damaging effects on stratospheric ozone. Indeed, the concentration of one of these gases, freon 11, peaked in 1994 and is now in a slow decline that should continue for the next century or so. The freon-12 concentration has not yet leveled off, but is expected to do so within the next few years. In terms of climatic effects, the main threat from CFCs comes from other long-lived compounds that may be used to replace the ones that have been phased out, and that could also act as greenhouse gases. Since these possibly-harmful replacement gases are as yet present in only small amounts, and since, as noted above, projected increases in CH_4 and N_2O are so much less severe, we shall for the rest of this discussion focus solely on the most important anthropogenic greenhouse gas, CO_2.

The Global Carbon Cycle

Like most other objects in the universe, the Earth holds a great deal of carbon, which is slowly and continually transported from the mantle to the crust and back again, in the course of volcanic outgassing and subduction. The portion that finds itself near the surface is continually exchanged and recycled among plants and animals and the soil and air and oceans. In some of these temporary storage places, carbon is more securely held, while in others it more readily combines with oxygen in the air to form CO_2. In order to predict how atmospheric CO_2 levels and climate may change in the future, we need to understand where carbon is stored and how it moves about.

Carbon Reservoirs

The carbon reservoirs that are most relevant to the global warming question are listed in Table 1, with the total amount of carbon, in *gigatons*, that they now contain. A gigaton is a billion (10^9) metric tons, 10^{12} kg, or about 2200 billion pounds.

In 1994, the atmosphere contained about 750 gigatons of carbon (Gt C) in the form of CO_2. This total amount of carbon corresponds to an average atmospheric *concentration* of CO_2 of 358 parts per million (ppm) by volume, although the actual CO_2 concentration varies slightly from place to place and from season to season. Notably, concentrations are slightly higher in the northern hemisphere than in the southern hemisphere because the main anthropogenic sources of CO_2 are located north of the equator. During the past decade, the average concentration of CO_2 has been increasing by about 1.5 ppm per year. At the start of 1999, the air will contain roughly 365 ppm, corresponding to about 765 Gt C.

Terrestrial vegetation—another carbon reservoir—contains by comparison about 610 Gt C, stored mostly as cellulose in the stems and branches of trees. Soils hold two to three times that much in the form of dead organic matter, or *humus*. The amount of carbon stored in fossil fuels is considerably larger—on the order of 5000 Gt—and the vast majority is in the form of coal. The oceans contain even more carbon—some 38,000 Gt—but the greatest part of these vast stores are held effectively out of circulation in the form of dissolved bicarbonate in the intermediate and deep ocean. Although the oceans cover so much of the Earth, they are very much limited in the amount of carbon dioxide they can absorb. As we shall see in a moment, it is the much smaller carbonate ion content of the ocean that determines its capacity to absorb CO_2.

That there is so much more carbon stored in fossil fuels than in the air is important, for it shows that burning these reserves—which releases carbon directly to the air in the form of carbon dioxide—can bring about some very large changes in atmo-

The World's Carbon Reservoirs	
Reservoir	**Size (Gt C)**
Atmosphere	750
Forests	610
Soils	1580
Surface ocean	1020
Deep ocean	38,100
Fossil fuels	
Coal	4,000
Oil	500
Natural gas	500
Total fossil fuel	5,000

spheric CO_2, especially if it occurs on a time scale that is faster than that of the natural removal processes.

Impacts of Burning All Remaining Fossil Fuel

We talk so often of the consequences of doubling the present levels of atmospheric CO_2 that some may think that this defines the ultimate threat. But a quick calculation reveals that if we were to burn all the world's fossil fuel reserves in a short period of time, atmospheric CO_2 would rise by about a factor of eight compared to its current value—which is not one, but three, doublings in what is presently there. The air around us would then hold almost ten times more CO_2 than was the case in pre-industrial times, when for millennia the concentration held relatively steady at 280 ppm.

Climate model calculations predict that each doubling of atmospheric CO_2 should produce an increase of 1.5 to 5° C (about 3 to 9° F) in the mean surface temperature of the Earth, so three of them could drive the temperature 4.5 to 15° C higher than what it is today. For comparison, during the warmest time interval of the past 200 million years—the Mid-Cretaceous Period, when dinosaurs dominated a far different and more tropical Earth—the mean temperature is thought to have been from 6 to 9° C above that of today. Thus, fossil fuels have the potential, in theory, of inducing a change in temperature that rivals anything that has occurred during recent geologic time.

This back of the-envelope calculation is obviously unrealistic, for all the coal and oil and natural gas will not be expended that quickly. At today's rates of consumption, burning all that is there would require several hundred years, which will allow natural processes time to dispose of a part of the added CO_2. As we shall see, however, Nature's CO_2 removal mechanisms are far from fast, and they get slower and slower as more and more CO_2 is added to the system. As a result, consuming what remains of fossil fuels could well lead to a 4- to 8-fold increase in CO_2.

Carbon In and Carbon Out

As we noted earlier, the world's supply of carbon is always on the move, passing back and forth among various natural reservoirs, although along no simple path. What is often described as the *global carbon cycle*, however, is more correctly a number of separate cycles that operate on different scales of time. At the most fundamental level of distinction are the *organic* and the *inorganic* cycles: the first involving compounds in which carbon atoms are attached to hydrogen or other carbon atoms (as in wood or living tissue) and the second limited to compounds in which carbon is attached to oxygen instead. . .

What is often described as the global carbon cycle, however, is more correctly a number of separate cycles that operate on different scales of time.

Plants and other photosynthetic organisms on land and in the water utilize the energy of sunlight to combine CO_2 from the atmosphere with water to form organic matter (composed of carbon, hydrogen, and oxygen) and to release oxygen to the air. Photosynthesis on land—most of which is accomplished in the leaves and needles of trees—removes CO_2 from the atmosphere at the prodigious rate of about 60 Gt C/yr, worldwide.

If the carbon cycle were that simple, there would be little concern about enhanced greenhouse warming, for whatever CO_2 we might add to the atmosphere would be completely removed by our friends the trees, in the span of but a dozen years or so. In reality, there are compensating flows in the opposite direction: photosynthesis on land is balanced, on average, by plant and animal respiration (that returns some of the water and CO_2 taken from the air), and by the decay of leaves and other vegetable matter (which also gives back CO_2 and water).

There is no question, today, that the global carbon cycle is out of balance.

Thus, to a first approximation, the terrestrial organic carbon cycle is "closed," in that it has no long-term, net effect. It does produce a pronounced seasonal modulation in global atmospheric CO_2 levels, diminishing them in northern hemisphere spring and summer—during the time when the majority of the world's plants are in leaf and thus at work—and driving levels up again in fall and winter, when the leaves of deciduous plants drop and decay.

In a similar way, CO_2 is rapidly exchanged between the atmosphere and the surface ocean (at opposing rates of about 90 and 92 Gt C/yr), and between the surface ocean and marine biota (at rates of about 40 and 50 Gt C/yr). These give-and-take flows of carbon were approximately balanced until our own activities began to tip the scales.

Human Perturbations to the Carbon Cycle

There is no question, today, that the global carbon cycle is out of balance. For some time we have been perturbing it in a variety of ways, the most telling of which is the burning of fossil fuels. The worldwide consumption of coal, oil (and its derivatives), and natural gas now releases CO_2 at a rate of about 5.5 Gt C/yr (Table 2).

Carbon dioxide is also being released by intensive deforestation in certain areas of the globe, mostly in the tropics, as forests are cleared for chiefly agricultural purposes. When trees are cut and burned and the land put under the plow, the carbon stored in the forests and in the underlying soils is released to the atmosphere. The rate at which this is happening is not well known, but is estimated at roughly 1.6 Gt C/ yr. The systematic clearing of trees is no newly-acquired penchant of humankind, nor one that is peculiar to tropical forests in faraway lands. In this century it has simply switched

Human Perturbations to the Global Carbon Budget

CO$_2$ sources	Flux (Gt C/yr)
Fossil fuel combustion and cement production	5.5 ± 0.5
Tropical deforestation	1.6 ± 1.0
Total anthropogenic emissions	7.1 ± 1.1
CO$_2$ sinks	Flux (Gt C/yr)
Storage in the atmosphere	3.3 ± 0.2
Uptake by the ocean	2.0 ± 0.8
Northern hemisphere forest regrowth	0.5 ± 0.5
Other terrestrial Sinks (CO$_2$ fertilization, nitrogen fertilization, climatic effects)	1.3 ± 1.5

Source: *Climate Change 1995*, published by the IPCC. Cited as Table 2 in original

its locus from Europe and North America—which were very heavily deforested in earlier times—to other areas that have more recently come under the pressures of population and economic growth.

Of the 7.1 gigatons of carbon released each year by fossil fuel burning and deforestation, about half, or 3.3 Gt C, accumulates in the atmosphere. The remainder is being removed by a combination of natural processes. Most of what Nature takes away is absorbed in the surface water of the oceans, which remove about 2.0 Gt C/yr. But the oceanic sink is difficult to quantify precisely because it depends on small differences between the dissolved CO$_2$ content of surface water and the amount that would be in equilibrium with the overlying atmosphere. Dissolved CO$_2$ concentrations vary both spatially and seasonally, so it is difficult to obtain enough measurements to define a precise global number for this loss process.

Finding the Missing Carbon

The remaining 1.8 Gt C/yr of anthropogenic CO$_2$—what we add minus what is absorbed in the air and oceans—is evidently being removed by increased carbon storage in forests and soils. This piece of the global carbon budget is the least understood, and for a number of years—not long ago—it was referred to as the *missing sink* for CO$_2$. What was deposited in the air each year was not balanced by the sum of what remained and what was known to be withdrawn, and no one knew for certain where the missing CO_2 had gone. Today, we are confident that what was unaccounted for is going into the terrestrial biosphere, and we have at least a qualitative understanding of the processes involved.

About a third of the "missing carbon" is being absorbed by regrowth of northern hemisphere forests that were cleared in the 1800s. In many instances, as in parts of New England and the Midwest today, the once-cleared farms or pastures have been now abandoned, to revert to trees. This process of forest recovery is particularly evident in the hills of central Pennsylvania, where this article is being written. Here, ridges that once were stripped clean of timber to support the steel and railroad industries are now returning to their original state.

Other factors that are thought to be contributing to CO_2 uptake by the terrestrial biosphere include the increased fertilization of plants by CO_2 and by anthropogenic nitrogen oxides.

The CO_2 *fertilization* effect seems particularly important. Most (though not all) plants grow faster in air that contains more CO_2. They also retain water more efficiently, since they do not need to open the pores, or *stomata*, on their leaves as wide to ingest the CO_2 that is needed for photosynthesis. Atmospheric CO_2 levels are known to have risen by about 25 percent since the early 19th century, and controlled experiments in greenhouses have demonstrated that this change should have stimulated a measurable increase in the growth rate of those plants that are not limited by availability of light, moisture, or other nutrients. This change should, in turn, increase the rate at which the terrestrial biosphere absorbs excess CO_2.

These particular responses may prove to be the good news of global warming, for most agricultural crops are among the plants that respond favorably to higher CO_2. What we do not know is what the net effect of increased CO_2 on world food production will be, for warming could at the same time diminish soil moisture and aid the spread of insect pests.

Limits on the Uptake of CO_2

Given the large uncertainties regarding the fate of CO_2 in the atmosphere today, can anyone say anything with confidence about how fast it will be removed, or how much will remain, in the future? The answer is "yes," but to understand why, we need to look more deeply at the several processes that each day remove carbon from the air.

The Terrestrial Biosphere as a Carbon Sink

The first one is the removal of CO_2 by the biosphere—and particularly the forests and the soil. At first look, this might

About a third of the "missing carbon" is being absorbed by re-growth of northern hemisphere forests that were cleared in the 1800s.

appear to offer means, within our control, to adjust the CO_2 content of the air, and thus compensate for whatever we might add, today or in the future. At present, the net effect of exchange with the terrestrial biosphere is small—that is, almost all the CO_2 that is taken in is soon released again, in the annual cycle of growth and decay or when forests are cleared and burned. If we could eliminate systematic deforestation, forests and soils could become a significant CO_2 sink, at least for a few decades until the growth of trees is compensated by their decomposition and decay. What is more, further increases in atmospheric CO_2 should add to the CO_2 fertilization of plants, thus increasing the rate at which carbon is sequestered in forests and soils.

Putting the brakes on deforestation, worldwide, may prove difficult, though, given the continuing increase in human population and economic development. If anything, pressures to convert forested areas to agricultural production are likely to grow as the demand for food and living space increases.

Climatic effects may also work against us. As the climate warms, rates of bacterial decomposition of organic carbon in soils can be expected to increase, releasing more CO_2 into the air. Should areas with temperate climates become subtropical in the future, the total biospheric carbon storage may decrease, even if trees are growing faster.

In short, it is not easy to say whether the CO_2 exchange with the terrestrial biosphere will increase or decrease in the future, much less to predict the rate at which it will change. Still, we can say something about the overall magnitude of the effect, simply by comparing reservoir sizes. The fossil fuel reservoir contains more than twice as much carbon as is now stored in forests and soils combined. Thus, even if we were able, somehow, to double the storage capacity of forests and soils, well over half of the potential fossil-fuel CO_2 would still need to be disposed of. And since doubling the amount of forested area seems entirely unrealistic, it is sad but true that the terrestrial biosphere is not capable of stabilizing atmospheric CO_2 for us.

How the Oceans Take in CO_2

The capacity of the world's oceans for absorbing CO_2 is also finite. Indeed, as noted earlier, a huge amount of dissolved carbon is sequestered there, amounting to roughly fifty times what is found in the atmosphere. Therefore, wouldn't an increase of but a few percent in what is stored in the oceans eliminate all concerns about possible global warming? Or a small error in our estimate of what the oceans now hold?

The answer to both questions, unfortunately, is no, and the reason is that the ability of the oceans to absorb anthropogenic CO_2 is controlled more stringently by chemical reactions than by the storage capacity of the oceans themselves.

The surface of the oceans absorbs CO_2 from the air by combining it with carbonate and borate ions, in a self-limiting *buffering* reaction that keeps the acidity of the oceans low enough to store dissolved carbon. The total uptake capacity of the ocean, as determined by its carbonate (and borate) ion concentration, is about 1800 Gt C, which is equal to only about one-third of the total fossil fuel inventory. This much-lower number moves the oceans from the major leagues into the minors, as far as global warming is concerned. Additional buffering capacity is available in the form of carbonate sediments that lie far below the surface, on the ocean floor. But since there is so little vertical circulation at such depths, it takes hundreds to thousands of years for any CO_2-enriched surface water to come within their reach.

The CO_2 that comes in contact with the sea surface is only slowly taken in, for there are long delays in even the ocean's normal buffering process, since most of the dissolved carbonate and borate is in the slowly-circulating deep ocean. Tracking with chemical tracers such as carbon-14 (radiocarbon) indicates that the time it takes for the deep ocean water to circulate to the surface ranges from a few hundred years in the North Atlantic to over 1500 years in portions of the Pacific. Thus waiting for the oceans to take their turn in absorbing anthropogenic CO_2 will require a kind of geologic patience.

Thus waiting for the oceans to take their turn in absorbing anthropogenic CO_2 will require a kind of geologic patience.

Calculating the Time Scales Involved

As much as scientists and policy-makers would love it, there is no single number that tells us how long anthropogenic CO_2, once introduced, will remain in the air, since what the oceans take in is limited by chemical reactions whose rates depend in part on how much CO_2 is introduced. The more we add, the more carbonate and borate ions are depleted near the surface ocean, the deeper the surface water must go to be dissolved, and hence the slower the process goes.

Sophisticated models that simulate ocean circulation to calculate the time required to dissolve pulses of CO_2 of various sizes have been run for many years. They all confirm that the process is slow, and that the larger the dose, the longer the time required. Such models indicate that 100 to 200 years would be needed to absorb about two-thirds of the carbon added since the dawn of the Industrial Revolution, were it injected all at once, and another 100 to 200 years to absorb two-thirds of what remains, and so on. For a dose that is ten times larger, 500 to 1500 years would be required to dissolve the first and subsequent two-thirds.

Projecting Future Atmospheric CO_2 Concentrations

To project the future course of CO_2 and its impact on global climate we need to know the sources, as well as the sinks, of CO_2, and to estimate how each of these will change in years to come. Anticipating future rates of fossil fuel burning and deforestation is difficult because both processes are influenced by many different factors, including population growth, economic growth, and future technology, all of which depend on human choices and priorities.

As a first step, we can bracket the problem by looking at a few possible, long-term outcomes. For this purpose, rather than attempting to make detailed projections of who will burn what, and why, we can simply ask the question: Suppose we were to burn up the entire fossil fuel reservoir, 5000 Gt C, over the next several centuries. What would be the likely effect on atmospheric CO_2 levels and on climate?

To answer even this, reliably, one needs a realistic, mathematical model of the carbon cycle which at a minimum simulates the vertical circulation in the world's oceans and the behavior of the terrestrial biosphere, including the effects of enhanced CO_2 fertilization.

. . .

Climate Implications

The results of the more realistic carbon cycle model, shown as the solid blue and black lines in Figure 2b, indicate that exploiting all the world's reserves of coal and oil and natural gas will drive atmospheric CO_2 to peak concentrations of roughly 1100 to 1200 ppm, which are about three times the levels of today. It also predicts that the maximum concentration that will be reached—some 400 to 800 years from now—depends far more heavily on the total amount of fossil fuel consumed than on the rate of burning.

A CO_2 concentration of 1200 ppm is equivalent to slightly more than two doublings of the pre-industrial level of 280 ppm: a stable, naturally-sustained plateau that is typical of the high CO_2, interglacial periods (like the present) of the last million years of Earth history. Two doublings, based on the logic given earlier, should raise the surface temperature from 3-10° C.

We need to point out, however, that our "more realistic" model was still far from real, for it used a one-dimensional representation of the real ocean that was designed to take in CO_2 as fast as is physically possible. It was also based on other highly optimistic assumptions about how much CO_2 will be absorbed by plants and soils. With better approximations of the real ocean and different assumptions about biospheric uptake, the projected peak atmospheric CO_2 levels could well exceed 2000 ppm, or nearly three doublings of the natural level. But regardless of these uncertainties, the exercise demonstrates that atmospheric CO_2 levels and global surface temperatures beyond the next century are likely to be significantly higher than anything that Earth has experienced in the last million years—if we consume all of the available fossil fuel. This is the prospect that should concern us.

The Economic Consequences of Long-term CO_2 Increases

What else would accompany an increase of 3-10° C in the mean surface temperature of the Earth, and how might our own or any nation be affected, economically?

Some Physical Consequences of Long-Term Warming

The political, economic, and humanitarian problems that could be involved in relocating environmental refugees on such a large scale can hardly be imagined.

Neither question is easily answered, in more than very general terms. Meteorologists have worked hard to identify the physical consequences of possible CO_2 doubling in the next 50 to 100 years, but not much effort has gone into evaluating the long-term consequences of even larger CO_2 increases. Among the likely physical effects, one of the more worrisome is the rise in sea level that would likely follow. A warming of 3-10° or more in the mean temperature of the Earth implies a larger change in surface temperature at higher latitudes. This will likely melt some of the polar ice and add to the more certain rise in sea level that will come about because of the natural expansion of the warmed water in the oceans.

The "permanent" Arctic and Antarctic ice caps hold enough water to raise sea level by many tens of meters, were a significant fraction of the ice to melt. And while the thermal inertia of these large masses of ice normally dampens the effects of short-term temperature excursions, were atmospheric CO_2 levels to remain substantially elevated year after year for several centuries . . . large increases in sea level would almost certainly ensue. Fully half of the world's people live on or near coastlines, and in some countries—for example, Bangladesh—nearly all the land area lies within a few meters of the present sea level. The political, economic, and humanitarian problems that could be involved in relocating environmental refugees on such a large scale can hardly be imagined.

Estimating the Economic Impacts

A great deal of effort has already been invested in estimating the economic effects of global warming over the next century, and indeed, the design and use of coupled climate-economy models has become something of a cottage industry among environmental economists. These models typically attempt to include the economic damages that might result from disruptions in agriculture, changes in energy demand, and modest increases in sea level, and the mitigation costs involved in switching from fossil fuels to alternative energy sources. Most of these estimates, not surprisingly, involve uncertainties which are even larger than those associated with climate change itself. To illustrate a fundamental point as simply as possible, I have chosen the economic assumptions adopted in the DICE (Dynamic Integrated Climate–Economy) model, developed at Yale University some years ago. The model, which has many strong points, treats the Earth as a whole, without attempting to make regional assessments. As such, it was widely used by economists to explore the economic implications of global warming, although there are now many, more elaborate models to choose from.

The main point to be made here, however, depends very little on the details of the economic model that is used. As I attempt to illustrate below, the assumption that most affects the outcome of any economic model of future global warming—no matter how elaborate it may be—is what is called the "discount rate."

Discount Rates

Economists, and most other people, are well aware that money tends to decrease in value as time progresses: a dollar today is worth a good deal more than a dollar ten years from now. Part of its decrease in value during that time is caused by inflation. Economic models can easily account for past or estimated future rates of inflation by doing calculations in constant dollars or, equivalently, by working in units of *consumption* nbsp; (of services purchased or goods consumed). A second and somewhat more subtle reason that money decreases in value is that per capita income is increasing, both nationally and globally, at a rate of a few percent per year. One dollar is worth more today than one dollar ten years from now, even after adjustment for inflation, in that it represents a larger proportion of one's income. This factor can also be removed from economic models by what is called *growth discounting*. The modeled calculations that are shown below include corrections for both of these factors.

There is a third reason why money is considered to be of greater value now than later: namely, that most people would prefer to buy (or consume) something sooner, rather than later. The degree to which people prefer consumption today as opposed to tomorrow is called their *personal rate of time preference*. From the study of past investment patterns, economists have inferred that in this regard, societies behave in much the same way as do individuals. Such studies suggest that, over the past few decades, this *social rate of time preference* has been about 3 percent per year: that is, people would just as soon have $100 in cash today as $103, adjusted for inflation, a year from now.

Although these concepts may seem unduly technical, they are absolutely critical for understanding the projected eco-

The assumption that most affects the outcome of any economic model of future global warming—no matter how elaborate it may be— is what is called the "discount rate."

nomic consequences of long-term environmental changes such as global warming. The reason is that, as with interest on savings, the effects of time-preference discounting are compounded each year. Thus, the cost or perceived gravity of an event fifty years in the future—for example, the complete infiltration of Miami's freshwater supply by sea water—will be *discounted* by a factor of $(1-0.03)^{50}$, or 0.97 to the 50th power, which is about 0.22. Thus, the financial impacts of an event that will come to pass in 2048 are reckoned at only a little more than a fifth as much as were the disaster to occur this year. This would not preclude the city of Miami from taking preventative action now, but it would lessen the urgency of doing so, based solely on a cost/benefit analysis. The city planners might reason that they would be better off taking the money that would be required for prevention, investing it, and using the returns to pay for importing freshwater when and if the anticipated disaster occurred.

The potential difficulties with time-preference discounting become more apparent when we consider problems, like global warming, that occur on even longer time scales. If we take the non-constant emissions scenario in Figure 2b (blue lines), the maximum CO_2 concentration (and therefore environmental impact) will not be reached until about 400 years from now. As a result, for the same 3 percent discount rate, the damages are discounted by $(1-0.03)^{400}$, or about 0.000005, which is a very small fraction indeed.

When the economic consequences are pared back this severely, only truly disastrous future economic damages are likely to suggest a need for preventative action. Is conventional, short-term economic discounting applicable to time periods of a century or more? One of the bases for this kind of discounting in economic projections is that one can put the discounted amount today in an investment fund that will guarantee the full amount at the end of the period of concern, thus insuring that the real costs of the eventuality will be met. But there is no global investment fund that will guarantee the needed return over a period of hundreds of years. Nor is it clear that society would be willing to set funds aside to cover something that will happen far in the future. No one living now, or even in the next several generations, will be alive at the time when the largest damages from global warming occur. To what degree are we bound to all future generations? Both practical and ethical issues separate the questions of short-term and long-term discounting, and they have not been resolved. What is justified, for practical reasons, on one time scale may well not apply on the other.

. . .

Implications for Energy Policy: A Personal View

If we consume a large fraction of the fossil fuels that today remain beneath the ground, atmospheric CO_2 levels will almost certainly increase by very large amounts, and as a result, the surface temperature of the Earth will warm significantly during the next several centuries. The prediction about CO_2 can be taken as robust, for it is a fundamental consequence of how much carbon is sequestered in the Earth's reserves of coal and oil and gas, and of the known limited capacity of the oceans and terrestrial biosphere to absorb the CO_2 that is released when these fuels are burned. Exactly how much the climate will warm as a result is uncertain, but there is no reason to believe that the uncertainty is any larger than the factor of three range indicated by current climate models.

Whether or not it is economically beneficial to reduce CO_2 emissions now depends to a large extent on how much we value the welfare of future generations compared to our own. From an ethical standpoint, many of us believe that we have such an inter-generational obligation and hence, we should begin as soon as possible to limit our use of fossil fuels.

What should these actions be? In the United States, some of the steps needed to cut back on CO_2 emissions—such as reducing our use of automobiles, for example—would require major changes in our transportation infrastructure and in our lifestyles as well, since people would need to live closer to their place of work. Voluntary deprivations are politically unpopular, to say the least, and in this case they could also prove very costly to implement. A large increase in the gas tax might indeed cause people to change their driving habits, but it seems unlikely that such a law can be passed in this country in the foreseeable future. For these reasons it is probably naive to think that changes of this fundamental sort might soon be realized.

But consumption of oil (and gasoline) is not the major problem in the long term, however, nor is natural gas, for as shown in Table 1, the amount of carbon stored in these two reservoirs is not that large. About 80 percent of fossil fuel carbon is in the form of coal. The known coal reserves contain more than five times as much carbon as is now in the air—and it is the burning of these large stores in years to come that could lead to the very large increases in atmospheric CO_2 and surface temperature that were cited here. In terms of maximum effect, our first and major effort should probably focus on coal.

Most of the coal that we burn in the U.S. is used to generate electric power. Another way to produce electricity that,

For these reasons it is probably naive to think that changes of this fundamental sort might soon be realized.

were it allowed, could replace coal at little or no increase in cost, is the use of nuclear reactors. While other methods, including the use of solar, wind, and geothermal power, are favored by most environmentalists, none of these has as yet the proven capacity to deliver large amounts of electricity at competitive costs to all areas of the country.

The cheapest source of electricity in this country, per kilowatt hour, is hydroelectric power, and the next is our (now aging) nuclear reactors. Admittedly, these comparisons do not include the cost of decommissioning nuclear plants, so the true costs of nuclear energy may be somewhat higher. But the widespread perception that nuclear power is exorbitantly expensive is almost certainly wrong.

The cost of constructing new nuclear plants has indeed been high in recent years, and no new ones are currently planned. But these costs could be reduced by adopting a standardized design and thereby streamlining the licensing process, as is done in other advanced countries where nuclear energy provides most of the electricity that is used. New reactor designs are now available that are "passively safe" (in the sense that should they malfunction, they will shut down, unattended, without the need for active human intervention) and these might help to win public acceptance for converting coal-fired generators to nuclear power. Disposing of radioactive waste is still a valid and serious concern, but it is probably a more tractable problem than global warming. In any case nuclear waste can be confined to certain designated storage areas, however environmentally discriminatory that may sound. Global warming, in contrast, will by definition affect everyone, for better or worse, no matter where he or she may live.

Nuclear power cannot be the only answer. Unless we turn to breeder reactors—a much riskier technology—our nuclear fuel reserves are relatively limited. Furthermore, it could prove a serious mistake to build nuclear plants in countries where there is insufficient technical infrastructure and expertise and where ensuring reactor safety could be far more difficult.

For all of these reasons we need to invest in the development of alternative energy sources that offer the possibility of becoming economical on a large scale several decades from now. Nuclear fusion and satellite solar power are two examples that come to mind, but there are many other ideas that deserve investigation. Much of the necessary research could be performed by utility companies, who would presumably compete vigorously with each other to find the most cost-effective solution, were coal-fired power plants to be restricted or banned. Since time is needed to develop these various other energy sources, we may well need to lean on nuclear power through the first decades of the next century, until something better comes along. But if we continue to rely so heavily on conventional fossil fuels, we may wait too long, and large-scale global warming could come to pass before we figure out how it might have been avoided.

Global Warming: The Origin and Nature of the Alleged Scientific Consensus[2]

Most of the literate world today regards "global warming" as both real and dangerous. Indeed, the diplomatic activity concerning warming might lead one to believe that it is the major crisis confronting mankind. The June 1992 Earth Summit in Rio de Janeiro, Brazil, focused on international agreements to deal with that threat, and the heads of state from dozens of countries attended. I must state at the outset, that, as a scientist, I can find no substantive basis for the warming scenarios being popularly described. Moreover, according to many studies I have read by economists, agronomists, and hydrologists, there would be little difficulty adapting to such warming if it were to occur. Such was also the conclusion of the recent National Research Council's report on adapting to global change. Many aspects of the catastrophic scenario have already been largely discounted by the scientific community. For example, fears of massive sea-level increases accompanied many of the early discussions of global warming, but those estimates have been steadily reduced by orders of magnitude, and now it is widely agreed that even the potential contribution of warming to sea-level rise would be swamped by other more important factors.

To show why I assert that there is no substantive basis for predictions of sizeable global warming due to observed increases in minor greenhouse gases such as carbon dioxide, methane, and chlorofluorocarbons, I shall briefly review the science associated with those predictions.

Summary of Scientific Issues

Before even considering "greenhouse theory," it may be helpful to begin with the issue that is almost always taken as a given—that carbon dioxide will inevitably increase to values double and even quadruple present values. Evidence from the analysis of ice cores and after 1958 from direct atmospheric sampling shows that the amount of carbon dioxide in the air has been increasing since 1800. Before 1800 the density was about 275 parts per million by volume. Today it is about 355 parts per million by volume. The increase is generally believed to be due to the combination of increased burning of fossil fuels and before 1905 to deforestation. The total source is estimated to have been increasing exponentially at least until 1973. From 1973 until 1990 the rate of increase has been much slower, however. About half

---

2. Article by Richard S. Lindzen from *Regulation* (on-line) 1992. Copyright © 1992 *Regulation*. Reprinted with permission.

the production of carbon dioxide has appeared in the atmosphere.

Predicting what will happen to carbon dioxide over the next century is a rather uncertain matter. By assuming a shift toward the increased use of coal, rapid advances in the third world's standard of living, large population increases, and a reduction in nuclear and other nonfossil fuels, one can generate an emissions scenario that will lead to a doubling of carbon dioxide by 2030—if one uses a particular model for the chemical response to carbon dioxide emissions. The Intergovernmental Panel on Climate Change Working Group I's model referred to that as the "business as usual" scenario. As it turns out, the chemical model used was inconsistent with the past century's record; it would have predicted that we would already have about 400 parts per million by volume. An improved model developed at the Max Planck Institute in Hamburg shows that even the "business as usual" scenario does not double carbon dioxide by the year 2100. It seems unlikely moreover that the indefinite future of energy belongs to coal. I also find it difficult to believe that technology will not lead to improved nuclear reactors within fifty years.

Nevertheless, we have already seen a significant increase in carbon dioxide that has been accompanied by increases in other minor greenhouse gases such as methane and chlorofluorocarbons. Indeed, in terms of greenhouse potential, we have had the equivalent of a 50 percent increase in carbon dioxide over the past century. The effects of those increases are certainly worth studying—quite independent of any uncertain future scenarios.

I also find it difficult to believe that technology will not lead to improved nuclear reactors within fifty years.

The Greenhouse Effect

The crude idea in the common popular presentation of the greenhouse effect is that the atmosphere is transparent to sunlight (apart from the very significant reflectivity of both clouds and the surface), which heats the Earth's surface. The surface offsets that heating by radiating in the infrared. The infrared radiation increases with increasing surface temperature, and the temperature adjusts until balance is achieved. If the atmosphere were also transparent to infrared radiation, the infrared radiation produced by an average surface temperature of minus eighteen degrees centigrade would balance the incoming solar radiation (less that amount reflected back to space by clouds). The atmosphere is not transparent in the infrared, however. So the Earth must heat up somewhat more to deliver the same flux of infrared radiation to space. That is what is called the greenhouse effect.

The fact that the Earth's average surface temperature is fifteen degrees centigrade rather than minus eighteen degrees centigrade is attributed to that effect. The main absorbers of infrared in the atmosphere are water vapor and clouds. Even if all other greenhouse gases (such as carbon dioxide and

It is still of interest to ask what we would expect a doubling of carbon dioxide to do.

methane) were to disappear, we would still be left with over 98 percent of the current greenhouse effect. Nevertheless, it is presumed that increases in carbon dioxide and other minor greenhouse gases will lead to significant increases in temperature. As we have seen, carbon dioxide is increasing. So are other minor greenhouse gases. A widely held but questionable contention is that those increases will continue along the path they have followed for the past century.

The simple picture of the greenhouse mechanism is seriously oversimplified. Many of us were taught in elementary school that heat is transported by radiation, convection, and conduction. The above representation only refers to radiative transfer. As it turns out, if there were only radiative heat transfer, the greenhouse effect would warm the Earth to about seventy-seven degrees centigrade rather than to fifteen degrees centigrade. In fact, the greenhouse effect is only about 25 percent of what it would be in a pure radiative situation. The reason for this is the presence of convection (heat transport by air motions), which bypasses much of the radiative absorption.

. . . The surface of the Earth is cooled in large measure by air currents (in various forms including deep clouds) that carry heat upward and poleward. One consequence of this picture is that it is the greenhouse gases well above the Earth's surface that are of primary importance in determining the temperature of the Earth. That is especially important for water vapor, whose density decreases by about a factor of 1,000 between the surface and ten kilometers above the surface. Another consequence is that one cannot even calculate the temperature of the Earth without models that accurately reproduce the motions of the atmosphere. Indeed, present models have large errors here—on the order of 50 percent. Not surprisingly, those models are unable to calculate correctly either the present average temperature of the Earth or the temperature ranges from the equator to the poles. Rather, the models are adjusted or "tuned" to get those quantities approximately right.

It is still of interest to ask what we would expect a doubling of carbon dioxide to do. A large number of calculations show that if this is all that happened, we might expect a warming of from .5 to 1.2 degrees centigrade. The general consensus is that such warming would present few, if any, problems. But even that prediction is subject to some uncertainty because of the complicated way the greenhouse effect operates. More important, the climate is a complex system where it is impossible for all other internal factors to remain constant. In present models those other factors amplify the effects of increasing carbon dioxide and lead to predictions of warming in the neighborhood of four to five degrees centigrade. Internal processes within the climate system that change in response to warming in such a manner as to amplify the response are known as positive feedbacks. Internal processes that diminish the response are known as negative feedbacks. The most important positive feedback in current models is due to water vapor. In all current models upper tropospheric (five to twelve kilometers) water vapor— the major greenhouse gas—increases as surface temperatures increase. Without that feedback, no current model would predict warming in excess of 1.7 degrees centigrade— regardless of any other factors. Unfortunately, the way current models handle factors such as clouds and water vapor is disturbingly arbitrary. In many instances the underlying physics is simply not known. In other instances there are identifiable errors. Even computational errors play a major role. Indeed, there is compelling evidence for all the known feedback factors to actually be negative. In that case, we would expect the warming response to carbon dioxide doubling alone to be diminished.

It is commonly suggested that society should not depend on negative feedbacks to spare us from a "greenhouse catastrophe." What is omitted from such suggestions is that current models depend heavily on undemonstrated positive feedback factors to predict high levels of warming. The effects of clouds have been receiving the closest scrutiny. That is not unreasonable. Cloud cover in models is poorly treated and inaccurately predicted. Yet clouds reflect about seventy-five watts per square meter. Given that a doubling of carbon dioxide would change the surface heat flux by only two watts per square meter, it is evident that a small change in cloud cover can strongly affect the response to carbon dioxide. The situation is complicated by the fact that clouds at high altitudes can also supplement the greenhouse effect. Indeed, the effects of clouds in reflecting light and in enhancing the greenhouse effect are roughly in balance. Their actual effect on climate depends both on the response of clouds to warming and on the possible imbalance of their cooling and heating effects.

Similarly, factors involving the contribution of snow cover to reflectivity serve, in current models, to amplify warming due to increasing carbon dioxide. What happens seems reasonable enough; warmer climates presumably are associated with less snow cover and less reflectivity— which, in turn, amplify the warming. Snow is associated with winter when incident sunlight is minimal, however. Moreover, clouds shield the Earth's surface from the sun and minimize the response to snow cover. Indeed, there is growing evidence that clouds accompany diminishing snow cover to such an extent as to make that feedback factor negative. If, however, one asks why current models predict that large warming will accompany increasing carbon dioxide, the answer is mostly due to the effect of the water vapor feedback. Current models all predict that warmer climates will be accompanied by

It is commonly suggested that society should not depend on negative feedbacks to spare us from a "greenhouse catastrophe."

increasing humidity at all levels. As already noted, such behavior is an artifact of the models since they have neither the physics nor the numerical accuracy to deal with water vapor. Recent studies of the physics of how deep clouds moisturize the atmosphere strongly suggest that this largest of the positive feedbacks is not only negative, but very large.

Not only are there major reasons to believe that models are exaggerating the response to increasing carbon dioxide, but, perhaps even more significantly, the models' predictions for the past century incorrectly describe the pattern of warming and greatly overestimate its magnitude. The global average temperature record for the past century or so is irregular and not without problems. It does, however, show an average increase in temperature of about .45 degree centigrade plus or minus .15 degree centigrade with most of the increase occurring before 1940, followed by some cooling through the early 1970s and a rapid (but modest) temperature increase in the late 1970s. As noted, we have already seen an increase in "equivalent" carbon dioxide of 50 percent. Thus, on the basis of models that predict a four degree centigrade warming for a doubling of carbon dioxide we might expect to have seen a warming of two degrees centigrade already. If, however, we include the delay imposed by the oceans' heat capacity, we might expect a warming of about one degree centigrade—which is still twice what has been observed. Moreover, most of that warming occurred before the bulk of the minor greenhouse gases were added to the atmosphere. . . . What we see is that the past record is most consistent with an equilibrium response to a doubling of about 1.3 degrees centigrade—assuming that all the observed warming was due to increasing carbon dioxide. There is nothing in the record that can be distinguished from the natural variability of the climate, however. If one considers the tropics, that conclusion is even more disturbing. There is ample evidence that the average equatorial sea surface has remained within plus or minus one degree centigrade of its present temperature for billions of years, yet current models predict average warming of from two to four degrees centigrade even at the equator. It should be noted that for much of the Earth's history, the atmosphere had much more carbon dioxide than is currently anticipated for centuries to come. I could, in fact, go on at great length listing the evidence for small responses to a doubling of carbon dioxide; there are space constraints, however.

Consensus and the Current "Popular Vision"

Many studies from the nineteenth century on suggested that industrial and other contributions to increasing carbon dioxide might lead to global warming. Problems with such predictions were also long noted, and the general failure of such predictions to explain the observed record caused the field of climatology as a whole to regard the suggested mechanisms as suspect. Indeed, the global cooling trend of the 1950s and 1960s led to a minor global cooling hysteria in the 1970s. All that was more or less normal scientific debate, although the cooling hysteria had certain striking analogues to the present warming hysteria including books such as *The Genesis Strategy* by Stephen Schneider and *Climate Change and World Affairs* by Crispin Tickell—both authors are prominent in support of the present concerns as well—"explaining" the problem and promoting international regulation. There was also a book by the prominent science writer Lowell Ponte (*The Cooling*) that derided the skeptics and noted the importance of acting in the absence of firm, scientific foundation. There was even a report by the National Research Council of the U.S. National Academy of Sciences reaching its usual ambiguous conclusions. But the scientific community never took the issue to heart, governments ignored it, and with rising global temperatures in the late 1970s the issue more or less died. In the meantime, model calculations— especially at the Geophysical Fluid Dynamics Laboratory at Princeton—continued to predict substantial warming due to increasing carbon dioxide. Those predictions were considered interesting, but largely academic, exercises—even by the scientists involved.

The present hysteria formally began in the summer of 1988, although preparations had been put in place at least three years earlier. That was an especially warm summer in some regions, particularly in the United States. The abrupt increase in temperature in the late 1970s was too abrupt to be associated with the smooth increase in carbon dioxide. Nevertheless, James Hansen, director of the Goddard Institute for Space Studies, in testimony before Sen. Al Gore's Committee on Science, Technology and Space, said, in effect, that he was 99 percent certain that temperature had increased and that there was some greenhouse warming. He made no statement concerning the relation between the two.

Despite the fact that those remarks were virtually meaningless, they led the environmental advocacy movement to adopt the issue immediately. The growth of environmental advocacy since the 1970s has been phenomenal. In Europe the movement centered on the formation of Green parties; in the United States the movement centered on the development of large public interest advocacy groups. Those lobbying groups have budgets of several hundred million dollars and employ about 50,000 people; their support is highly valued by many political figures. As with any large groups, self-perpetuation becomes a crucial concern. "Global warming" has become one of the major battle cries in their fundraising efforts. At the same time, the media unquestioningly accept the pronouncements of those groups as objective truth.

The present hysteria formally began in the summer of 1988, although preparations had been put in place at least three years earlier.

As most scientists concerned with climate, I was eager to stay out of what seemed like a public circus.

Within the large-scale climate modelling community—a small subset of the community interested in climate—however, the immediate response was to criticize Hansen for publicly promoting highly uncertain model results as relevant to public policy. Hansen's motivation was not totally obvious, but despite the criticism of Hansen, the modelling community quickly agreed that large warming was not impossible. That was still enough for both the politicians and advocates who have generally held that any hint of environmental danger is a sufficient basis for regulation unless the hint can be rigorously disproved. That is a particularly pernicious asymmetry, given that rigor is generally impossible in environmental sciences.

Other scientists quickly agreed that with increasing carbon dioxide some warming might be expected and that with large enough concentrations of carbon dioxide the warming might be significant.

Nevertheless, there was widespread skepticism. By early 1989, however, the popular media in Europe and the United States were declaring that "all scientists" agreed that warming was real and catastrophic in its potential.

As most scientists concerned with climate, I was eager to stay out of what seemed like a public circus. But in the summer of 1988 Lester Lave, a professor of economics at Carnegie Mellon University, wrote to me about being dismissed from a Senate hearing for suggesting that the issue of global warming was scientifically controversial. I assured him that the issue was not only controversial but also unlikely. In the winter of 1989 Reginald Newell, a professor of meteorology at the Massachusetts Institute of Technology, lost National Science Foundation funding for data analyses that were failing to show net warming over the past century. Reviewers suggested that his results were dangerous to humanity. In the spring of 1989 I was an invited participant at a global warming symposium at Tufts University. I was the only scientist among a panel of environmentalists. There were strident calls for immediate action and ample expressions of impatience with science. Claudine Schneider, then a congressman from Rhode Island, acknowledged that "scientists may disagree, but we can hear Mother Earth, and she is crying." It seemed clear to me that a very dangerous situation was arising, and the danger was not of "global warming" itself.

In the spring of 1989 I prepared a critique of global warming, which I submitted to *Science,* a magazine of the American Association for the Advancement of Science. The paper was rejected without review as being of no interest to the readership. I then submitted the paper to the *Bulletin of the American Meteorological Society,* where it was accepted after review, rereviewed, and reaccepted—an unusual procedure to say the least. In the meantime, the paper was attacked in

Science before it had even been published. The paper circulated for about six months as samizdat. It was delivered at a Humboldt conference at M.I.T. and reprinted in the *Frankfurter Allgemeine.*

In the meantime, the global warming circus was in full swing. Meetings were going on nonstop. One of the more striking of those meetings was hosted in the summer of 1989 by Robert Redford at his ranch in Sundance, Utah. Redford proclaimed that it was time to stop research and begin acting. I suppose that was a reasonable suggestion for an actor to make, but it is also indicative of the overall attitude toward science. Barbra Streisand personally undertook to support the research of Michael Oppenheimer at the Environmental Defense Fund, although he is primarily an advocate and not a climatologist. Meryl Streep made an appeal on public television to stop warming. A bill was even prepared to guarantee Americans a stable climate.

By the fall of 1989 some media were becoming aware that there was controversy (*Forbes* and *Reader's Digest* were notable in that regard). Cries followed from environmentalists that skeptics were receiving excessive exposure. The publication of my paper was followed by a determined effort on the part of the editor of the *Bulletin of the American Meteorological Society*, Richard Hallgren, to solicit rebuttals. Such articles were prepared by Stephen Schneider and Will Kellogg, a minor scientific administrator for the past thirty years, and those articles were followed by an active correspondence mostly supportive of the skeptical spectrum of views. Indeed, a recent Gallup poll of climate scientists in the American Meteorological Society and in the American Geophysical Union shows that a vast majority doubts that there has been any identifiable man-caused warming to date (49 percent asserted no, 33 percent did not know, 18 percent thought some has occurred; however, among those actively involved in research and publishing frequently in peer-reviewed research journals, none believes that any man-caused global warming has been identified so far). On the whole, the debate within the meteorological community has been relatively healthy and, in this regard, unusual.

Outside the world of meteorology, Greenpeace's Jeremy Legett, a geologist by training, published a book attacking critics of warming—especially me. George Mitchell, Senate majority leader and father of a prominent environmental activist, also published a book urging acceptance of the warming problem (*World on Fire: Saving an Endangered Earth*). Sen. Gore recently published a book (*Earth in the Balance: Ecology and the Human Spirit*). Those are just a few examples of the rapidly growing publications on warming. Rarely has such meager science provoked such an outpouring of popularization by individuals who do not understand the subject in the first place.

The activities of the Union of Concerned Scientists deserve special mention. That widely supported organization was originally devoted to nuclear disarmament. As the cold war began to end, the group began to actively oppose nuclear power generation. Their position was unpopular with many physicists. Over the past few years, the organization has turned to the battle against global warming in a particularly hysterical manner. In 1989 the group began to circulate a petition urging recognition of global warming as potentially the great danger to mankind. Most recipients who did not sign were solicited at least twice more. The petition was eventually signed by 700 scientists including a great many members of the National Academy of Sciences and Nobel laureates. Only about three or four of the signers, however, had any involvement in climatology. Interestingly, the petition had two pages, and on the second page there was a call for renewed consideration of nuclear power. When the petition was published in the New York Times, however, the second page was omitted. In any event, that document helped solidify the public perception that "all scientists" agreed with the disaster scenario. Such a disturbing abuse of scientific authority was not unnoticed. At the 1990 annual meeting of the National Academy of Sciences, Frank Press, the academy's president, warned the membership against lending their credibility to issues about which they had no special knowledge. Special reference was made to the published petition. In my opinion what the petition did show was that the need to fight "global warming" has become part of the dogma of the liberal conscience—a dogma to which scientists are not immune.

At the same time, political pressures on dissidents from the "popular vision" increased. Sen. Gore publicly admonished "skeptics" in a lengthy *New York Times* op-ed piece. In a perverse example of double-speak he associated the "true believers" in warming with Galileo. He also referred, in another article, to the summer of 1988 as the Kristallnacht before the warming holocaust.

The notion of "scientific unanimity" is currently intimately tied to the Working Group I report of the Intergovernmental Panel on Climate Change issued in September 1990. That panel consists largely of scientists posted to it by government agencies. The panel has three working groups. Working Group I nominally deals with climate science. Approximately 150 scientists contributed to the report, but university representation from the United States was relatively small and is likely to remain so, since the funds and time needed for participation are not available to most university scientists. Many governments have agreed to use that report as the authoritative basis for climate policy. The report, as such, has both positive and negative features. Methodologically, the report is deeply committed to reliance on large models, and within the report models are largely verified by comparison with other models. Given that models are known to agree more with each other than with nature (even after "tuning"), that approach does not seem promising. In addition, a number of the participants have testified to the pressures placed on them to emphasize results supportive of the current scenario and to suppress other results. That pressure has frequently been effective, and a survey of participants reveals substantial disagreement with the final report. Nonetheless, the body of the report is extremely ambiguous, and the caveats are numerous. The report is prefaced by a policymakers' summary written by the editor, Sir John Houghton, director of the United Kingdom Meteorological Office. His summary largely ignores the uncertainty in the report and attempts to present the expectation of substantial warming as firmly based science. The summary was published as a separate document, and, it is safe to say that policymakers are unlikely to read anything further. On the basis of the summary, one frequently hears that "hundreds of the world's greatest climate scientists from dozens of countries all agreed that . . . " It hardly matters what the agreement refers to, since whoever refers to the summary insists that it agrees with the most extreme scenarios (which, in all fairness, it does not). I should add that the climatology community, until the past few years, was quite small and heavily concentrated in the United States and Europe.

While the International Panel on Climate Change's reports were in preparation, the National Research Council in the United States was commissioned to prepare a synthesis of the current state of the global change situation. The panel chosen was hardly promising. It had no members of the academy expert in climate. Indeed, it had only one scientist directly involved in climate, Stephen Schneider, who is an ardent environmental advocate. It also included three professional environmental advocates, and it was headed by a former senator, Dan Evans. The panel did include distinguished scientists and economists outside the area of climate, and, perhaps because of this, the report issued by the panel was by and large fair. The report concluded that the scientific basis for costly action was absent, although prudence might indicate that actions that were cheap or worth doing anyway should be considered. A subcommittee of the panel issued a report on adaptation that argued that even with the more severe warming scenarios, the United States would have little difficulty adapting. Not surprisingly, the environmentalists on the panel not only strongly influenced the reports, but failing to completely have their way, attempted to distance themselves from the reports by either resigning or by issuing minority dissents. Equally unsurprising is the fact that the *New York Times* typically carried reports on that panel on page 46. The findings were never

Nonetheless, the body of the report is extremely ambiguous, and the caveats are numerous.

subsequently discussed in the popular media—except for claims that the reports supported the catastrophic vision. Nevertheless, the reports of that panel were indicative of the growing skepticism concerning the warming issue. Indeed, the growing skepticism is in many ways remarkable. One of the earliest protagonists of global warming, Roger Revelle, the late professor of ocean sciences at Scripps Institution of Oceanography who initiated the direct monitoring of carbon dioxide during the International Geophysical Year (1958), coauthored with S. Fred Singer and Chauncy Starr a paper recommending that action concerning global warming be delayed insofar as current knowledge was totally inadequate. Another active advocate of global warming, Michael McElroy, head of the Department of Earth and Planetary Sciences at Harvard, has recently written a paper acknowledging that existing models cannot be used to forecast climate.

Differences between expectations of unmeasurable changes of a few tenths of a degree and warming of several degrees are conveniently ignored.

One might think that such growing skepticism would have some influence on public debate, but the insistence on "scientific unanimity" continues unabated. At times, that insistence takes some very strange forms. Over a year ago, Robert White, former head of the U.S. Weather Bureau and currently president of the National Academy of Engineering, wrote an article for *Scientific American* that pointed out that the questionable scientific basis for global warming predictions was totally inadequate to justify any costly actions. He did state that if one were to insist on doing something, one should only do things that one would do even if there were no warming threat. Immediately after that article appeared, Tom Wicker, a *New York Times* columnist and a confidant of Sen. Gore, wrote a piece in which he stated that White had called for immediate action on "global warming." My own experiences have been similar. In an article in Audubon Stephen Schneider states that I have "conceded that some warming now appears inevitable." Differences between expectations of unmeasurable changes of a few tenths of a degree and warming of several degrees are conveniently ignored. Karen White in a lengthy and laudatory article on James Hansen that appeared in the *New York Times Magazine* reported that even I agreed that there would be warming, having "reluctantly offered an estimate of 1.2 degrees." That was, of course, untrue.

Most recently, I testified at a Senate hearing conducted by Sen. Gore. There was a rather arcane discussion of the water vapor in the upper troposphere. Two years ago, I had pointed out that if the source of water vapor in that region in the tropics was from deep clouds, then surface warming would be accompanied by reduced upper level water vapor. Subsequent research has established that there must be an additional source—widely believed to be ice crystals thrown off by those deep clouds. I noted that that source too probably acts to produce less moisture in a warmer atmosphere. Both

processes cause the major feedback process to become negative rather than positive. Sen. Gore asked whether I now
rejected my suggestion of two years ago as a major factor. I
answered that I did. Gore then called for the recording secretary to note that I had retracted my objections to "global
warming." In the ensuing argument, involving mostly other
participants in the hearing, Gore was told that he was con-
fusing matters. Shortly thereafter, however, Tom Wicker published an article in the *New York Times* that claimed that I
had retracted my opposition to warming and that that warranted immediate action to curb the purported menace. I
wrote a letter to the *Times* indicating that my position had
been severely misrepresented, and, after a delay of over a
month, my letter was published. Sen. Gore nonetheless
claims in his book that I have indeed retracted my scientific
objections to the catastrophic warming scenario and also
warns others who doubt the scenario that they are hurting
humanity.

Why, one might wonder, is there such insistence on scientific unanimity on the warming issue? After all, unanimity in
science is virtually nonexistent on far less complex matters.
Unanimity on an issue as uncertain as "global warming"
would be surprising and suspicious. Moreover, why are the
opinions of scientists sought regardless of their field of
expertise? Biologists and physicians are rarely asked to
endorse some theory in high energy physics. Apparently,
when one comes to "global warming," any scientist's agreement will do.

The answer almost certainly lies in politics. For example, at
the Earth Summit in Rio, attempts were made to negotiate
international carbon emission agreements. The potential
costs and implications of such agreements are likely to be
profound for both industrial and developing countries. Under
the circumstances, it would be very risky for politicians to
undertake such agreements unless scientists "insisted." Nevertheless, the situation is probably a good deal more complicated than that example suggests.

The Temptation and Problems of "Global Warming"

As Aaron Wildavsky, professor of political science at Berke-
ley, has quipped, "global warming" is the mother of all environmental scares. Wildavsky's view is worth quoting.
"Warming (and warming alone), through its primary antidote of withdrawing carbon from production and consumption, is capable of realizing the environmentalist's dream of
an egalitarian society based on rejection of economic growth
in favor of a smaller population's eating lower on the food
chain, consuming a lot less, and sharing a much lower level
of resources much more equally." In many ways Wildavsky's
observation does not go far enough. The point is that carbon
dioxide is vitally central to industry, transportation, modern
life, and life in general. It has been joked that carbon dioxide

*Apparently,
when one comes
to "global
warming," any
scientist's agree-
ment will do.*

controls would permit us to inhale as much as we wish; only exhaling would be controlled. The remarkable centrality of carbon dioxide means that dealing with the threat of warming fits in with a great variety of preexisting agendas—some legitimate, some less so: energy efficiency, reduced dependence on Middle Eastern oil, dissatisfaction with industrial society (neopastoralism), international competition, governmental desires for enhanced revenues (carbon taxes), and bureaucratic desires for enhanced power.

The very scale of the problem as popularly portrayed and the massive scale of the suggested responses have their own appeal. The Working Group I report of the Intergovernmental Panel on Climate Change suggested, for example, that a 60 percent reduction in carbon dioxide emissions might be needed. Such a reduction would call for measures that would be greater than those that have been devoted to war and defense. And just as defense has dealt with saving one's nation, curbing "global warming" is identified with saving the whole planet! It may not be fortuitous that this issue is being promoted at just the moment in history when the cold war is ending.

Clearly, "global warming" is a tempting issue for many very important groups to exploit.

Major agencies in the United States, hitherto closely involved with traditional approaches to national security, have appropriated the issue of climate change to support existing efforts. Notable among those agencies are NASA, the Department of Defense, and the Department of Energy. The cold war helped spawn a large body of policy experts and diplomats specializing in issues such as disarmament and alliance negotiations. In addition, since the Yom Kippur War, energy has become a major component of national security with the concomitant creation of a large cadre of energy experts. Many of those individuals see in the global change issue an area in which to continue applying their skills. Many scientists also feel that national security concerns formed the foundation for the U.S. government's generous support of science. As the urgency of national security, traditionally defined, diminishes, there is a common feeling that a substitute foundation must be established. "Saving the planet" has the right sort of sound to it. Fundraising has become central to environmental advocates' activities, and the message underlying some of their fundraising seems to be "pay us or you'll fry."

Clearly, "global warming" is a tempting issue for many very important groups to exploit. Equally clearly, though far less frequently discussed, are the profound dangers in exploiting that issue. As we shall also see, there are good reasons why there has been so little discussion of the downside of responding to "global warming."

A parochial issue is the danger to the science of climatology. As far as I can tell, there has actually been reduced funding for existing climate research. That may seem paradoxical, but, at least in the United States, the vastly increased number of scientists and others involving themselves in climate as well as the gigantic programs attaching themselves to climate have substantially outstripped the increases in funding. Perhaps more important are the pressures being brought to bear on scientists to get the "right" results. Such pressures are inevitable, given how far out on a limb much of the scientific community has gone. The situation is compounded by the fact that some of the strongest proponents of "global warming" in Congress are also among the major supporters of science (Sen. Gore is notable among those). Finally, given the momentum that has been building up among so many interest groups to fight "global warming," it becomes downright embarrassing to support basic climate research. After all, one would hate to admit that one had mobilized so many resources without the basic science's being in place. Nevertheless, given the large increase in the number of people associating themselves with climatology and the dependence of much of that community on the perceived threat of warming, it seems unlikely that the scientific community will offer much resistance. I should add that as ever greater numbers of individuals attach themselves to the warming problem, the pressures against solving the problem grow proportionally; an inordinate number of individuals and groups depend on the problem's remaining.

In addition to climatologists, are there other groups that are at risk? Here, one might expect that industry could be vulnerable, and, indeed, it may be. At least in the United States, however, industries seem to be primarily concerned with improving their public image, often by supporting environmental activists. Moreover, some industries have become successful at profiting from environmental regulation. The most obvious example is the waste management industry. Even electric utility companies have been able to use environmental measures to increase the base on which their regulated profits are calculated. It is worth noting that about 1.7 trillion dollars have been spent on the environment over the past decade. The environment, itself, qualifies as one of our major industries.

If Wildavsky's scenario is correct, the major losers would be ordinary people. Wealth that could have been used to raise living standards in much of the world would be squandered. Living standards in the developed world would decrease. Regulatory apparatuses would restrict individual freedom on an unprecedented scale. Here too, however, one cannot expect much resistance to proposed actions—at least not initially. Public perceptions, under the influence of extensive, deceptive, and one-sided publicity, can become disconnected from reality. For example, Alabama has had a pronounced cooling trend since 1935. Nevertheless, a poll among professionals in Alabama found that about 95 percent

If Wildavsky's scenario is correct, the major losers would be ordinary people.

of the participants believed that the climate had been warming over the past fifty years and that the warming was due to the greenhouse effect. Public misperceptions coupled with a sincere desire to "save the planet" can force political action even when politicians are aware of the reality.

What the above amounts to is a societal instability. At a particular point in history, a relatively minor suggestion or event serves to mobilize massive interests. While the proposed measures may be detrimental, resistance is largely absent or coopted. In the case of climate change, the probability that the proposed regulatory actions would for the most part have little impact on climate, regardless of the scenario chosen, appears to be of no consequence.

Modelling and Societal Instability

Even supercomputers are inadequate to allow long-term integrations of the relevant equations at adequate spatial resolutions.

So far I have emphasized the political elements in the current climate hysteria. There can be no question, however, that scientists are abetting this situation. Concerns about funding have already been mentioned. There is, however, another perhaps more important element to the scientific support. The existence of modern computing power has led to innumerable modelling efforts in many fields. Supercomputers have allowed us to consider the behavior of systems seemingly too complex for other approaches. One of those systems is climate. Not surprisingly, there are many problems involved in modelling climate. For example, even supercomputers are inadequate to allow long-term integrations of the relevant equations at adequate spatial resolutions. At presently available resolutions, it is unlikely that the computer solutions are close to the solutions of the underlying equations. In addition, the physics of unresolved phenomena such as clouds and other turbulent elements is not understood to the extent needed for incorporation into models. In view of those problems, it is generally recognized that models are at present experimental tools whose relation to the real world is questionable.

While there is nothing wrong in using those models in an experimental mode, there is a real dilemma when they predict potentially dangerous situations. Should scientists publicize such predictions since the models are almost certainly wrong? Is it proper to not publicize the predictions if the predicted danger is serious? How is the public to respond to such predictions? The difficulty would be diminished if the public understood how poor the models actually are. Unfortunately, there is a tendency to hold in awe anything that emerges from a sufficiently large computer. There is also a reluctance on the part of many modelers to admit to the experimental nature of their models lest public support for their efforts diminish. Nevertheless, with poor and uncertain models in wide use, predictions of ominous situations are virtually inevitable— regardless of reality.

Such weak predictions feed and contribute to what I have already described as a societal instability that can cascade the most questionable suggestions of danger into major political responses with massive economic and social consequences. I have already discussed some of the reasons for this instability: the existence of large cadres of professional planners looking for work, the existence of advocacy groups looking for profitable causes, the existence of agendas in search of saleable rationales, and the ability of many industries to profit from regulation, coupled with an effective neutralization of opposition. It goes almost without saying that the dangers and costs of those economic and social consequences may be far greater than the original environmental danger. That becomes especially true when the benefits of additional knowledge are rejected and when it is forgotten that improved technology and increased societal wealth are what allow society to deal with environmental threats most effectively. The control of societal instability may very well be the real challenge facing us.

A Dying Planet? How the Media Have Scared the Public[3]

The air is polluted, the rivers and lakes are dying, and the ozone layer has holes in it.
(Ann Landers)

Most environmental, economic and social problems of local, regional, and global scale arise from this driving force: too many people using too many resources at too fast a rate.
(Blue Planet Group)

ACCORDING TO a CBS News Survey before Earth Day 1990, "The American public has an almost doomsday feeling about the national seriousness of environmental problems." The press, environmental organizations, and the public say that pollution in the United States and the world is not just bad, but getting worse.

One could cite prominent scientists, politicians of every stripe, and religious leaders of every denomination. In 1991, the nation's Roman Catholic bishops "acknowledged that overpopulation drains world resources." They asked Catholics "to examine our lifestyles, behaviors and policies, to see how we contribute to the destruction or neglect of the environment." Even the Pope issued a 1988 encyclical "In Sollicitude Rei Socialis" and a 1990 New Year's message on this theme of environmental "crisis" and "plundering of natural resources," and "the reality of an innumerable multitude of people." Luckily, the Pope apparently has "gotten religion" and turned back since then.

The environmentalist ideal has suffused the Jewish community, too. Consider a "Consultation on the Environment and Jewish Life" in Washington, intended as "a Jewish communal response to the world environmental crisis." The italicized second paragraph of that invitation letter says: "We appreciate the many important issues on the Jewish communal agenda. But the threat of ecological catastrophe is so frightening and universal that we believe we must mobilize our community's considerable intellectual and organizational resources as soon as possible." The signers of the invitation included just about every big name in the organized Jewish community.

Even grammar-school texts and children's books fill young minds with unsupported assertions that mankind is a destroyer rather than a creator of the environment. A couple of decades ago, parents and schools began to present chil-

3. Article by Julian Simon. From *The Ultimate Resource 2*. Copyright © 1996 Princeton University Press. Reprinted with permission.

dren with material like this from Golden Stamp Book of *Earth and Ecology.*

Our Dirty Air—The sea of air in which we live—our sky—is no longer sparkling clean. Once the smoke from chimneys was whisked away by winds and soon became lost in a clear sky. Then we believed that the sky could hold all the wastes we could pour into it. By some sort of miracle, we thought, the sky kept itself clean.

Now there are too many chimneys pouring smoke, ashes, and poisonous fumes into our sky. Where the land has been scoured of grass and forests and there are no crops planted to hold the soil, the slightest breeze whips up choking clouds of dust that spill the dirt into the air. Hour after hour, fumes from millions of automobiles' exhausts are spewed into the air....

In many large cities, there are no clear days at all now. Over portions of the earth, there is a haze, darkest where the population is greatest. Each year air pollution becomes worse as we dump greater loads into the sky.

Yet, this is the air we must breathe to live. You can survive for days or even weeks without food, but without air, you will die in only a few minutes. Right now you are probably breathing polluted air. It is air containing poisons. Some of these poisons are kinds that do not kill immediately. They take their toll over the years, and more and more people are becoming victims of respiratory ailments. . . .

"No more Clean Waters—Once the United States was a land of pure, sparkling waters. . . . But in the few hundred years since America's discovery, its waters have been almost totally spoiled by pollution. The greatest damage has come in very recent years.

Still, the people in many cities must drink the water from these lakes and rivers. They make it drinkable by loading it with purifying chemicals. But the chemicals make the water taste bad. There is also a point at which the chemicals used to purify water become poisonous to people, too.

Streams in the United States have indeed become open sewers carrying away wastes from industries and dwellings. The wastes are really only moved downstream to the next town or city, where more wastes are added, until the pure stream becomes little more than a sluggish stench.

Now Lake Erie is dead—killed by pollution.

Lake Michigan may be the next of the Great Lakes to be killed by man. Even sooner, a much larger body of water appears to be doomed-the giant Gulf of Mexico!

National Wildlife Magazine Judgments about Environmental Quality

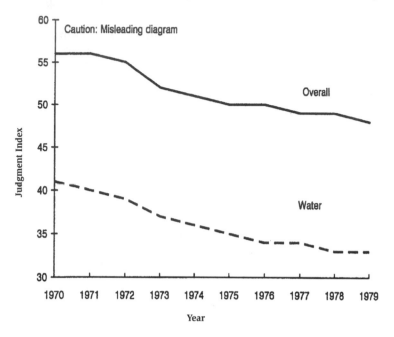

By now we have reached the stage that *50 Simple Things Kids Can Do to Save the Earth* has sold almost a million copies (this book retails meaningless and false information to kids-for example, instructing them to use water-based instead of oil-based paint); *This Planet Is Mine* is another best-seller in this new genre. It is a sign of the times that "more Pennsylvania high school students are taking environmental education classes than physics."

The schools' teachings are having a powerful effect. The consensus view of an informal *Fortune* survey of high-schoolers on this "issue on which almost everyone agreed" was "If we continue at the pace we're going at now, the environment is going to be destroyed completely" A 1992 poll found that 47 percent of a sample of 17 year olds said that "Environment' is among the "biggest problems in our country these days"; 12 percent mentioned "Economy" as a distant runner-up. Compare the almost opposite results by their parents: 13 percent "Environment" versus 56 percent "Economy."

Just about all of these assertions of rising pollution are nonsense, as we shall see—but they are dangerous nonsense.

A revealing sequence of events:

From 1970 to 1984, the widely reported Environmental Quality Index of the National Wildlife Federation gave numbers purporting to show that environmental conditions were getting worse, as seen in [the figure above]. In a typical year, *the New York Times* headline for the Index was "Environmental quality Held Down," and the story began, "The nation's overall environmental well-being declined slightly in 1976. . . ."

Despite the impressive name of the index and its numerical nature, it was, according to the National Wildlife Federation, which prepares and disseminates it, "a subjective analysis [that] represent[s] [the] collective thinking of the editors of the National Wildlife Federation Staff." That is, the Environmental Quality Index represented casual observation and opinion rather than statistical facts. It included such subjective judgments as that the trend of "living space" is "down . . . vast stretches of America are lost to development yearly." In 1984, as it got harder and harder to reconcile the real facts and the foolish numbers, National Wildlife dropped the numbers and retreated to words only, which are less easy to confute and make ridiculous with the actual data. I hope that my criticism in the first edition helped sink the numerical index by making it seem ridiculous. Several types of public opinion polls confirm the above anecdotal evidence of rising public concern:

1 People's answers to poll questions about whether environmental conditions have been getting better or worse during (say) the past twenty years show that many more people believe that there has been deterioration than believe that there has been improvement. A 1988 survey found that eight in ten Americans (81 percent) were convinced that "the environment today is less healthful than the environment in which my parents lived." In 1990, 64 percent said that pollution increased in the past ten years, and 13 percent said it decreased. Another 1990 poll found that when asked, "Compared to twenty years ago, do you think the air you breathe is cleaner today or more polluted?" 6 percent said cleaner and 75 percent said "more polluted." With respect to the "water in the lakes, rivers, and streams," 8 percent said "cleaner" and 80 percent said "more polluted," but these polls were taken in the midst of the Earth Day publicity. In 1991, 66 percent of Americans responded "Worse" to "Overall, do you feel the environment has gotten better; gotten worse, or stayed the same over the past 20 years?" and only 20 percent said "better."

2. The trends in proportions of people expressing worry about pollution problems show large increases over recent years. In Harris polls (a) the proportion who said that air pollution by vehicles was "very serious" rose from 33 percent in 1982 to 59 percent in 1990; (b) the proportion who said that "Air pollution from acid rain, caused by sulfur dioxide emissions in power plants" was "very serious" rose from 42 percent in 1986 to 64 percent in 1990; (c) there was an increase from 30 percent in 1986 to 49 percent in 1990 saying "very serious" for "Air pollution by coal-burning electric power plants." (However, a 1991 Roper poll found that people thought that the environment would be cleaner five years

hence than at the poll date, unlike a similar comparison in 1980. And people's assessment of the environment "At the present time" was less positive in 1991 than in 1980.

3. People expect worsening. In 1990, 44 percent said they "Expect pollution to increase," and 33 percent expected decrease."

4. A survey of high school students found that "the only interviews who didn't share the perspective . . . that the environment is going to be destroyed completely . . . were the worst educated of the inner-city youth." . . . It is consistent with the fact that such powerful abstract thinkers as Bertrand Russell, John Maynard Keynes (who wrote a famous book on statistical logic in addition to his work in economics), and several Nobel prize winners in mathematical economics such as Paul Samuelson, Wassily Leontief, and Jan Tinbergen arrived at exactly the same wrong conclusions as did Malthus about the effect of population growth on food and natural resource supplies. In this subject one will arrive at sound understanding and predictions only if one pays much attention to historical experience and does not allow oneself to be carried away by elegant deductive and mathematical constructions such as exponential growth in a finite system. Education in large quantities would seem to increase one's propensity to rely on such abstractions. (I hope to write more on the nature of the thinking involved in these subjects in a coming book.)

One might wonder whether less-well-educated persons are less responsive to environmental issues simply because they know less. But surveys that ask whether "pollution increased in the past ten years," or "decreased," or "stayed about the same" show that answers are not related to amount of education (The only striking difference is that females were more likely than males to say "increased" and less likely to say "decreased"—72 percent versus 56 percent and 8 percent versus 19 percent, respectively. There also was a slight gradient downward in "increased with older groups."

Consider this important piece of conflicting evidence, however: When asked about the environmental conditions in their own area—whose conditions they know personally—as well as conditions in the country as a whole, respondents rate the local environment more highly and indicate a much lower degree of worry about it than about the environment in the country as a whole. When asked before Earth Day 1990 whether pollution is "a serious problem that's getting worse" for "the country as a whole," 84 percent said "serious," but with respect to "the area where you live," only 42 percent said "serious." As the *Compendium of American Opinion* put it, "Americans are primarily concerned about the environment in the abstract . . . most Americans are not worried about environmental problems where they live . . . most Americans do not feel personally affected by environmental problems." In this instance, people feel that the grass is greener on *his* or *her* side of the street—or more precisely that the grass is browner on the other person's side of the street which the comparer has never even seen. This cuts the logical ground out in under the abstract aggregate judgments, because they are not consistent with the sum of the individual judgments.

That is, there is a distinction between public belief and . . . scientifically established facts . . . The discrepancy between the public's beliefs about the environment that they *first-hand*, and about the areas that they only know *second-hand*, is most revealing. The respondents view the situation they know first-hand more positively than the situation at large. The only likely explanation is that newspapers and television—the main source of notions about matters which people do not experience directly-are systematically misleading the public, even if unintentionally. There is also a vicious circle here: The media carry stories about environmental scares, people become frightened, polls then reveal their worry and the worry then is cited as support for policies to initiate actions about the supposed scares, which then raise the level of public concern. The media proudly say "We do not create the 'news,' we are merely messengers who deliver it." These data show that the opposite is true in this case.

. . . Pollution was no worse in 1970 than in 1965, but the proportion of the population that named it one of the three most important governmental problems rose from 17 percent in 1965 to 53 percent in 1970 (and fell thereafter), marking the media attention to the 1970 Earth Day. Erskine, a long-time student of public opinion, labeled this 'a miracle of public opinion,' referring to the 'unprecedented speed and fluency with which ecological issue have burst into American consciousness.'"

These data show the speed with which public opinion can change—or really, be changed, because here there is no possibility that the actual conditions changed radically (and indeed, if they changed, if was for the better, as we shall see).

A very strange poll result emerged from a November 1993 poll conducted by the *Los Angeles Times*. Various groups of elites, and the general public, were asked, "I'm going to read you a list of dangers in the world and after I finish, tell me which one of them you think is most dangerous to world stability." Eighteen percent of the public responded "environmental pollution" and 10 percent, "population growth." But of the "science and engineering" members of the National Academy of Sciences, only 1 percent said "environmental pollution"—but an extraordinary 51 percent said "population growth." (The latter is not a typographical error; the percentages add to 100.) The only explanation I can guess at is that many of those NAS members are biologists, whose attitudes

Consider this question and the answers to it over just five years:
Compared to other parts of the country how serious, in your opinion, do you think the problem of air/water pollution is in this area—very serious, somewhat serious, or not very serious?

Very Serious or Somewhat Serious

Year	Air	Water
1965	28%	35%
1966	48%	49%
1967	53%	57%

toward population growth have long tended to be very negative. (In passing, notice how population growth is simply
assumed in the poll to be a danger, which biases the results,
of course.) . . .

Summary

The public believes that pollution in the United States is
bad, and has been getting worse. These beliefs can be seen
to be connected to writings in the press and statements on
television. The poll results showing popular belief that pollution at large is bad are logically contradicted and thereby
undermined by poll results showing that what respondents
know best-conditions in their own areas—are reported as
much better than conditions in the nation at large.

Coverage of Pollution Issues in Newspapers and Magazines

 — · — Number of air pollution reports and articles in The Times (of London)

 —— Number of pollution articles in eight American mass circulation magazines

----- Number (scale x 20) of air pollution articles in Toronto newspapers

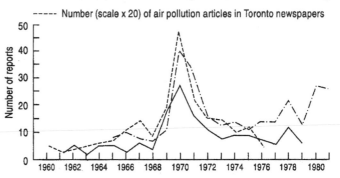

Impacts of a Projected Depletion of the Ozone Layer[4]

Life on Earth depends in part on a thin shell of gaseous ozone that stretches from about 10 to 25 miles above our heads, encompassing the planet like an invisible, protective shield. At this altitude, it lies well above the height at which normal commercial aircraft fly, and far beneath the orbital paths of spacecraft. The ozone layer is the main barrier between us and the hazardous ultraviolet radiation that streams toward the Earth, day in and day out, from the burning surface of the Sun. Ozone—a form of oxygen—is selective in what it takes from sunlight: screening out, through a process of atomic absorption, only the more energetic ultraviolet rays while allowing the visible light and the warm infrared to pass through, untouched.

A HISTORY OF OZONE

Oxygen itself came into the Earth's atmosphere some two billion years ago as a product of photosynthesis in early forms of plant life. It is now an ever-present component of the air, from the surface of the Earth to the outer reaches of the atmosphere. Toward the top, in the rarefied upper atmosphere, the stream of highly energetic ultraviolet (UV) radiation from the Sun impinges on molecules of ordinary oxygen (O_2), splitting them into the two atoms (O) of which they are made. In a perpetual dance the molecules and atoms of oxygen swirl together to form ozone (O_3), which reverts in time to more stable O_2 molecules. Only to be hit and split apart again. Through this delicate balance a stratospheric ozone layer is maintained. At any time, however, very little ozone is there: enough to form a layer a mere 3 mm (a tenth of an inch) in thickness were it compressed under the conditions that exist at ground level.

The part of the UV spectrum of solar radiation that splits O_2 apart in the upper atmosphere lies in what is shown as the highly energetic "ultraviolet-C" or UVC range. The ozone that is subsequently created is itself a strong absorber of the remaining UVC and of much of the adjacent region of the UV, closer in wavelength to visible light, that is called the ultraviolet-B or UVB. Sandwiched between the UVB and the violet end of the visible spectrum is the less energetic UVA.

Atmospheric oxygen screens out all of the short wave UVC; the ozone layer—thin as it is—prevents longer wave UVC and most of the solar UVB radiation from reaching the Earth's surface. This is highly beneficial, for UVC and short

---

4. Article by Frank R. de Grujil from *Consequences* vol. 1, no. 2. Reprinted with permission.

wave UVB radiations blocked by ozone are particularly damaging to organisms, because these wavelengths are absorbed in living matter by essential molecules, such as DNA, and damage them. Thus, by a magnificent coincidence the biosphere has created its own protective, atmospheric UV filter under which life could evolve and exist on the surface of the planet.

Human intervention and response

In the 1930s commercial laboratories developed compounds of chlorine, fluorine and carbon (called chlorofluorocarbons, or CFCs) and similar bromine-related compounds as convenient, non-corroding, non-toxic and non-flammable gases which subsequently found a wide range of industrial applications, including everyday use in spray cans, refrigerators and air conditioners. In a sense, these fruits of human ingenuity turned out to be too good: by design these so-called *halocarbon* gases are so stable that they react with almost nothing—until, that is, they slowly rise into the sky: climbing high enough, after a period of years, to be hit by direct UV radiation from the Sun. They then break apart and release chlorine or bromine which can react with the ozone that is there, pushing the delicate balance of natural photochemical reactions in the direction of ozone destruction. Thus, the ozone layer—an evolutionary heritage of a billion years of time—has come under serious threat in but the last few decades of industrial activity.

The ozone layer—an evolutionary heritage of a billion years of time—has come under serious threat in but the last few decades of industrial activity.

This startling realization came to light in 1974, based on the laboratory work of Sherwood Rowland and Mario Molina. By then the wheels had been already set in motion for the gradual deterioration of the protective ozone layer. Industry—the world's only source of halocarbon gases—was from a business point of view understandably reluctant to immediately halt production and use of these versatile compounds; nor were there any immediate replacements available. Corrective action awaited wider attention and momentum in public and political arenas. The threat of ozone-depleting gases needed to be substantiated further, and possible adverse effects needed to be weighed against the practical costs of reducing or stopping production. In the process, industry began to capitalize on the growing public concern by producing "ozone friendly" spray cans.

Computer models of atmospheric circulation and chemistry subsequently confirmed the threat of ozone depletion by these compounds, yielding more quantitative estimates of ozone reduction which were continually refined. But although it was well established that UV radiation damages proteins and DNA, very little was known of the actual severity and scale of effects under even natural levels of UV radiation. Forecasting the consequences of increases in ambient UV radiation thus became a formidable task.

The one exception appeared to be the expected increase in skin cancer in light-skinned people. Here increased incidence could be estimated quantitatively, based on higher levels of UVB, and these estimates were also refined by subsequent research. Figures regarding skin cancer and the concern about other potentially grave impacts proved daunting enough to initiate actions to limit the commercial production of CFCs and other ozone-depleting substances.

Something the atmospheric models had not forecast was the dramatic, early springtime depletion of stratospheric ozone over the South Pole of the Earth, later termed the "ozone hole," that was discovered almost through accident in routine measurements taken in Antarctica. Further measurements established that the phenomenon was the result of increased amounts of chlorine in the stratosphere in its most reactive form, intensified by the unique circulation of air near the Earth's poles and the presence of ice crystals in the peculiar stratospheric polar clouds. It was as though Mother Nature were performing a little experiment, in her basement, to emphasize that the consequences of adding chlorine in the ozone layer was not a figment of scientific imagination, and that an anthropogenic increase in gaseous chlorine compounds was not a good idea. This finding brought a sense of urgency to policy makers, and measures were repeatedly stepped up to phase out the production of CFCs and other ozone degrading substances, through a series of unprecedented international protocols in 1987, 1990, and 1992.

CHANGES IN ATMOSPHERIC OZONE

The thin layer of ozone that surrounds the Earth is neither uniform nor constant. It is naturally thinner at the equator than over the poles, and it exhibits substantial temporal variations—as much as +/-20% at any place, as a result of changing solar intensity and atmospheric circulation. These natural variations can mask any subtle, long-term changes in ozone concentrations, making it necessary, if global trends are sought, to carry out an extended series of reliable measurements that cover all of the Earth.

Spaceborne and other measurements have documented downward trends in stratospheric ozone which are greatest in winter and early spring and strongest in polar regions—especially in the Southern hemisphere. Globally averaged losses have totaled about 5% since the late 1960s. Although the rate of loss has now been slowed, total ozone is expected to continue to drop through the present decade, when the decrease at mid latitudes in the Northern hemisphere in summer and fall should maximize at 6 to 7%. A reduction in ozone of this amount would correspond to a resulting 6 to 12% increase in the average annual dose of biologically-harmful UV radiation. In addition to increases in annual UV dosage, transient depletions in ozone in the spring may cause invisible "UV storms" which could prove particularly harmful to vulnerable young plants and animals in very early developmental stages, such as fish in shallow water. A striking finding was that in the vicinity of the Antarctic ozone hole (64° South latitude) the DNA-damaging UV radiation can exceed the summertime maximum at San Diego (32° N) where because of the lower latitude, the Sun climbs higher in the sky and there is less atmospheric absorption.

Natural events can also affect the pace at which chlorine depletes ozone. Relatively low levels of global ozone documented by satellite measurements during 1992 and 1993 may have been related to the June 1991 eruption of Mt. Pinatubo in the Philippines. The volcanic eruption introduced clouds of dust particles into the stratosphere, thereby enhancing the chemical destruction of ozone by chlorine. In 1994, ozone amounts measured in the stratosphere were relatively normal. In January 1995, however, levels in the northern hemisphere dropped again by 10 to 25%: a change that cannot be attributed to volcanoes. On the whole, one has to be careful and not attach too much weight to ozone levels at any particular time at any particular location, because the ozone layer as a component of the atmosphere has an inherently chaotic behavior. Of greater import are trends in large scale averages of ozone levels over long periods of time.

The same ozone that is "good up there" can be "bad down here."

Good and bad ozone

Ozone is also found in the air near the ground but in amounts that are highly variable from place to place and that constitute at most a tenth of what exists in the stratosphere. In polluted areas, especially where there are high levels of nitrogen oxide in the air—as in congested traffic zones—the residual solar UVB radiation that reaches ground level can cause increased levels of ozone, which is a major constituent of photochemical smog. As in the stratosphere there is a give and take between the production of ozone by the UVB in sunlight and the blocking of the same UV by the ozone itself, and by the sulfur dioxide that is also prevalent in polluted air. Direct exposure to ozone is known to be harmful, and dramatically so in photochemical smog: it causes respiratory complaints and can seriously exacerbate asthma. It is also damaging to plants, as can sometimes be seen in trees that bound busy freeways. Hence, the same ozone that is "good up there" can be "bad down here." Moreover, an ozone depletion in the stratosphere will lead to an increase in the "bad ozone down here" in polluted areas because of the extra UVB radiation that will reach the ground to create it.

Even with full compliance with the now internationally agreed phase-out of ozone-degrading chemicals such as CFCs, the Earth's stratospheric ozone layer is expected to continue to decline, reaching maximum depletion around the turn of the century, and then gradually return to 1970 levels in about 50 years' time. During this period the biosphere will be exposed to higher levels of harmful UV radiation.

EFFECTS ON HUMAN HEALTH

Although the ozone layer blocks most of the damaging UVB radiation received from the Sun, a small amount slips by, damaging our skin in the form of sunburns and "suntans." UVB radiation is strongly absorbed in the skin and in the outer layers of the eye, and does not penetrate any deeper into the human body.

Like most organisms exposed to sunlight, the human skin has developed various defense mechanisms against the damaging effects of UV radiation. The skin adapts to increased exposure to UV by thickening its outer layer (the *epidermis*) and by developing pigmentation that serves to shade the more vulnerable and deeper residing dividing cells. Molecular damage is dealt with in the body through repair or replacement. Overly damaged cells will normally self destruct through a process called *apoptosis*, and if this fails, the immune system should get rid of any resulting aberrant cells. As explained below, it is when these natural safeguards fail or are overcome that real trouble can ensue.

Quite apart from its damaging effects, UVB radiation can also be beneficial: in the skin it initiates the production of vitamin D3 that helps build and maintain our bones. Very little UVB radiation is needed for this purpose, however, and the process of production is self limiting.

Damage to the eyes

The human eye is less well protected by internal safeguards than the skin, but it is also less exposed thanks to the shielding provided by the brow and eye lids. Under certain circumstances, such as bright reflection from snow-covered ground, the surface of the eyeball can develop a painful "snow blindness" (or *photokeratu-conjunctivitis*). One such episode is, however, usually sufficient for people to take precautions the next time.

Long-term damage to the eyes by UV radiation is more difficult to prevent because there is no feeling of pain or early warning. People usually become aware of the effect when it is too late. Chronic UV exposure can cause *pterygium* (an outgrowth on the most superficial cell layer of the eyeball) and climatic droplet *keratopathy* (a degeneration of the fibrous layer that covers the lens); both afflictions can reduce clarity of vision and even cause blindness. *Cortical cataracts*—one of several forms of the cataracts that cloud the lens of the eye—can also result from UV radiation.

A lack of firm knowledge regarding wavelength and UV dose dependencies make it difficult to estimate the impact of an ozone depletion on any of these long term ocular effects,

UVB radiation is strongly absorbed in the skin and in the outer layers of the eye, and does not penetrate any deeper into the human body.

beyond a tentative estimate of about a 0.5% increase in cataract incidence for every persistent 1% decrease in average ozone concentration. Thus, based on the estimated 6-7% total drop in ozone during summertime, as noted above, the incidence of cataracts might be expected to rise by up to 3% in the early part of the next century.

Skin cancer

As mentioned earlier, UV radiation damages DNA, the molecule that builds the genes that in turn carry the genetic information used by the cell to build up the proteins it needs for its normal functions. After a sunny day on the beach a single, typical exposed cell in the epidermis has developed some 100,000 to 1,000,000 damaged sites in its DNA. In spite of a formidable DNA repair system, some damage may persist, resulting in faulty replication of DNA in a daughter cell. In some instances, a series of such events may cause certain crucial genes (called *oncogenes* and tumor-suppressor genes) to malfunction, in which case a cell is altered, causing it to grow independently into a tumor or cancer. Recent research is beginning to unravel these steps in more detail.

Non-melanoma skin cancer (mainly *squamous* and *basal cell carcinomas*) is among the most frequently diagnosed and most rapidly rising forms of cancer in white populations; in the U.S. alone, about 600,000 cases are diagnosed each year, twice as often in men than in women. Only about 1% of these skin tumors prove lethal: because of their moderate growth rate and early detection (though small, they are cosmetically apparent as red nodules or blotches) they are well treatable. At the same time, adequate treatment can result in mutilation of the skin or of facial features where they are often found.

The connection between non-melanoma skin cancer and exposure to the Sun is well established from both epidemiological data and from experiments with laboratory animals, in which chiefly squamous cell carcinomas have been induced. The types of alterations found in recent studies of the "p53" tumor suppressor gene in human non-melanoma skin cancers clearly identify UV radiation as the cause. Moreover, it has long been known that people with *xeroderma pigmentosum* (a rare disease that impairs the ability of cells to repair DNA damage induced by UVB radiation) run a 1,000 times higher risk of skin cancer than healthy people.

Such causal relationships are further confirmed by experimentally UV-induced skin cancers in mice. Based on the plausible assumption that the UV-cancer forming processes are basically the same in mice and men, and by combining animal and epidemiological data, quantitative estimates can be made of the consequences of an ozone depletion: the incidence of non-melanoma skin cancer is expected to increase by approximately 2% for every persistent 1% loss in average ozone concentration.

For the U.S. the reduction in ozone—down to as much as -7% in summertime by the end of the century—is expected to result in a steady increase in non-melanoma cancers in ensuing years. By mid-century incidence could rise to as many as 100,000 extra cases per year, when compared to the 1960s. Accumulated over the next century the overall effect of the temporary ozone dip may total 3 to 5 million additional cases in the U.S., and a further delay in the return to 1960 levels of ozone can increase this number substantially. Based on present epidemiological data, the increases would be found most in lower latitudes where the Sun is higher in the sky and where there are more sunny days, as in the American Southwest and Florida. Globally the highest incidence of all forms of skin cancer is found among red-haired and fair-skinned people who have immigrated from more overcast regions of northern Europe to sunnier and lower-latitude Australia.

It is almost impossible to detect the initial increase in non-melanoma skin cancer that might be attributed to the slight decline in ozone over the last decades, because of the incomplete manner in which incidence is customarily reported. Another difficulty in detecting an ozone-related change is the background against which it must be measured: there has been a steep increase in skin cancer, almost worldwide, in the last few decades—most likely due in large part to societal trends in dress and work habits and in the sun-seeking behavior of many modern people. These trends (and the use of sun-tanning parlors) amount to a voluntary increase in risk for those involved, and campaigns have been launched to counter them. An ozone reduction, on the other hand, imposes a population-wide involuntary increase in risk.

Melanoma

In the mid-1980s the relationship between solar UV radiation and skin cancer of the pigment cells (or melanocytes), known as *melanoma*, was still heavily debated, in part because these more serious cancers are not limited to parts of the body that are the more exposed to direct sunlight. However, epidemiological data from the last decade have substantiated a relationship with solar exposure, and animal experiments have shown that UV radiation can at the very least enhance the development of these more lethal tumors. Although the incidence of melanoma is much lower than that of non-melanoma skin cancer (about 17,000 males and 12,000 females are now diagnosed each year with melanomas in the U.S.), the mortality is much higher, amounting to about 20% of all cases diagnosed.

Interviews with melanoma patients and healthy people have suggested that the risk of melanoma may be related to a history of sporadic over-exposure to UV radiation. Epidemiological studies (and particularly those involving migration) have further demonstrated the particularly insidious relationship between high exposure to the Sun during childhood and a dramatic increase in risk of melanoma skin cancer later in life. Exposure to high levels of UV radiation as a child is also associated with the later development of large numbers of moles, which in the form of *dysplastic nevi* may sometimes be rather large, very irregularly shaped and pigmented, and reddish due to a higher blood content; a large number of moles (typically over 50 that are more than 2 mm or a tenth of an inch in diameter) is a well established risk factor for melanoma skin cancer.

As yet, however, it is still not possible to produce confident quantitative estimates of the impact of an ozone depletion on the incidence of melanoma. Experiments with laboratory animals have yielded ambiguous information on even the part of the UV that is responsible: a test with opossums, for example, indicates that UVB-induced DNA damage is important, whereas one with fish has shown that solar UVB radiation could be less important than the more prevalent and weaker radiation in the UVA region of the spectrum. Were UVA radiation, acting independently of UVB radiation, to prove the primary cause of melanoma in humans, a reduction in atmospheric ozone would have very little impact, since ozone—though effective in blocking the UVB—is almost transparent to the UVA.

It is still not possible to produce confident quantitative estimates of the impact of an ozone depletion on the incidence of melanoma.

Immunological effects

Laboratory experiments have established that a skin tumor removed from a mouse that was chronically exposed to UVB will usually be rejected when the tumor is implanted in a genetically identical mouse that was not subjected to UV radiation. After a series of UVB exposures, however, the second mouse will accept the implanted tumor cells and allow the tumor to grow, well in advance of any subsequent UVB-induced tumors. The obvious conclusion is that exposure to UVB takes away the animal's natural ability to fight off these cancers of the skin. The tumor implants are also accepted when the immune system of the mouse is generally suppressed. In analogy, it has been found in humans that patients on immunosuppressive medication for kidney transplants run a dramatically increased risk of cancer in sun-exposed skin.

Further experiments showed that a prior series of UVB exposures can block attempts to immunize a laboratory animal to react against a foreign compound or infectious agent put in contact with its skin. As is the case for the UV-induced skin tumors, the animal may then develop a particular susceptibility to skin infections from such compounds. While the mechanisms responsible for this kind of selective lack of response to immunization are as yet not clear, the significant finding from animal experiments is that natural immunity to various kinds of infectious diseases is weakened by UVB radiation, including, in some studies, oral infections that do not involve the skin. A special concern is that UVB radiation may also lower the effectiveness of preventive vaccinations, as, for example, against tetanus.

It has also been shown that UV radiation can suppress immune reactions in humans, including blacks, although chiefly through a transient inability to immunize through the part of the skin that was exposed. In 10 to 30% of the cases, however, the immunity failure was not transient. In these instances the subject became lastingly *immuno-tolerant*, in the sense of being incapable, following a series of UV exposure sufficient to cause mild to notable sunburn, of mounting an adequate immune response against the particular compound with which the trial immunization was carried out. Interestingly, the trait to develop a UV-induced immunotolerance appeared to be particularly prevalent among people who had had skin cancers removed. These and other experiments have established that our natural immune system is affected by UV radiation at dosages experienced by many people today; data from other animals have proven that there is a genuine risk for increased severity of infections.

As yet there is no information from medical research on the present impact of ambient UV radiation on infectious diseases and vaccination programs. Acquiring the necessary epidemiological data is no easy task; still, its complete lack should be embarrassing when one considers the potential scale of the impact on people worldwide and the fact that for over a decade such studies have been identified as of high priority among needed research on the effects of an ozone depletion. Today even the crudest quantitative estimates of effects of an ozone depletion on infections and vaccinations seem still a long way off.

IMPACTS ON ECOSYSTEMS

All animals and plants and other organisms that are exposed to the Sun, though well shielded by the ozone layer, have developed ways to cope with and protect themselves from the small fraction of solar UVB radiation that normally reaches the Earth's surface. Even a small amount of UVB radiation can have a significant effect on ecosystems. In the tropics, for example, where a thinner ozone layer and a higher Sun result in systematically stronger UV dosage, certain trees have been found to be restricted in their growth by current levels of solar UV radiation. In ecosystem studies, as in medicine, science has not yet reached the point where any practically useful assessments of the consequences of increased dosages can be made. Research has thus far been mainly limited to more rudimentary studies in laboratories and greenhouses that test the sensitivity of different plant species to enhanced UV radiation. Only a few field investiga-

Even a small amount of UVB radiation can have a significant effect on ecosystems.

tions have been performed on an appreciable scale, and proper ecological studies are still in their infancy.

In general, it appears that plant species can react in widely different ways to increased levels of UVB radiation: some may be clearly limited in their growth; other varieties may be insensitive or rapidly become so by adaptive mechanisms; and still others may even exhibit enhanced growth. Under added stress, as through drought, the differences in UV sensitivity may be completely lost. The majority of plant species that have been tested were agricultural plants; trees appear to run a higher risk of accumulating UV damage over their far longer lifetimes.

In addition to direct effects on photosynthesis and growth, there may also occur more subtle changes, such as a delay in flowering, a shift in the distribution of leaves, a change in leaf structure, or a change in a plant's metabolism. As verified in field studies, such subtle changes may have far-reaching consequences by causing a plant to loose ground to neighboring plants with whom they compete. Thus, dramatic shifts in plant populations and in biodiversity may ensue.

These potentially significant disturbances at the basis of terrestrial and marine food webs may have a domino effect that could ultimately affect mankind.

Similar processes can occur in the marine ecosystems that exist at shallow depths in photosynthetically active zones. UV radiation can penetrate tens of meters into clear ocean water. It has been found that phytoplankton—the minuscule, plant-like organisms that float on or near the surface of the ocean and that serve as the base of the entire marine food chain—are sensitive to the levels of UVB radiation that penetrate the ocean's surface. Recent studies have focused particularly on the waters that bound the Antarctic continent, directly under the ozone hole, and rates of phytoplankton production were indeed found to be depressed relative to other similar areas.

These potentially significant disturbances at the basis of terrestrial and marine food webs may have a domino effect that could ultimately affect mankind. Moreover, loss of biodiversity due to enhanced UV radiation may render an ecosystem more vulnerable to the other stresses such as are expected to accompany greenhouse-induced climate change. Higher levels of UVB levels could also reduce the global plant cover that serves as a sink for CO_2, thus enhancing climatic change.

Unfortunately, at this time scientific research has produced only limited and widely varying data on possible impacts on single plants or species, and much remains to be done to quantify the possible effects on any marine, terrestrial, or agricultural ecosystem. Ecosystems may be further disturbed by deleterious effects of UV radiation on animals, especially in vulnerable, early stages of life such as larvae or the eggs of frogs in shallow water.

A PERSONAL VIEW

The integrity of the Earth's ozone layer has been a subject of concern for over 20 years. In the U.S. the issue was first raised in about 1970 by what seemed then to be the likely prospects of the intrusion of commercial fleets of supersonic jets (like today's Concorde) that would fly at higher altitudes than conventional aircraft and perturb the natural chemistry of the stratosphere. Later the greater threat of CFCs and bromine-related gases came into the limelight, in time resulting in the international agreements on production limits that now serve as an example of effective worldwide policy response to environmental threats.

As a result of actions taken, ozone-depleting gases in the atmosphere are increasing less rapidly and the ozone layer is probably degrading less rapidly. We should all be encouraged by the collective willingness to take protective measures with significant economic impacts, even in the face of uncertainty regarding the ultimate effects of what is to be avoided, and by the choice that was made to err on the environmentally safe side. Behind the actions taken in the Montreal Protocol of 1987 and the London and Copenhagen amendments of 1990 and 1992 were atmospheric models and atmospheric measurements, including specific campaigns to Antarctica and Greenland. In addition, many countries have in recent years started to monitor the ground-levels UV radiation. Behind all of these actions were perceived impacts on the biosphere, and on human health in particular. Yet we are still not very sure of what the effects would have been had we not phased out the production of these compounds.

Surprisingly little effort has been expended in studies of any of the potential *effects* when compared to that given to the *causes* of the loss of ozone. There are several reasons that may explain the imbalance, including the inherent difficulties in funding and accomplishing research that spans the chasms between physical, biological and medical science; the more instant gratification, on the part of policy makers, of regulatory action as compared to longer-term monitoring and research; and the dilemma—so common to the environmental concerns of today—of long-term problems in a short-term world.

The International Council of Scientific Unions has long sponsored a Scientific Committee on Problems of the Environment (SCOPE) which has emphasized in its recent reports that the impacts of an ozone depletion call for the full utilization of the existing capacities of research, and preferably a major expansion. The UNEP Panel on Environmental Effects of Ozone Depletion concludes in its 1994 report that present reality is far from the goal of defining impacts, and that funding of research on UVB effects is still very low and does not even allow full utilization of the existing research capacity. There may be added hope in a recent decision of the Environmental Research Programme of the European Union to stimulate and support UVB radiation-related environmental research. This may provide a basis for a growing, coherent and well-directed European research program on the effects of solar UV radiation on health and our environment, and serve as an example for other countries of the world.

To justify the initial action to curb ozone-depleting gases it has apparently been sufficient to bring forward and substantiate one or two seriously adverse effects, but full and in-depth knowledge of all effects is needed for a complete and well-balanced assessment, and especially, for subsequent adequate mitigating action. What is clearly needed now is a well-directed, long-term research program aimed at defining possible impacts on human health and on the environment which can provide policy makers with information that is today in very short supply. Hand in hand with such a program must go continued efforts to monitor compliance with the accords. The UNEP committee, pursuant to the Montreal protocol, has the task of providing regular updates (at least every 4 years) on the current knowledge regarding the effects of a depletion of stratospheric ozone, in order to provide the information needed to control the release of ozone degrading substances, and if necessary, to allow well-guided intervention schemes to mitigate the effects of the residual ozone depletion.

By even the most optimistic scenarios the adverse effects of UVB radiation due to residual ozone depletion will persist far into the next century.

The danger at this time is that policy makers and others involved with matters of the environment may come to believe that the existence of formal international agreements marks the end of the troubling subject of ozone layer protection, and with it all concerns regarding possible impacts. In fact, by even the most optimistic scenarios the adverse effects of UVB radiation due to residual ozone depletion will persist far into the next century.

CONCLUSION: A SUMMARY OF POTENTIAL HUMAN HEALTH IMPACTS

Any persistent drop in the amount of protective ozone resident in the stratosphere will increase the amount of solar ultraviolet radiation that reaches the surface of the Earth, at the risk of direct and deleterious effects on human health: that much is known with certainty. Likely effects include permanent clouding of the lens of the eye, which is particularly sensitive to the UVB exposure: a reduction of 7% in the amount of stratospheric ozone (the maximum expected in summer for middle latitudes by the end of the century) could increase the incidence of cataracts in sun-exposed people by 3 to 4%. Even more liable to damage is the sun-exposed skin, in the form of increased skin cancer. A total reduction of 7% in ozone in summertime would probably increase the incidence of non-melanoma skin cancer by about 16%. The incidence of more deadly melanoma could also rise. Chronic exposure to the increased UVB that would accompany any persistent loss in ozone would also affect the natural immune system, with an increased potential for infection and disease.

These changes and associated risks . . . serve as rough indications of what could follow in the course of the early part of the next century after the presently-projected maximum in man-made ozone depletion. If the ozone layer were indeed restored to a thickness characteristic of the 1960s, the risks to human health would also be reversed, although with a delay in time. On the other hand, were present ozone-protective measures to prove inadequate, the effects may persist and even reach appreciably higher levels.

Do We Still Need Nature? The Importance of Biological Diversity[5]

Our reliance on the Earth's non-renewable resources of oil and other fuel and non-fuel minerals is well understood by most people. Yet, when caught in the tide of technological advances that seem to dominate our everyday lives, we can easily forget the extent to which the modern, industrial world still depends on the biological world: on both the ecological systems that we have already learned to manage, such as farms and orchards, and on those we have not.

A fundamental property of ecological systems is a certain mixture, or *diversity* of living things: we cannot expect to find deer or ducks in the wild in the absence of the interconnected web of other plants and animals on which their lives depend. Biological diversity, or *biodiversity*, is a term that is now commonly used to describe the variety of living things and their relationships to each other and interactions with the environment.

The notion of biodiversity encompasses several different levels of biological organization, from the very specific to the most general. Perhaps the most basic is the variety of information contained in the genes of specific organisms, be they petunias or people. Different combinations of genes within organisms, or the existence of different variants of the same basic gene are the fundamental "stuff" of evolution. At the next level is the variety of different species that exist on the Earth: a concept that includes the relationship of different groups of species to each other. Biodiversity also describes the varied composition of ecosystems, and the variety of different sorts of ecosystems that are found in regions of study that biologists call *landscapes.*

It has been clear for some time that at all of these levels of organization the rich biodiversity that has always characterized the natural world is today declining. The extinctions or threatened extinctions of many species are but the most visible and well-known manifestation of a deeper and more far-reaching trend. What has been less obvious to many people are the potential consequences of these changes.

5. Article by Anthony C. Janetos from *Consequences* vol. 3, no. 1. Reprinted with permission.

OUR DEPENDENCE ON BIODIVERSITY

Our lives depend on biodiversity in ways that are not often appreciated. A case in point is agriculture. Society has learned a tremendous amount about techniques to maximize crop yields, both in temperate climates such as the grain belt of the U.S. and Canada, and in subtropical and tropical environments, where the "green revolution" that gained initial momentum in the 1960s vastly increased yields of rice and other crops. In both cases, the advances relied in part on biodiversity, and specifically on the availability of diverse strains of cereal grains capable of responding positively to heavier applications of fertilizer. The need continues, for we are still learning how to sustain tropical agriculture and to minimize adverse environmental impacts of fertilizers and pesticides while maintaining high yields, and how to sustain the highly-managed agro-ecosystems on which we more and more depend.

Much of today's world is also dependent on wild resources, of which the best known examples are probably marine fisheries. The industrial nations of the world support large and technologically-advanced fleets whose sole purpose is to harvest wild fish for human consumption, either directly or indirectly as fishmeal for fertilizers, cattle feed, and aquaculture. Averaged globally, people derive about 16 percent of their total animal protein from marine fisheries. Many developing nations also support a combination of open-ocean fishing industries and intensive coastal and local fisheries, upon which coastal populations depend both for food and for their economic livelihood. About a sixth of the world's population, much of it in the developing world, derives more than a third of their total protein from marine fisheries.

Our long-standing dependence on the natural world for wood is another example that is still much in evidence around the world. Only a small fraction of the timber that is cut in the U.S., for instance, is harvested from plantations: most is taken from natural forests that are not intensively managed. Worldwide, an even greater fraction comes from trees grown in the wild: by far the most important source is unmanaged or lightly managed forest stands. The use of wood for fuel, while of little consequence in technologically advanced countries like our own, is an abiding staple in many developing nations, and the twin demands for shelter and fuel have led to extensive deforestation in many parts of the world, such as Madagascar and Indonesia.

Four out of every five of the top 150 prescription drugs used in the U.S. have had their origins in natural compounds. An example is aspirin—a derivative of salicylic acid which was first taken from the bark of willow trees. Today aspirin and many other drugs are synthesized more efficiently than they can be extracted from the wild, but they were first discovered in naturally occurring compounds, which then formed the basis for subsequent improvement. The process of discovery still continues. For example, *taxol*, a promising anti-cancer drug, was first extracted from a tree found in the wild: the Pacific yew. The chemical substance from which taxol came has since been discovered in close relatives of that species, thus reducing pressures for harvesting what is already a small population.

Other economic gains derive from our interaction with the natural world, of which the best known example may be the economic value of tourism. Much, although obviously not all vacation travel comes under the rubric of "eco-tourism," driven by a desire to see and experience the natural world. The total economic activity generated by tourists of this kind has been recently estimated by the United Nations at nearly $230 billion each year. Even on regional and local scales, the revenue generated by tourism can be substantial, and a major component of local and regional economies.

Each of the activities cited above provides resources and economic gains for citizens in all societies. Yet each is at risk due to the continued erosion of the resource on which they are based, which is biodiversity. In what follows we review what is known of the forces that are reducing biodiversity and some of the possible consequences of this loss, and suggest areas in which additional research and policy analyses are most needed.

THE WINDS OF CHANGE

The recent Global Biodiversity Assessment of the United Nations Environment Program (UNEP) has identified four major causes of the present decrease in biodiversity, and a fifth which may yet prove to be important.

Land Use

Changes in how the land is used are probably the principal contributor to the current decline in biodiversity. About 1 to 2 percent of the land surface of the Earth is now devoted to urban use, but other changes in land cover and land use far exceed the direct impact of the small fraction that is paved or developed for homes and factories and other buildings. *Homo sapiens* has already converted about a quarter of all the land surface to agricultural uses. By some estimates we now appropriate directly or indirectly about 40 percent of what biologists call the *primary production* of the Earth's biota (the products of photosynthesis on which all other life depends), and the percentage that comes under our control in this way is increasing.

The pressures on terrestrial resources and land depend very much on population growth and the demands of early stages of economic development. Moreover, land acquisition, especially for agriculture and forestry, focuses initially on those areas with the most fertile soils and equable climates, which are often the areas of greatest biological diversity.

Deforestation in the humid tropics is probably the best-known current example of rapid land-use change. During the decade of the 1970s, vast areas of tropical forest in South America, Africa, and Southeast Asia were cleared and converted to agriculture and other uses. In the middle-to-late 1980s, the rates of deforestation in South America slowed dramatically, largely due to economic and tax policy changes in Brazil, but the pace of cutting in Africa and Southeast Asia, though poorly quantified, remains high. Globally, the rate of loss of tropical forests for the 1980s has been estimated at about 1 percent per year, but there is still considerable uncertainty. The rates of extinction of local species that accompany these rapid changes in land cover may soon be far in excess of what is found today, reaching as high as 10,000 times the natural background rate.

In the industrialized nations of the Northern Hemisphere the most rapid and widespread conversion of forest to other uses took place over the last several hundred years. In this time, much of the northeastern U.S., for example, was deforested at least once, in connection with the rise of agriculture and timber industries. But as regional and national economies changed, many previously cleared areas were left to return to their natural vegetation. As a result, forests have reappeared in parts of the Northeast, and indeed the country as a whole has probably gained forested land over the last several decades.

The current trend of most concern with respect to tree-cover in the U.S. is a shift to smaller parcel sizes. What once were continuously forested landscapes are now a quilt of small patches of trees, criss-crossed with roads, subdivisions, agricultural tracts, and a variety of different land-uses and land-covers: a scene that is familiar to anyone who has looked out an airplane window. The average size of tree-covered parcels is smaller than was the case twenty, fifty, or a hundred years ago, resulting in a landscape that is highly fragmented and partitioned.

The difference in terms of the natural world is great, and several studies now point with concern to the biological impacts of the shift to less continuous landscapes. The known consequences of these changes are reduced numbers of both plants and animals and a greater possibility of the outright loss of some of them—when in effect, they are painted into a corner with nowhere left for them to go. The interweaving of favorable and unfavorable habitats also curtails the ability of organisms to disperse, and makes recolonization of distant areas more difficult.

An analogous pattern of fragmentation can be found in parts of South America where deforestation was previously extremely rapid. Although the amount of new cutting appears to have fallen from that of previous decades, it seems to be increasing again in the rain forest of the Amazon, and the deforested, newly colonized regions now have their own distinctive appearance. Patchworks of active fields, orchards, abandoned fields, second growth forest, and primary forest are the norm. But the scene is ever changing through an interplay of active use by initial colonizers, abandonment, partial recovery through natural processes, and as then often happens, subsequent re-use. Analyses of potential impacts on biodiversity that are based on simple measures of deforested area can provide little more than very general conclusions.

Many of the best documented cases of individual species being driven to extinction or near-extinction by humans are those of over-exploitation.

Deforestation is not the only land-use change of interest or concern. Another with broad implications for biodiversity is the intensification of agriculture and grazing on those lands that have been traditionally devoted to these purposes. Of particular importance for biodiversity are the secondary impacts of intensive agriculture. Heavy applications of fertilizers and pesticides have the potential of creating additional environmental problems as well as affecting the abundance and viability of the other plants and animals and micro-organisms in the same or adjoining areas.

The adverse effects of non-point-source pollution due to the run-off of pesticides and herbicides from intensively-used fields are well-known. In addition, because of the understandable tendency to put the best land into production first, the expansion of agriculture into less fertile areas typically requires heavier applications of chemicals, more extensive site preparation, and other forms of more intensive management. The typical result is increased chemical run-off to the landscape, and with ensuing degradation, additional pressure for expansion, and so on. It is such a cycle that has led to widespread desertification in some parts of the world, primarily through overgrazing that can be compounded by naturally occurring droughts.

Over-exploitation

Many of the best documented cases of individual species being driven to extinction or near-extinction by humans are those of over-exploitation.

The passenger pigeon—a species that resembled the smaller, mourning dove—was in the early 1800s the most abundant bird in North America, and so plentiful that migrating flocks of a billion or more individuals would darken the skies of parts of the eastern U.S. for days at a time. By the end of the last century it had been hunted to the brink of extinction, and in September of 1914, in a Cincinnati zoo, the passenger pigeon disappeared forever with the death of the last remaining bird. The American bison, or buffalo, of the Great Plains was also nearly hunted out of existence in the same century, and its larger, woods-dwelling relative was driven to extinction.

As many as a quarter of all the bird species in the world may have similarly vanished in the course of the last 1000 years with the expansion of human populations through the islands of the South Pacific. The spread of early people through the New World, about 10,000 years ago, was probably responsible for the extinction of many of the large mammals that were originally here: now-extinct mammoths, sloths, and cave bears are known to have been hunted by those who first walked through North and South America. The same impact was felt by large mammals in Australia, New Zealand, and Madagascar. The current and rapid loss of tropical hardwoods in many regions due to high commercial demand, low rates of successful replacement, and the long periods of growth necessary to produce new, marketable resources has raised concern about over-exploitation of some species, such as rosewood, although none of the trees are known to have been driven to extinction.

Over-exploitation is also a major factor in reducing the natural biodiversity of marine fisheries through major reductions in populations, although again, no extinctions have been documented. During the last two decades, the world has seen the collapse of a number of marine fisheries. Some of these have recovered, but others, such as the cod and haddock fisheries in the North Atlantic, have not. Even for those that recover, the consequences of the original over-exploitation on population dynamics and genetic diversity are now only poorly understood. What is often apparent is a systematic decrease in the size, and hence age, of the individuals that are harvested. The selective loss of larger fish has significant impacts on those that remain. If fertility is strongly related to body size, as is the case for many fish species, over-exploitation not only reduces the abundance of a species, but it may also make recovery more difficult in systematically removing the most fecund individuals. The ensuing consequences for overall ecosystem functioning and biodiversity are as yet not well understood.

Whole ecosystems can also be affected by over-exploitation. For example, a reduction in organic carbon and nutrients, including phosphorus or nitrogen, as may occur in intensively farmed areas, decreases the fertility of soils. When losses are severe, the resulting depletion can lead to either more intensified use by adding more fertilizers and then herbicides and pesticides to control weeds and pests (in the cycle noted above), or to abandonment. If abandoned, the land will probably not recover its original component of plant and animal species because of the depleted nutrients. Through this chain of happenings, an over-exploitation of the soil for agricultural gain can have long term, negative impacts on the biodiversity of the region.

Alien introductions

Introductions and invasions of alien species of plants and animals is a long-recognized problem, as detailed in an earlier issue of CONSEQUENCES. We have only limited ability to predict quantitatively the results of any particular intruder, including its capability of establishing a permanent, reproducing population. What is certain is that some areas are by nature more susceptible. Continental forests are reasonably resistant to newly introduced tree species, except in cases where they have been disturbed by heavy cutting or partial clearing. Native meadows and prairies, when disturbed, have also proven particularly susceptible to intruders, as is the case for the many grasslands around the world that have been converted to pasture or cultivated land. For example, many of the now common grasses in the intermontane western U.S. and southwestern Canada are transported Eurasian weeds. These species were able to invade and become established because the original perennial tussock grasses were unable to support the intensification of grazing from large-scale cattle ranching.

Freshwater lakes and streams have little immunity to invading species. Alien plants or animals seem able to establish reproducing populations relatively easily, and the new species often have significant impacts on biotic composition, and on a variety of ecosystem processes. Two examples of the kind of changes that can result from even well-meant introductions are the purposeful introduction of game fish to many lakes and streams throughout the world that replaced native varieties, and the ecological havoc that followed the introduction of the Nile perch in Lake Victoria in 1960 to benefit commercial fishing. In less than thirty years, the appetite of the Nile perch, whose food is smaller fish, led to the extinction of about thirty species of fish that were native to the lake.

In terrestrial ecosystems, the largest changes occur when the intruder brings quite different traits from those of native species. The best documented example is that of the introduction of the exotic tree, *Myrica faga*, into Hawaii, which has resulted in large changes in ecosystem dynamics. The significant difference, in this case, was the ability of the introduced tree—a legume like peas and beans and clover—to convert atmospheric nitrogen to ammonia, a characteristic not previously present in those ecosystems. This ability of the introduced tree increases the nitrogen

If abandoned, the land will probably not recover its original component of plant and animal species because of the depleted nutrients.

content of soils, and thus alters the raw materials on which many other plant species depend.

Introduced species with characteristics that are not qualitatively different from those of native species, can through force of numbers have large and long-lasting effects on them. About 100 European starlings were released in New York City in 1890–91 by a collector bent on establishing all the birds mentioned in the writings of William Shakespeare. The result, evident throughout the country today, is a diminished number of many native American songbirds, through competition for nest-sites, in which the aggressive and now very abundant starling has been extremely successful.

Pollution and toxification

The widespread increase of various pollutants and poisonous or toxic substances in the environment has had obvious local impacts on biodiversity in acutely affected areas. In western industrialized countries the more severe instances of air and water pollution are for the most part now being addressed through regulation and clean-up. In many developing nations, however, the financial resources needed to correct acute pollution problems are not available, and air-and water-borne pollution continue to pose great environmental problems, including local reductions in the diversity of living species.

In many parts of the industrialized world, long-term chronic pollution of air, water, and soil pose problems that are difficult to resolve and rectify. The degree to which chronic, low-level pollution constitutes a risk to biodiversity is less clear than for acute exposures, but several facts are worth noting. One is that the transport of many pollutants has been surprisingly wide and rapid. Organic compounds of chlorine such as DDT, for example, can literally be found all over the world due to atmospheric transport, even though many of these substances have long been banned in western industrialized countries, and they often remain and accumulate in parts of both terrestrial and aquatic food chains.

Another concern is that long-term pollution, at even low levels, can affect whole ecosystems, with resultant impacts on biodiversity that bring about additional changes in how ecosystems operate. The chain of events through which central European forests have responded to acid deposition is a ready example. There, the chronic deposition of airborne acidic substances from industrial effluents affects both chemical processes and essential microorganisms in the soil, lowering the vitality of trees and ground-cover and making groundwater, streams, and lakes more acidic.

A third concern is that pollutants in soils and ground water, once introduced, remain there for a long time, due both to the chemical stability of many of the compounds

In many parts of the industrialized world, long-term chronic pollution of air, water, and soil pose problems that are difficult to resolve and rectify.

involved, and the extremely slow rates at which ground water is circulated or exchanged. A fourth arises through the fact that many insecticides work by a process of mimicry—copying the behavior of vital hormones in the species they are designed to attack. But hormones that regulate the physiological functions of non-target species, especially the reproductive functions, can also be mimicked by the same insecticides. This raises the concern that the ever-increasing load of these compounds in natural systems may impact wildlife in general, and even humans. The recent discovery of prevalent reproductive anomalies in some forms of wildlife, such as some frogs and toads, is believed by some scientists to be due to hormonally active substances introduced into the environment.

Climate change

Natural variations in climate are among the more important causes of past changes in biodiversity, both locally and for the Earth as a whole. The prospect of human-induced changes in the climate adds new concerns, however, particularly if the rate of change should prove as rapid as many now foresee.

Current projections of general circulation models imply rates of change of the global climate system that exceed those of almost any natural variation in the geologic past.

Current projections of general circulation models imply rates of change of the global climate system that exceed those of almost any natural variation in the geologic past. These rapid changes in surface temperature and other weather parameters could lead to severe mismatches between regional conditions and the physiological requirements of many plant species. Were the average surface temperature to rise by several degrees C, that warming would probably be followed by potentially large re-organizations of some ecological communities. For example, some model simulations suggest that with such a change, much of deciduous forest in the eastern U.S. could be replaced by savanna-like vegetation, composed of mixtures of open park land and grasses. Similarly, some forest ecosystem models have suggested that rapid and extensive diebacks of certain trees could occur over much of their current range. Were this to happen, there would undoubtedly be an associated wave of changes in the fauna as well.

By itself, a systematic change in predominant vegetation, which has happened before in the geologic past, would not necessarily imply an increase in the rate of species extinctions. At the same time, with global warming some species will find less optimal habitat than before, particularly in higher latitudes. Plants and animals that now inhabit montane and alpine habitats—and which are there through an evolved dependence on cooler temperatures and higher altitudes—may with warming of these regions have nowhere else to go. The combination of potentially rapid climate change with the increased fragmentation of land cover is especially troubling: while it would be conceivable for some organisms to disperse to climatically more favorable habitats, the shift could in practice carry them across many unfavorable regions.

The recent consensus findings of the Intergovernmental Panel on Climate Change of a now detectable signature of anthropogenic influences on the physical climate system adds new impetus to examine the probable impacts of continued global warming on living things, and biodiversity in particular.

THE LOSS OF SPECIES

Species extinctions have received the lion's share of the attention in debates regarding biodiversity and the need to sustain it. The loss of individual species in ecosystems, such as frogs in wetlands or ferns in a forest, can certainly affect the ways in which those systems work together to cycle essential nutrients and water and process energy. Since we have only limited ability to predict how ecosystems will respond in terms of replacement or built-in redundancy to the possible loss of a specific species, there is some reason to be concerned when any are threatened by extinction.

At the same time, the same degree of concern should apply to reductions in the populations of species, even if they are not reduced to disappearance altogether. The role that classes of organisms play in ecosystems depends not only on what they do in terms of material cycling and energy flow, but on how many are there to do it. Reductions in abundance of an essential species can clearly affect overall system functioning, and therefore the degree to which ecosystem services will continue to be provided.

Some, known as *keystone species*, play a role in ecosystems that seems out of proportion to their number, such that even small changes in their abundance may have great impacts on the ecosystems in which they live. A common example is the sea-otter, a marine mammal that lives along the coasts of the northern Pacific Ocean. They dive and prey on sea-urchins that principally feed, in turn, on large seaweed called kelp. When sea otters are present, the number of urchins is kept sufficiently low that stands of kelp—which are of commercial value as a source of potash and iodine—can become established and thrive. When otters vanish from the scene, the resulting growth in urchin populations effectively prevents the plant's successful regeneration, and eventually leads to the loss of kelp forests.

In time, all classes of living things—like the dinosaurs, or, we must presume, our own species—must face extinction. But the disappearance of any of them is a critical endpoint, marking the end of 3.5 billion years of evolutionary development. In Nature it represents a permanent depletion of biodiversity and a loss of genetic information on which evolution is based. In terms of people and nations, it

In time, all classes of living things . . . must face extinction. But the disappearance of any of them is a critical endpoint, marking the end of 3.5 billion years of evolutionary development.

counts as a loss of potential economic value in terms of services or products. Each species is a reservoir of unique genetic information that cannot be reproduced once it is gone. In this broader sense, any extinction, however trivial it may seem, represents a permanent loss to the biosphere as a whole.

What we need to know for informed policy decisions are the ecosystem services that a threatened species provides; the degree to which it offers opportunities for direct economic benefit; how expected benefits weigh against costs of preservation; and on a more general level, how present or expected rates of extinction compare to what might be expected through natural changes. The telling questions are whether and by how much the present rate of species loss differs from the rate that Nature would exact, were we not here, and whether the species that are lost play important keystone roles. The challenge is that this sort of information is only rarely available. Nor do we have, as yet, a predictive theory of keystone species.

Rates of loss

The UNEP Global Biodiversity Assessment has recently reviewed the methods that have been used in the literature to calculate natural, or background extinction rates and have compared them against current trends. The results, which are intentionally conservative, are sobering. Best estimates are that current extinction rates for well-documented groups of primarily, but not exclusively, vertebrates and *vascular* (in general, seed-bearing and fern-like) plants are at least 50 to 100 times larger than the expected natural background. There is no good reason to expect these rates to differ very much for plant or animal groups that are less well-studied.

On the basis of recent estimates of land-use change, largely in the tropics, there is a reasonable expectation that extinction rates in the very near future could rise, worldwide, to as much as 10,000 times the natural level. Extinctions of this number and extent would approach, and possibly surpass, the major mass extinctions of the geologic past, as when dinosaurs and other life forms disappeared, about 65 million years ago.

The total number of species that inhabit the planet is unknown. The UNEP Global Biodiversity Assessment uses an estimate of about 13 million, but the range varies from 8 to 50 million or more. Only about 2 million species have been described scientifically, and they are distributed very unevenly among different taxonomic groups (Table 2). While important in its own right, the number need not be precisely known to be concerned about the rates at which the better documented species are now disappearing. In today's world, most extinctions will occur before the species have even been named and described, much less known ecologically.

THE SERVICES THAT BIODIVERSITY PROVIDES

Assessments of the economic benefits of biological diversity have been based primarily on our ability to generate revenue from biodiversity, through activities that produce measurable results in current markets, such as pharmaceuticals or tourism. But there are additional benefits from biodiversity that are not so easily included in commercial market analyses, and that come under the name of ecosystem services. These are the end results of natural biological processes that either improve the overall quality of the environment, or provide some benefit to the human users of the landscape—such as improvement of water quality and reduction of flooding. The concept of ecosystem *services* is unabashedly tilted toward human uses.

The study of ecosystem services is relatively new, but what is known points consistently in one direction: maintaining diversity on a variety of levels of ecological and biological organization—within forests, or among the trees that are there, or even within the genes of a single variety—is critical if services are to be maintained on a sustainable basis.

Ecosystem services can be provided in a variety of forms. One example is the purification of water that generally occurs by flowing through forested ecosystems and wetlands, which is an extremely important function from the standpoint of human populations that live downstream. The presence of living vegetation provides an efficient sink for many atmospheric pollutants as well. The regulation of stream flow by vegetation in the upper reaches of watersheds has long been recognized as an important ecosystem service, and watershed managers manipulate both the amount and type of vegetation in watersheds to help control sedimentation, floods, and sometimes stream flow.

The services that ecosystems provide often depend on the underlying physical structure of the habitat, such as the conditions for feeding and breeding that may be needed for the continued survival of an important animal species. What is often required is a diversity of habitats over an entire landscape. Ecosystem services may also depend on the presence of a particular species, as is the case in highly co-evolved plant-pollinator systems, or in highly managed agroecosystems that rely on specific pollinators, such as honeybees.

Biodiversity also plays an important role in maintaining ecosystem services over long periods of time, through the ups and downs of natural variations. Ecosystems that have lost either genetic or species diversity are less resistant to the effects of environmental perturbations, such as droughts, and are slower to recover when disturbed. Diver-

Biodiversity also plays an important role in maintaining ecosystem services over long periods of time, through the ups and downs of natural variations.

sity is a form of ecosystem health insurance: those ecosystems that include several species that serve the same or similar functions tend to be more resistant to environmental stress and recover faster from perturbations.

THE ECONOMIC VALUE OF ECOSYSTEM SERVICES

The economic value of ecosystem services is difficult to calculate, and this raises several important problems when we look at biodiversity in the context of public policy. How can we measure the economic value of ecosystem services such as water purification, or resistance to environmental disturbances? Since the maintenance of biodiversity involves choices and ultimately, costs, how can markets reflect and distribute these values appropriately?

The task may be somewhat easier in the case of new products and materials that are derived from the natural world. Prospecting for new pharmaceuticals is the most publicized, but not the only example. New food crops are also a possibility, although to date there have been very few such introductions that have achieved more than regional importance, either dietarily or economically. More intriguing, perhaps, is the use of genetic engineering to extract biochemical processes from the natural world. Research of this kind has found application in biological clean-up, or *bioremediation* of toxic waste and oil spills. An even more promising and somewhat more controversial opportunity is found in harnessing processes at the most fundamental levels of biological structure.

The pool of resources hidden in the genetic resources of living things is potentially huge. An example is the *polymerase chain reaction* (PCR) that is used in genetic research and in commercial applications to manipulate DNA. The ready availability of substances that speed up the rate at which the cells replicate—the catalysts that in living matter are proteins known as enzymes—has literally made genetic engineering practical on industrial scales.

The enzymes used to catalyze PCR were first isolated from bacteria that can survive only in high temperatures, and the source from which they were taken was natural hot springs in Yellowstone National Park. In this case, to say that an entire new industry depended on the diversity of organisms and habitats in the National Park system is no exaggeration. Substantial prospecting is now underway in these and other extreme environments to find enzymes that will catalyze other, industrially-useful reactions.

WHAT LIES AHEAD?

The population of the Earth will likely double by the year 2050, resulting in a world of at least 10 billion people, the largest number of whom, by far, will live in tropical and subtropical Asia, Africa, and South America. These are as well the regions in greatest need of economic development,

The population of the Earth will likely double by the year 2050, resulting in a world of at least 10 billion people, the largest number of whom, by far, will live in tropical and subtropical Asia, Africa, and South America.

and the twin pressures of population growth and economic expansion can only increase the demands on biological resources. We can anticipate an ever-increasing competition among different uses of the available land, and the maintenance of biodiversity may not rank high in the face of other, more obvious demands.

Many of the existing policies of our own country that have been enacted to preserve biodiversity have been focused on threatened species, or to preserve striking or unique ecosystems, such as Yellowstone National Park. The Endangered Species Act, the Convention on International Trade in Endangered Species, and our system of National Parks will continue to help in preserving biodiversity. But there are other areas of public policy that are as useful and important. In fact, it may well be that lands and waters that are necessarily exploited for their natural resources will hold the key for practical strategies to maintain biodiversity, for parks and preserves, alone, are inadequate for the task.

In truth, much that happens to preserve or decrease biodiversity arises through secondary effects of policies that are enacted for other reasons. Fisheries policies that aim to maintain fishery harvests; forestry policies that seek to maximize the economic yield of marketable timber; agricultural policies that maintain subsidies for keeping land in production that might be used for other beneficial purposes; and policies for the management of public lands that encourage overgrazing by maintaining artificially low grazing fees all have important negative effects on biodiversity, although not by design.

Other existing policies have impacts that work in the other direction. But unless the impacts on biodiversity of private acts or public policies are understood, and until there exists a broader consensus regarding the relative value of biodiversity, there is little hope, in this or any country, of holding the line at the levels that are needed for almost any use or service. We all need to be more aware of the direct benefits, indirect benefits, services, and future potential that biodiversity offers for both private gain and public benefit. We need greater awareness and coordination of policies that affect biodiversity, and national goals that go deeper than the protection of endangered species and the preservation of public parks.

From an economic perspective, much more work needs to be done to put a fair and meaningful valuation on biodiversity. The service aspects of biodiversity must be understood, and market mechanisms put in place to include these very real factors in both policy and business decisions.

From a scientific perspective, we need to learn more, and more quickly, about the role that biodiversity plays in the working of ecosystems. Gaps in our present knowledge of these connections now limit our assessments of the risks imposed when biodiversity declines, and preclude more complete economic evaluations.

In all of this, calls will be heard to defer action until we have in hand a more complete and reliable inventory of the present extent and variety of life on Earth, in terms of the number of species of plants and animals. Although counting must go on, it is now clear that waiting to learn the full extent of biodiversity before acting to stem so precipitous a decline is not a prudent choice, for both ecological and economic reasons.

Last, but certainly not least, are the issues of stewardship and ethics. In the long run, we must be concerned about maintaining the capability of the biological world to adapt, through adjustment and evolution, to changes in the physical environment. In addition, many would agree that as a society we bear the ethical obligation to protect the habitability of the planet, and to act as responsible stewards of its biological riches for the present and future welfare of the human species. To do that requires an appreciation of the value of biodiversity—both what it provides for the natural world and the ways that we can use it—and a commitment to preserve it so that our children and their children will continue to realize the benefits of a biologically rich Earth. Surely such a challenge demands the attention of scholars and policy-makers alike.

III. Personal Testimonies

Editor's Introduction

Over the years, some of the most engaging writing about ecology has come from adventurous souls who have ventured both near and far afield to write first-hand reports of nature in its exotic and even its mundane wonder. Thoreau's observations in *Walden*, and Charles Darwin's voyages on the *H. M. S. Beagle*, for example, still excite readers for their precision of observation and rich descriptions of flora and fauna. The three articles in this section present an opportunity to move away briefly from scientific or political discussion for a more immediate experience of global ecology through the eyes of folk who are passionately concerned about the survival of the Earth in all its fragile wonder.

Not all the articles in this section are romantic paeans to wild, untampered-with nature. Walter T. Anderson's "There's No Going Back to Nature" debunks the neo-Luddite dogmatism seen in some circles. "The idea that people should somehow learn to 'leave nature alone' has an aura of commendable humility," writes Anderson, "and it's the easiest thing imaginable to put into words, but it's quite impossible to put into practice in today's world." Originally published in the counter-cultural *Mother Jones* magazine, the article might conceivably have upset the conventional wisdom of some of that publication's readers, as when he writes: "Don't look for a great surge toward Green parties, or a worldwide burst of enthusiasm for deep ecology or bioregionalism. That back-to-nature sort of environmentalism seems to be enjoying a certain vogue at the moment, but actually the future will likely belong to what I call proactive environmentalists--people who are able to use information and technology, who don't mind living in this world as it is, and who are unafraid to engage in the hands-on management of ecosystems." The author examines attempts to "repair" the Florida Everglades, to "restore" grasslands on the Great Plains, and to develop new food sources in seawater-farming ventures.

Another article relates how an early exposure to the Peruvian rain forest had a formative impact on the life and career of its author. In "Requiem for Nature: The Making of a Dissident," John Terborgh of Duke University recounts his visit to the rainforest in Peru's Apurìmac Valley some thirty years ago at the beginning of his career as a tropical biologist. Terborgh's personal observations of the region's fragile ecosystem since the early 1970s have reinforced his resolve to preserve the environment in the face of technical and political challenges. He writes in an idiom that borders on reverence, as in these words: "At close range, the passing river emitted an audible hiss, the sound of roiling gravel being swept along the bottom by a powerful current . . . Tier upon tier of forest-clad ridges mount into the cloud-shrouded distance, creating extravagant vistas of wild inaccessibility that I found irresistibly alluring. For me, a tropical biologist at the beginning of my career, to be in the heart of such a wholly pristine scene was both sublime and exhilarating." Shades of nineteenth-century Transcendentalism, in which "the sublime" would be an antidote to neurasthenia?

In Jim Motavalli's interview, "Conversations with Paul and Anne Ehrlich," America's two leading population experts comment on the impacts of human overpopulation on global ecology since the publication, some thirty years ago, of Paul Ehrlich's book *The*

Population Bomb. In their new book, *Betrayal of Science and Reason*, the Ehrlichs write: "Around the world, we have watched humanity consuming its natural capital and degrading its own life-support systems." The Ehrlichs also advance the not-surprising argument that as women become empowered in traditional societies, fertility rates will decrease. Still, they project a world population of some eight to 12 billion by the middle of the twenty-first century.

The personal testimonies presented here remind us that ecology is not just a collection of dry statistics, but an experience of the world through the flesh-and-blood bodies of men and women who perhaps feel their connections to the Planet a little more deeply than the rest of us. Human beings are the only self-reflective species. These reflections and self-reflections remind us that humans are a part of the global ecology both as active shapers and as passive participants. Not everyone is swayed by data, however carefully collected and presented. Sometimes it takes a poet or a naturalist or a hiker to alter and deepen our perceptions of living in and with nature.

There's No Going Back to Nature[1]

We are not in—nor about to be in—a world with a small human population living simply and leaving nature alone. The future belongs to proactive environmentalists who use information and technology to make ecosystems.

Some futurists say we are entering the "environmental century," and this will probably turn out to be right for a lot of reasons—some good and some bad. The good news is, more and more people are beginning to understand that a healthy environment is essential to everything we do. The bad news is, we're likely to have an ample enough supply of nasty problems to keep the environment on everybody's mind for a long time to come.

This doesn't mean the future is going to be terrible—far from it. It only means that there will be tough challenges, things for people and societies to work on and learn about. And it doesn't mean, either, that environmentalism—at least all the varieties of it that we hear about today—will be a potent force in this global civilization. Don't look for a great surge toward Green parties, or a worldwide burst of enthusiasm for deep ecology or bioregionalism. That back-to-nature sort of environmentalism seems to be enjoying a certain vogue at the moment, but actually the future will likely belong to what I call proactive environmentalists—people who are able to use information and technology, who don't mind living in this world as it is, and who are unafraid to engage in the hands-on management of ecosystems.

It's really amazing—especially in a society said to have reached the end of ideology almost 40 years ago—that the various strains of back-to-nature environmentalism such as deep ecology, bioregionalism, ecofeminism, and neo-Luddism have congealed so quickly into what any student of politics would recognize immediately as another ideology. It certainly has all the earmarks of one—a philosophy, a political movement, and enough jargon to gag a Washington speechwriter. Its dogma includes opposition to "anthropocentric"—i.e., human-centered thought or action, a hands-off approach to nature, a deep suspicion of all things technological, a passion for the primitive, and a desire to get back to some kind of decentralized world in which people live and work within their bioregions, preferably with native plants and animals.

---

1. Article by Walter Truett Anderson for *Mother Jones* Sep./Oct. 1996. Copyright © Foundation for National Progress. Reprinted with permission.

This hankering for the past is one of the chief badges of membership in the movement. Some Americans—such as farmer-author Wendell Berry—merely want to get back to the agricultural lifestyles of a few decades past, before the midcentury wave of mechanization. Many European Greens revere the medieval era. The real high rollers scorn agriculture altogether and yearn for the good old life of hunting and gathering. This last position was eloquently expressed by a former Earth First! Journal editor who wrote that "many of us...would like to see human beings live much more the way they did 15,000 years ago..." Such ideas as these are remarkably popular on the campuses and in the coffee shops—and remarkably irrelevant to most of the valuable environmental work that is being done now and will be done in the future.

And that's the problem: The world is changing very quickly, and we desperately need a vision that engages this new world honestly and creatively, with daring and hope and perhaps even a touch of optimism. The appealing fantasies of back-to-nature environmentalism have the same effect on public dialogue that Gresham's law has on the economy. Bad money drives out good, and muzzy slogans drown out serious thinking. We simply are not in, nor about to be in, a world that resembles the bioregionalist dream of a small human population, most folks happily living simple lives in the country and leaving nature alone. It might be nice if we were, or it might not. But that really doesn't matter, because events aren't headed in that direction. The world is becoming more densely populated, not less; more urbanized, not less; more technological, not less. Most important of all, human beings are exerting ever more—not less—power in nature, having a greater impact on ecosystems. This is our world, and this is our work.

The idea that people should somehow learn to "leave nature alone" has an aura of commendable humility, and it's the easiest thing imaginable to put into words, but it's quite impossible to put in to practice in today's world.

The idea that people should somehow learn to "leave nature alone" has an aura of commendable humility, and it's the easiest thing imaginable to put into words, but it's quite impossible to put into practice in today's world. Proactive environmentalism—which deserves greater support and understanding from progressives—involves managing ecosystems, sometimes in ways that totally transform them. Every ecosystem, every population of wild animals, is, in one way or another, managed by human beings right now. Sure, there are different kinds of management, some of them trying to keep ecosystems relatively pristine and protect wildlife. But everywhere conservation is an active business that involves much more than merely battling exploitation. It also involves understanding information, using technology, and often making decisions that change ecosystems and affect the evolutionary future of species. Restoration is one of the most important pieces of the new environmentalism. People are rebuilding rivers and streams and ponds and beaches, reconstructing forests and prairies and deserts, sometimes coaxing populations of near-extinct species back to a sustainable size. I don't know whether to call ecological restoration an art or a science or a technology, because it's a bit of all those; but it's sure as hell not a matter of leaving nature alone. In most places, certainly in the more developed parts of the world, you don't get a restored ecosystem by fencing it off and doing nothing. Do that, and the result will be a lot of native plants and animals coexisting more or less peacefully with a lot of non-native ones. Many such mixed ecosystems can be found in national, state, and regional parks, and in the privately held rural areas that are not-too-accurately called "nature preserves." And there's nothing wrong with that; they maintain open space, habitat, and watershed, and they're valuable and beautiful and productive in many ways.

But a true restoration project—like the piece of American prairie that the great naturalist Aldo Leopold and his associates began carving out of a Wisconsin cornfield about 60 years ago—is a deliberate human creation. Those pioneer restorationists hauled in tons of soil, ripped out everything that didn't have proof of citizenship, and planted thousands of native seeds and seedlings they had found in various places more or less close to the site. Nowadays we have lots of small restoration projects, even in urban areas. Volunteers in Marin County, near San Francisco, pitch in to restore local salmon streams where construction work and erosion from neighboring pastures have ruined spawning beds. Work crews spend their weekends making small check dams on the tributaries to prevent sediment from spilling into the creeks, wrestling rocks into place along the cattle-damaged banks, and rebuilding the spawning areas.

You can also find similar projects undertaken on a larger scale by professional restorationists such as the "river doctors" who work in places like Washington and Montana and Colorado, bringing back streams that have suffered badly at the hands (and feet) of miners, cattle herds, and developers.

Larger yet is the project to repair the Florida Everglades, which—if it's carried out as currently proposed—will be the largest water-system restoration in history. Most of the work will be done by the U.S. Army Corps of Engineers, which in the past has taken a beating from environmental writers, myself included. But the corps' mindset is changing. Instead of master-planning everything, the restorers are using what they call "adaptive management," which means proceeding with a general objective, trying some things (different ways of modifying levees, for example), and seeing what works best. It's a pragmatic and flexible approach that, while far from "hands-off" restoration, certainly isn't the same as the heavy-handed replumbing of ecosystems so often practiced in the past.

The Everglades are not, of course, going to be restored to what they were a few hundred years ago—not in southern Florida with its enormous agricultural areas, its cities with millions of inhabitants, and God knows how many tourists coming to fish and take romantic boat rides through the sloughs. But restorations—even "true restorations" like the Wisconsin prairie—are never perfect reproductions of a past ecosystem. They are different because of what's not there— species that have become extinct—and also because of what is there: Inevitably, some bird, insect, or plant newcomer succeeds in sneaking in and making itself at home. Also, the restorationist always has to make a choice about what past state to emulate. The image of homeostasis—like much of the rest of the pop ecology that informs the back-to-nature mystique—is inaccurate. "Undisturbed" ecosystems change too, sometimes dramatically, and any restoration project mimics a certain era, much as an "old town" mimics a certain stage in a city's history. You have to decide what nature to go back to—which is yet another way of saying you can't get away from human agency. Furthermore, restored ecosystems don't stay restored unless somebody puts in a lot of work keeping them that way.

A restoration project, then, is a technique of environmental management in the present and not a return to the past. Some restoration projects are about improving the depleted soil of farmlands. Some are about restoring populations of certain plant or animal species, like the controversial return of the wolves now roaming in and around Yellowstone National Park. Others—like Holistic Resource Management (HRM), which includes a style of cattle ranching being tried out in many parts of the American West—are essentially techniques for using natural resources without using them up.

HRM ranching begins with the somewhat startling proposition that grasslands should be periodically trampled down and fertilized by big herds of hoofed animals—as they once were by buffalo and elk. This breaks up hard crusts, keeps the soil porous and receptive to rain, helps decompose dried grass stalks and other such materials, and works minerals into the soil. The tricky part is that buffalo herds moved around, whereas most cattle herds stay in one place, overgraze, and produce erosion. The "holistic" solution is to simulate the behavior of the long-gone native herds by bunching the grazing animals together, letting them feed for a while in one place, then moving them and giving the just-grazed area an opportunity to recover. I'm not yet convinced that Holistic Resource Management is the solution to soil damage from cattle ranching, but at the very least it is turning out to be a peacemaker in the range wars between ranchers and environmentalists. And it may be the key to the large-scale restoration of bison populations in the American West.

In forestry, a lot of attention is being paid now to the "reactive" kind of environmentalism—stopping the clear-cutters, saving the rainforests—and those are indeed worthwhile and necessary efforts. But most of the effective forest protection today, and nearly all of the reforestation, is active management. Agroforestry—which means either growing trees as crops or integrating tree-growing into other crops—is essential.

In Tanzania, where deforestation is so severe people have to travel miles to find wood, some farmers are using an agroforestry technology known as "rotational woodlots." They plant trees, mostly varieties of Australian acacia, alongside their regular food crops. The farmers continue to grow and harvest food for two or three years until the trees take over. Then the field becomes a woodlot and a source of fuelwood, poles for buildings, and fodder for animals—meanwhile restoring fertility to the soil like any fallow—until the farmers clear-cut it and go back to growing crops between the stumps.

In other parts of the world, farmers are planting the New Zealand-bred "super trees." These tall trees, sometimes called "kiwi willows," sprout like mad. They are grown for energy, fodder, or timber, and may help forests store carbon dioxide. Since they are hybrids, they're sterile and don't produce seeds that can escape and take over an ecosystem.

But bioregional purists don't like these kinds of agroforestry: Super trees are not exactly natural and Australian acacias don't ordinarily grow in Africa.

Some of the most interesting and really innovative projects going on now—like the coastal desert developments in which crops are irrigated with seawater—don't fit neatly into any category.

Some of the most interesting and really innovative projects going on now—like the coastal desert developments in which crops are irrigated with seawater—don't fit neatly into any category. They don't meet even the most spacious definition of restoration, because they thoroughly make over sizable pieces of real estate, turning them into ecosystems of a sort that never existed before.

Fly over the coastline of the Arabian Sea or the Gulf of California, and here and there you can look down and see seawater farms—green circles on the parched land. They are the advance guard of an entirely new kind of agriculture, now being developed by a team of scientists at Planetary Design Corp. in Arizona. CEO Carl Hodges and his associates studied hundreds of saltwater plants and then began to focus on salicornia, which grows along marshy coastlines and produces a crunchy, pleasant-tasting stalk—kind of like a lightly salted string bean.

Salicornia, under various names, has been known as an edible plant for centuries—it was a favorite snack of George Washington—but was never bred or cultivated. The scientists began breeding new strains, hoping to get one that could produce high-quality oil and meal. Eventually they got two promising varieties. They plan to use salicornia not only for sea-water–based food production, but also for soil-building, stimulating new urban development along coastal deserts, and taking CO2 out of the atmosphere. Salicornia will be a piece, perhaps a small piece or perhaps a very large one, of the effort to feed the world during the next 50 years or so of continuing population growth. And it will also be a piece of the attempt to find methods of development that are not only locally sustainable, but active contributors to environmental management on a large—indeed, global—scale. Hodges calls it "climate defensive food production."

Salicornia farming is an excellent example of proactive environmentalism. First of all, it starts with recognizing and accepting the present and near-future global situation. The world in which the salicornia enthusiasts expect to do their work is not ecotopia. It is a densely populated, urbanizing, developing world with vast amounts of land already degraded by erosion, depleting freshwater supplies, and an ever-increasing need for fossil fuels.

Farming salicornia is not chemical intensive, because the seawater provides most of the nutrients needed for growing the crops, but otherwise it violates most of the ideals of small-scale bioregional agriculture: It's commercial farming; it needs a good-sized capital investment; it uses sophisticated irrigation technology; and it is based on a plant native to few of the places where the crops now grow.

Projects such as this inspire enthusiasm from most people—but are scornfully dismissed as "technological fixes" by back-to-nature true believers.

Projects such as this inspire enthusiasm from most people—but are scornfully dismissed as "technological fixes" by back-to-nature true believers.

The term technological fix deserves some attention here, since it's one of the staples of ecotopian rhetoric, along with the promiscuous overuse—to the point of meaninglessness—of the word "natural." The argument against simply fixing up something with a technological repair job may well apply in some specific cases—if, for example, a person is presented with the choice between having a quadruple bypass and adopting a healthy lifestyle—but it really doesn't have much relevance to most current environmental concerns. The world is not faced with a simple choice of either adopting more environmentally sensitive attitudes or applying new technologies. Rather, we are seeing both a rapid evolution of technology away from heavy industrialism and value shifts about the environment.

Most of the other back-to-nature terms are similarly pumped-up and carelessly repeated concepts that have a certain amount of reasonableness if taken in moderation. That great favorite, "anthropocentrism," for example. This isn't just a challenge to the habit of valuing plants and animals only for their usefulness to humans—which is something that needs challenging. The self-described "deep ecologists" are not interested in any such sensible objective. They escalate the rhetoric and prescribe that human beings learn how to live in equality with all other living things. However charming this might sound, it has utterly nothing to do with a world that is about to have 6 billion people in it, whether we like it or not.

Bioregionalism, too, is a useful idea in some contexts—such as governance of air basins. But it becomes pure nonsense when people begin to advocate it—as Kirkpatrick Sale does in his book *Dwellers in the Land*—as a solution to be imposed on the whole world, by relocating people from the cities to rural areas where they would then take up ecologically correct lifestyles. There are indeed people who remain in one place, don't get hooked into the global economy, and rarely travel—all parts of the bioregional answer—and that's a perfectly fine way to live. The trouble is in turning it into a universal mandate and a political agenda—a crusade to get everybody living that way. Not everybody does, not everybody wants to, and not everybody can.

Even the people who talk bioregionalism don't live that way—and don't seem to notice the gap between what they say and how they live. Some years back, *Sierra* magazine ran an interview with poet Gary Snyder, in which he advised all of us: "Quit moving. Stay where you are . . . become a *paysan, paisano, peón.*" He then proceeded directly, with no evident sense of irony, to telling of his recent trips to China and Alaska. A bit further on he added: "I've been traveling eight or 10 weeks a year, doing lectures and readings at universities and community centers around the United States. I'm able to keep a sense of what's going on in the country that way."

I don't think this makes Snyder a hypocrite. I think he's a perfectly honest guy who would rather recycle green platitudes for admiring listeners than think hard about what it really means to live in a global civilization.

Probably the most serious weakness of pop ecophilosophy is its Luddite tilt. Technology isn't just a thing—it is human thought, action, information, and invention, and a living part of who and what we are. Some applications of technology are lousy and some are wonderful. But simply taking sides for or against technology is the lowest common denominator of public discourse.

Some technologies are and will always be central to environmental protection. I doubt that most people realize how important information technologies are in environmental management today.

We worry about the hole in the ozone layer—and we should worry about it—but don't appreciate the exquisite technology involved in detecting it, monitoring its ebbs and flows, projecting its future. Nobody *sees* a hole in the ozone. Like many other major environmental issues, it is accessible to our understanding only through the use of monitoring technologies.

An enormous environmental information system has grown, spreading and connecting around the world. The living Earth is now inseparable from this ever-expanding complex of satellites, transmitters, relay towers, computers, and software. With these devices, people observe the condition of the ozone, speculate on the future of the world's climate, study tectonic movements deep below the surface, brood over the oceans, track the migrations of wild animals and the changes in forests and deserts. This is technology that doesn't fit into any simplistic pro vs. con debate. It is neither the malevolent cause of our problems nor their magical solution—just an essential means of acquiring information. And it will play a larger part in bringing greater environmental awareness than the collected works of all the writers and philosophy professors who push deep ecology and bioregionalism.

Biotechnology has become the Great Satan for the back-to-nature ideologists.

So far most of the buzz about the "information revolution" has focused on its organizational, economic, and cultural impact, with far less attention paid to its biological side. It's high time we recognized that we are becoming not just an information society but a bioinformation society. And a global one. Ecological information will play a central role in everything people do in this society, and so will biotechnology.

Biotechnology has become the Great Satan for the back-to-nature ideologists. But their crusade against it is a tangle of misperceptions, flaws, and half-truths. Let me mention five of the big ones:

1. *Biotechnology is the same as the biotechnology industry.* This is a correct perception of who controls most of the biotechnological research and development—at least in the United States and Europe—but it isn't an accurate perception of what biotechnology is. It is a far-reaching scientific revolution that is transforming all the life sciences and being applied all over the world, by all kinds of people. You get a whole different picture of biotechnology if you go to one of the conferences that bring together scientists who are working on agriculture in Africa, Asia, and Latin America. Most of their research is supported by governments and foundations rather than by large corporations and entrepreneurial start-ups. They are using the new biotechnologies to improve local crops such as sweet potatoes, yams, rice, corn, and bananas. They don't talk of technological fixes, pro or con; they just apply the best tools to the problems at hand.

2. *Biotechnology is naturally opposed to organic farming and sustainable development.* Some new biotechnologies— such as cell and tissue culture—are already being applied in crop plants grown by organic farmers. And, as the various tools and insights of biotechnology gradually spread through all of agricultural research, they will contribute to sustainable development around the world. Most of this work has to

do with rather unspectacular modifications of crop plants to improve their nutritional value or resistance to pests and diseases. Mexican scientists, for example, are genetically modifying potatoes for virus resistance. The potatoes are different, but the farming methods will be about the same—the commercial growers just won't have to use pesticides against the insects that carry the virus, and the small subsistence farmers, who couldn't afford pesticides in the first place, will get more food from their crops. But sometimes you do hear of more radical possibilities, leapfrog jumps into the 21st century. "Pharming"—using genetically modified plants and animals to produce medicine—will become increasingly important in some developing countries. People who have traditionally raised goats may start raising transgenic goats as a source of medicines—which is more practical than building and operating high-tech factories to produce those same medicines. Some researchers have already developed potatoes that can confer immunity to cholera and various other diarrhetic diseases, and are now engineering the same traits into bananas. This means people can produce vaccines locally, getting around the storage and refrigeration problems that so often hamper immunization efforts in tropical countries.

3. *Biotechnology is opposed to environmentalism.* Research in biotechnology is producing useful environmental applications such as bioremediation (microbes that take chemical pollutants out of water; plants that take up mercury from the soil), and new kinds of materials including genuinely biodegradable plastics. There are plenty of pro-biotechnology environmentalists and ecologists now (the Ecological Society of America published a declaration of support for biotechnology some years ago), and I expect that in the future the new biotechnologies will be seen as more similar to the solar technologies than to nuclear power.

4. *Biotechnology is inherently dangerous.* Yes, there are risks that we need to watch out for. One is the possibility of getting allergenic substances into food products. Another has to do with developing crops with built-in pest resistance: Pests might evolve resistance to the resistance, or (in areas where there are wild relatives of the crop plants nearby) the pest resistance could spread to the weeds. I'm glad some environmental organizations—such as the Environmental Defense Fund—have biotechnology specialists who concern themselves with these problems, and who can speak up on regulatory issues, countering the industry's representatives. But this is much different from opposing biotechnology as a whole. That brings us to the fifth fallacy:

5. *If you oppose biotechnology strongly enough, you can make it go away.* You can't. What you can do—as Jeremy Rifkin demonstrates admirably—is poison the dialogue, confuse the public, and get your name in the papers. You can

also discourage the leaders of environmental organizations from demanding more research in areas such as bioremediation. But biotechnology is inseparable from the rest of biological science and an irreversible evolutionary transition, and it is not about to go away. It will—and has already to a far greater extent than most people suspect—become an integral part of research in agriculture and medicine, and a basic part of the fabric of all our lives. Most people now neither know nor care that they are eating cheese manufactured with rennin produced by genetically engineered microbes. Sooner or later we will all understand that it makes no sense to be simply for or against biotechnology, any more than it does to be simply for or against technology. The real arguments—the ones we should be having—will be about how we use the tools and who gets access to them.

The back-to-nature mystique is based on opposition to human power in nature, and its followers are always reluctant to acknowledge having any themselves.

We are going forward into an interesting few decades. With a bit of wisdom and good will—not to mention luck—we will reach the latter part of the next century with population on the decline, new opportunities for restoration and ecosystem management, and a great tool kit of technology and bioinformation. But along the way, we will have to come to terms with power. The back-to-nature mystique is based on opposition to human power in nature, and its followers are always reluctant to acknowledge having any themselves. This pose has its advantages: If you say you don't have such power and don't want anybody else to have it, you both establish your own personal goodness and duck all the problems that come with having it. But the truth is that we all have a lot of power—both individually, and collectively as a species—and will have more as time goes on.

In his book *Power and Innocence*, Rollo May eloquently dissected the psychology of "pseudoinnocence"—a willful inability to deal maturely with power. "We cannot develop responsibility," he wrote, "for what we don't admit we have." He was talking about interpersonal relations, but the observation applies equally well to the larger human undertaking of learning our way into the 21st century. We have to admit to having power, face the impossibility of leaving nature alone, and cultivate our environmental ethics and policies accordingly. And as that happens, we may begin to develop some genuinely deep ecology.

The Making of a Dissident[2]

When I first laid eyes on Peru's Apurìmac valley, I declared it to be the most beautiful place I had ever seen. The sinuous Apurìmac River sparkled in the bright sunshine, radiating an intense blue color as it coursed swiftly over beds of sand and gravel between towering walls of virgin forest. At close range, the passing river emitted an audible hiss, the sound of roiling gravel being swept along the bottom by a powerful current. Soaring ranges of the Andes frame both sides of the fertile valley through which the Apurìmac flows. Tier upon tier of forest-clad ridges mount into the cloud-shrouded distance, creating extravagant vistas of wild inaccessibility that I found irresistibly alluring. For me, a tropical biologist at the beginning of my career, to be in the heart of such a wholly pristine scene was both sublime and exhilarating.

More than thirty years have passed since I began a career of studying tropical forests in the Apurìmac valley. The valley then had few inhabitants, but those few had already irrevocably altered the status quo. These self-proclaimed pioneers had claimed the best sites in the valley. The indigenous Campa Indians, once sovereign over the whole region, had been displaced from the fertile valley floor and had retreated into the foothills. To the Campas, the pioneers were alien invaders and usurpers. To the pioneers, Indians didn't count. By the criteria of the pioneers, the forest was unclaimed wilderness because it had not been cleared. Ownership could be claimed only of cleared land on which someone had obviously toiled. Everything else was up for grabs.

To be sure, the first pioneers were intrepid souls, for reaching the valley in those days entailed a grueling seven-day trek over the Andes with a train of pack animals. These first settlers to breach the wilderness were driven not by a love of solitude and nature but by the lure of fertile land and what it promised for the future. These were ambitious people, determined to create wealth out of virgin nature.

The completion of a road into the valley brought the wilderness idyll to an abrupt and jolting end. Financed by the Alliance for Progress (Alianza para el Progreso), President John F. Kennedy's much ballyhooed international economic development program, the road opened the floodgates to a second wave of invaders. These were not the scions of wealthy landowning families, as the first pioneers had been, but landless and illiterate peasants from the Andean highlands. In the vanguard of a demographic explosion that continues to drive people into rain forests the world over, these *colonos* (settlers) veritably poured into the valley. Every arriving truck carried several families perched atop the load.

---

2. Article by John Terborgh from *Requiem for Nature.* Copyright ©
1999 Island Press. Reprinted with permission.

With little more than their clothing, an ax, and a machete, they set off into the forest in search of a dream, land they could call their own. Many of them had never seen a tropical forest before.

With the weekly arrival of scores of families encouraged by a government-sponsored land distribution program, the frontier melted away in what was, in retrospect, no more than the blink of an eye. An impromptu shantytown sprang up where the road ended on the riverbank. The once proud but now demoralized Campas retreated into the distance, always one jump ahead of the *colonos*.

By 1972, the year I last saw the Apurìmac valley, the population of *colonos* had swollen to more than a hundred thousand and was still growing steadily. By then, hardly a tree remained of the magnificent forest that had so recently filled the valley bottom. Plantations of coffee, cacao, and coca and slash-and-burn patches had replaced the forest and were appearing on the lower slopes of the mountains, a sign that the fertile valley floor had all been claimed.

When I decided to leave the valley, I knew I would not return. I left because the wild nature that had drawn me there had been extinguished in just seven years. What has happened to the Apurìmac valley in the years since my last visit concentrates in one small region all the passions and violence that frontier zones inspire. The soils and climate of the valley are ideally suited to the cultivation of coca. Coca was widely grown there during my time, but it was treated as any other agricultural commodity and sold in the legitimate market. To be sure, there were traders who smuggled bales of coca leaf out of the valley on the backs of mules, but only to avoid the government tax. Coca leaves have been chewed in the Andes for centuries; they are appreciated by workers for their ability to assuage hunger and to numb the pain of hard labor. Peru has always condoned a legitimate market for coca leaf, but not for refined cocaine. Cocaine is a vice of the modern world.

By the mid-1970s, the dark clouds of the drug boom had begun to gather, and one by one the friends I had made in the Apurìmac were forced to flee for their lives. The entire valley was gripped in terror as innocent citizens became inextricably caught up in the struggle between government forces and increasingly powerful bands of narcotraficantes. It was impossible to remain neutral in this struggle. Government forces routinely threatened people at gunpoint, demanding that they serve as informers. Anyone called in for questioning by government investigators was suspected of having divulged information and risked reprisals from the other side. Anyone involved in producing, processing, or transporting *pichicata* (cocaine) viewed anyone who was not as a threat. If you weren't with them, you had to be against them. There was no in-between. Bodies lying beside the road

What has happened to the Apurìmac valley in the years since my last visit concentrates in one small region all the passions and violence that frontier zones inspire.

or floating down the river served as frequent reminders that like it or not, everyone was involved.

With the rise of the Sendero Luminoso revolutionary move-ment in the early 1980s, the alignment of forces in the valley shifted, but the struggle continued. The revolutionaries found natural bedfellows in the narcotraficantes. The Sen-deristas cared about ideology but not about drugs, whereas the narcos cared about drugs but not about ideology. Com-plementarity of interests led to an unholy alliance in which the guerrillas tied down the police and military, confining them to heavily fortified positions at night and leaving the narcos free to pursue their business unhindered. In return, the narcos shared their profits with the Senderistas, who used the funds to finance their movement. Throughout the entire period from the late 1970s through the early 1990s, when the government of Alberto Fujimori finally restored security to Peru, the Apurìmac valley, a peaceful wilderness only a short time before, was too dangerous a place for the likes of me—or, for that matter, any outsider.

Being witness to the explosive destruction of rain forest carried out in the name of development, the blatant disre-gard of indigenous rights, the corrupting influence of drug traffic, and the abject fear that gripped Peru during the hey-day of the Sendero Luminoso has profoundly influenced my thinking about conservation. These experiences, and many others I shall relate, have convinced me of the extreme chal-lenges ahead in the effort to conserve some bits of tropical nature for posterity. Poverty, corruption, abuse of power, political instability, and a frenzied scramble for quick riches are common denominators of the social condition of devel-oping countries around the world. It is in this vastly different social context, contrasting in nearly every respect with the comfortable conditions we enjoy in the United States, that tropical nature must be conserved if it is to be conserved at all.

Poverty, corrup-tion, abuse of power, political instability, and a frenzied scramble for quick riches are common denomi-nators of the social condition of developing countries around the world.

Tropical forests have been a consuming passion for me throughout my career as an academic scientist. I have spent nearly a third of my adult life in the forest, living in make-shift bush camps or at a rustic research station in Peru's Manu National Park, which I discovered in 1973 after fleeing the Apurìmac valley. Located in a distant corner of the upper Amazon basin, the Manu is relatively inaccessible and so represents tropical nature largely as it existed before humans intruded into the scene.

Beyond my experiences in the Manu, I have had occasion to visit tropical forests all over the world and to view the problems of tropical conservation at first hand. These experi-ences have given me a global perspective on biological pres-ervation that few people are privileged to have. What I have seen convinces me that the conventional wisdom now being applied to the conservation of tropical nature is misguided and doomed to failure.

As a tropical biologist, I have been invited to serve on the boards of directors of a number of international conservation organizations. Such organizations typically appoint a token scientist or two to provide a point of view that would otherwise be lacking. Serving on these boards has been an eye-opening experience for an ivory-tower academic who is most at home in the rain forest and the classroom. As a naïve outsider ushered into the company of some of the titans of society-politicians, bankers, chief executive officers, heads of foundations, the fabulously wealthy—at first I felt out of my depth. But after sitting through a few meetings, I realized that some of the organizations were rudderless ships, lacking both vision and knowledge. Many of my fellow board members had barely stepped into the developing world, and then only to visit game parks or to dine with presidents and government ministers. Few, if any, of them had seen how a developing country looks from the bottom. Moreover, none of them, including me, was a conservation professional. Most of them specialized in financial management and the bottom line.

The world suffers no shortage of conservation crises.

Board meetings were largely devoted to lengthy discussions of the financial state of the organization: what was being done to raise money; whether budget goals could be achieved; what the president's compensation should be; which public relations firm should be hired for the next campaign; whether to rent more office space or construct a new building; and endless matters of this sort. Where were the deep discussions of conservation policy and strategy? They simply were not on the agenda.

It is said that some corporate executives can't see beyond the next quarterly report, an attitude that prevails to an unfortunate degree on the boards of conservation organizations. Boards want to see results. Goals therefore cannot be too distant, and above all, they should be concrete or, better yet, quantifiable. Approaches and directions are often fad or crisis driven, reflecting the public's short attention span and the organizations' unending need to attract new members.

The world suffers no shortage of conservation crises. Elephants, rhinoceroses, and tigers are under relentless assault for their highly valued body parts. Around the world, it is easy to raise the alarm for a disappearing parrot here, a rare crane there, a vanishing tortoise somewhere else. Conservation emergencies such as these are the stuff of fundraising campaigns, but they don't add up to a coherent plan for saving nature.

To be fair, the officers of conservation organizations are obliged to walk a tightrope between the shifting whims of a fickle public on one side and the narrow agendas of major donors, such as the billion-dollar foundations, the U.S.

Agency for International Development (USAID), and the World Bank, on the other. The freedom from financial concerns needed to enable them to sit down, chart a course, and then stick to it simply does not exist. Conservation organizations thus become prisoners of the bottom line, much as corporations are.

Faced with constantly shifting fads in conservation policy, a desire to impress directors with short-term results, an unending need to respond to crises, and an almost obsessive preoccupation with the demands of fund-raising, officers of conservation organizations are distracted from thinking deeply about ways in which conservation can be achieved over the long term. Yet no other institutions capable of crafting a global conservation strategy exist.

Seeing all this from an insider's point of view has filled me with apprehension. What can be done to ensure that nature survives the twenty-first century? That is the central question of this book, to which each chapter provides a partial answer. But from this one question come others. Is conservation being successfully implemented in the areas where most of the earth's biological wealth resides? If not, what will be required to ensure success, when success is defined as preserving the earth's wealth of wild species for the next 100 years, just to start? Can science provide adequate guidance? What types of institutions should champion the cause? How many obstacles lie in the way of our creating institutions that can sustain nature through the twenty-first century? Can the obstacles be diminished or removed? Having spent much of my adult life in tropical South America, I am perhaps more keenly aware than most people of what the challenges are. But no one, including me, has a magic wand that will make the challenges disappear. I can only offer some suggestions and hope that conservation organizations and governments will respond by designing programs robust enough to endure a century of unprecedented social and technological change.

Conversations: Paul and Anne Ehrlich[3]

Paul and Anne Ehrlich, Stanford University professors and population control advocates, don't suffer fools gladly, as this frank discussion with them makes clear. As in their new Island Press book, *Betrayal of Science and Reason*, the Ehrlichs rely on hard scientific data, not rosy speculation and optimistic fantasy. They have been the country's best-known population authorities for 30 years, since Paul Ehrlich published *The Population Bomb*, which argued forcefully that the planet was positioning itself for catastrophic human overcrowding, food shortages and mass starvation.

It was while doing field study on butterflies, reef fish and birds in the 1950s that the Ehrlichs first began to think about human population impact on a rapidly disappearing ecosystem. "Around the world," they write in *Betrayal*, "we have watched humanity consuming its natural capital and degrading its own life-support systems. Virtually everywhere—be it the Conoros Islands or California, Dehli or Detroit, Antarctica or Alaska, Fiji or Florence, Tanzania or Tokyo, Australia or the Amazon, Beijing or Bora Bora—we've seen the results of gradually building pressures caused by increasing human numbers, overconsumption, and the use of environmentally damaging technologies and practices."

The Ehrlichs have their critics, who point out that the worst of their doomsday predictions haven't come to pass, but the weight of scientific evidence clearly supports their point of view—that humanity has only briefly postponed a catastrophic collision with the consequence of runaway population growth.

E: *It's now been almost 30 years since your book* The Population Bomb *was first published. It had enormous impact on many people who probably had not thought much about population issues before, and I think it ultimately led to a downsizing of the American family. But now you would say that Americans need a second waking up regarding population?*

PAUL EHRLICH: Yes, population has become more a part of the standard discourse, but one of the things people still don't understand is how big a connection there is between environmental problems and population size. There is a lot of concern about immigration, which is basically people flowing up a gradient of wealth, but there is almost no concern about consumption control in the United States. We

---

3. Interviewed by Jim Motavalli. Reprinted with permission from *E/ The Environmental Magazine*, Subscription Department: P.O. Box 2047, Marion, OH 43306; Telephone: (815) 734-1242. Subscriptions are $20 per year.

have a dual problem: the third-largest population in the world and this incredibly high level of per-capita consumption, serviced very often by sloppy technologies. I'm afraid that most Americans who are aware of population problems tend to think of them in terms of poor countries.

Do you think of population as a sheer numbers problem? Is there a definitive carrying capacity of the Earth?

PAUL EHRLICH: The carrying capacity of the Earth depends on the behavior of the individuals. At current behavior we're clearly above the carrying capacity because we're reducing the capacity of the planet to support people in the future. Now that doesn't mean that, in theory, if you worked out a system by which everyone was vegetarian and nobody went anywhere, you might be able to permanently support something like the present population—although few scientists who look at all the factors think that would be possible. By almost any standard, we are beyond carrying capacity now; but that doesn't mean we can't still go beyond that capacity for some time.

ANNE EHRLICH: We're well past carrying capacity now, but a lot depends on what kind of lifestyle people are living and what kind of technologies we'll have. There's always the possibility that new technologies will support more people, but you can't put your money on them before they show up. The Green Revolution [which spread fertilizer technology to the Third World in the 1960s] created a small miracle in doubling and tripling small crops, but there's no reason to think that will be repeated. There are biological limits to what you can get in terms of crop yields.

Your most recent book, **The Stork and the Plow,** *takes a rather vivid look at the environmental degradation we've experienced in the last couple of decades. Do you think that's a major factor in carrying capacity? I know that Lester Brown of Worldwatch Institute raised a big furor when he wrote that China may not be able to feed itself in a few years.*

ANNE EHRLICH: Lester Brown is right to focus on China, because no other country has a population of one billion and an economic growth rate of 10 percent a year. India is almost as large [in population] but its economy is growing at a much smaller rate. No one could foresee an increase in demand there that would parallel China.

PAUL EHRLICH: We're not able to support the present population on income from our natural capital; we're only doing it by exhausting our capital. That's a one-way street. In other words, we are getting rid of deep, rich agricultural soils through erosion, by creating pavement, and we are getting rid of our fossil ground waters by overpumping them, by paving over recharge areas, by permanently poisoning them with industrial effluents. So we're running into severe water constraints, and water is a non-substitutable resource in

We have a dual problem in the U.S.: the third-largest population in the world and this incredibly high level of per capita consumption, serviced very often by sloppy technologies.

most uses. We're also getting rid of biodiversity. I think most knowledgeable scientists believe we've now launched the biggest extinction episode since the one that wiped out the dinosaurs about 95 million years ago.

I believe anthropologist Richard Leakey calls it the "sixth extinction"?

PAUL EHRLICH: There have been a series of very large extinction episodes through geologic times, and unless things change very rapidly, this one will match the earlier ones. Of course, there were no human beings when the earlier ones were going on. People do not seem to understand that their fates are imminently intertwined with the other organisms of the planet. That is, they are working parts of the life support system, the eco-systems that supply our economy with absolutely irreplaceable services. In other words, if we lose most biodiversity, we will also lose our industrial civilization.

What do you say to the people Leakey calls "the anti-alarmists," who say that a lot of the really horrible things population critics talk about haven't happened, that species are always dying out?

PAUL EHRLICH: The one resource that we will never run out of is imbeciles. The new book Anne and I wrote basically takes on all of the arguments of the "don't worry, the environment is in great shape, all we need is unconstrained capitalism and everything will be fine"–crowd and we take the arguments one after another and present the scientific community's consensus on it. But it's like creationism, you just can't put some of these things down. There's just an anti-intellectual, anti-science trend that is very serious in the United States, fed by idiots who just keep publishing this nonsense. You may have seen Gregg Easterbrook's *A Moment on the Earth*; it's got hundreds of serious scientific errors.

On population in particular? How is it wrong?

PAUL EHRLICH: Easterbrook says that if you travel east from San Francisco, you quickly get into areas that have "barely known" disturbance from human beings. Now, moving east from San Francisco you go through the polluted San Francisco Bay, which has had virtually all of its wetlands destroyed; then through the polluted and developed East Bay Foothills; then into the solid agricultural Central Valley; then into the over-grazed, logged and no-top-predators-left Sierras; then into the over-grazed and full-of-exotic-plants Great Basin. If you go all the way around the world east from San Francisco you won't find any area that hasn't seen some major intrusion from human beings, and most of it is significant. The book is very popular, but it's just dead wrong from one end to the other.

A lot of people are looking ahead to the coming age of environmental goodness or something. Well fine, but unfortunately scientists are charged with presenting their best diagnosis of the situation, and they're not necessarily right. I make mistakes, all of my colleagues have made mistakes, but one of the things that we're forced to do is get our stuff carefully reviewed by our colleagues before we publish it so we maintain our scientific reputations. You're not going to get the credibility of the scientific community unless you have your stuff reviewed, unless you avoid childish errors.

But some of this pseudo science is just amazing. [Ehrlich arch-nemesis] Professor Julian Simon says in the 1994 book *Scarcity or Abundance* that we now have in our minds and libraries enough information to keep the human population growing for...guess how many years.

Thirty? Fifty?

PAUL EHRLICH: You're a little low. Seven *billion* years. Well, I did a little calculation. The world population is currently doubling about every 40 years. But if you give Simon a break and calculate it at a millionth of the current rate, that is, doubling every 40 million years, for seven billion years, there would be more people than there are electrons in the universe. I mean, this is the sort of crap they put out and yet these people are taken seriously. If I believed something like that, they'd throw me out of the National Academy of Science, I'd lose my tenure at Stanford, my colleagues would laugh at me wherever I went.

In E, we have published ads from a group called Negative Population Growth (NPG) promoting immigrations curbs. Some of our readers wrote in to say the ads were racist, and that what groups like that really want is to keep out Third World people or people of color.

PAUL EHRLICH: We do live in a racist society, but one can't say that all people who are opposed to immigration are opposed for racist reasons. I think some of them are. The facts of the case are fairly simple. Immigration to the United States is a disaster for the entire world, because immigrants take on the characteristics of Americans and become super consumers and add to the most over-populated, environmentally destroying country in the world. What we should have, and NPG is exactly right, is a birth-plus-immigrants rate that is lower than our death-plus-immigrants rate. We should have slightly fewer people moving into the population than are moving out, and keep it that way for a long time until we can get down, maybe in a century, to a sustainable population.

ANNE EHRLICH: I think it's perfectly reasonable to be tough on illegal immigrants, with stricter border controls and other measures. And beyond that, our quotas for legal immigration are much too high; they should be cut back by a quarter, though I'd prefer not to commit to an absolute number. We have the fastest-growing population of the developed countries, over one percent a year when you add together

Immigration to the United States is a disaster for the entire world, because immigrants take on the characteristics of Americans and become super consumers and add to the most over-populated, environmentally destroying country in the world.

one million legal immigrants, 2.5 million babies born and continuing illegal immigration.

I was wondering how important you saw the role of religion as a damper in preventing population control. You wrote in The Stork and the Plow *that President Reagan and the Pope had formed something of an unholy alliance to both keep down family planning funding and to stop the spread of abortion services.*

PAUL EHRLICH: There is a very big difference between religion, which I think is very helpful to a lot of people and in most cases does not affect reproductive behavior at all, and the political actions of the Pope and the Catholic hierarchy. If Paul Ehrlich tells people to have fewer babies, they don't necessarily listen. If the Pope tells them to have more babies, they don't necessarily listen either, as is evidenced by the fact that the average family size in Italy is 1.2 children, the lowest in the world. There is no Catholic problem in the population issue; there is a problem of the Pope making it much more difficult for governments to provide contraceptive services.

Could you make some projections of population, what it would be in the year 2025 or 2050?

PAUL EHRLICH: Projections show something in the vicinity of eight to 12 billion by the middle of the next century. All the assumptions are that we won't see a significant rise in death rates and in birth rates. The median assumptions would lead you to something like 10 or 11, assuming a continuing decline in birth rates. We'll be very lucky in some ways to get to eight or nine billion without having a bad die off, and it's going to rely very heavily on the effects of widespread land use changes; how bad the climate changes induced by global warming will be, and other factors. We're running a vast experiment on ourselves and taking out no significant insurance against destroying our life-support systems.

You actually have some optimistic passages in The Stork and the Plow. *You talked to parents in India who, 20 years ago, would have had four or five kids, but now only have one or two.*

PAUL EHRLICH: In the last 20 years, we've seen very clearly that one way to get birth rates down is to empower women, particularly to make them literate. The state of Kerala in India has a tradition of women being empowered and literate, and their fertility rate is lower than that of the United States now. Unfortunately, the resources are not being made available in many places that would help get that job done, due in no small part to former President Ronald Reagan and some of the meatballs in the Congress at the present time.

ANNE EHRLICH: Study after study shows that the more autonomy women have, the more likely they will be to

> *In the last 20 years, we've seen very clearly that one way to get birth rates down is to empower women, particularly to make them literate.*

accept birth control, limit families and keep them healthy. When women have decision-making power, that's what they do.

Are you at all hopeful that what you saw in India will snowball and counteract the rapid population growth that you'd see happening otherwise?

PAUL EHRLICH: We are getting some progress in that area, it's just not fast enough. What I would hope for is that people would realize that their basic security is environmental security, that there are just too many people in the world, all trying to consume much too much using very sloppy technologies, and that something will finally have to be done about that.

ANNE EHRLICH: I'm not necessarily pessimistic. World population is now growing at 1.5 percent a year, where 30 years ago it was over two percent. Some of the higher population projections are really scary, but some of the lower ones are also possible and we should shoot for them.

IV. Some Solutions to the Ecology Crisis

Editor's Introduction

There are no easy solutions to the complex and wide-ranging challenges presented by the global ecology crisis. As we have seen in the essays in this collection, political, economic, social, and cultural factors are as daunting as technical ones. In this section are presented proposals by three experts concerned with the impact of climate change, species survival, and other environmental issues. This is not to say that their suggestions are the only solutions; indeed, there may be many viable approaches to the problem. These three proposals offer thoughtful and sometimes challenging solutions that should be part of the global dialogue on this vital issue.

As the developed nations move into a postindustrial economy, it is important to realize that many developing nations look to the old Western models of industrialization based on large-scale uses of nonrenewable resources. Richard C. Rockwell, in "From a Carbon Economy to a Mixed Economy: A Global Opportunity," critically examines the role of carbon as the "element of choice" for the world's industrial economies. Rockwell advocates, among other things, an end to the inefficient and ecologically unsound "urban spawl" that has come to characterize life in the United States. He fears that future generations will fault us for the "long time it took science to make itself heard" in this debate, "and the ensuing decades of delay in acting on a solid theory that was supported by mounting empirical evidence." On a hopeful note, he comments that the concept of "goods" is being increasingly applied not just to manufactured products, but to non-material "goods" like "the quality and protection of the environment."

Randy Hayes of the Rainforest Action Network takes a more activist viewpoint in promoting his "Five Hundred Year Plan" for sustainable economic development that includes comprehensive changes in approaches to land use and restrictions on the logging industry. Hayes argues that "the world's deforestation to date and its rate of increase have given rise to a state of global emergency." Logging is one of the most sensitive ecological issues today, whether in Oregon or Brazil. The industry claims that logging is necessary to sustain a viable economy and to assure long-term employment of its workers. Critics of this viewpoint--sometimes branded as "tree huggers"—think that this is a short-sighted approach, since the long- and even short-term benefits of deforestation are devastating to local and global ecological systems. The issue is fraught with emotion and complexity. Granted, Hayes takes an activist's stance. He writes with passion and determination, as his thesis statement that "The world's deforestation to date and its rate of increase have given rise to a state of global emergency. Yet an effective response to this problem could, more than anything else, help us build a sustainable society in our lifetime. The 500 year sixfold approach is offered as a framework to halt deforestation and its consequences."

Finally, Ronald L. Trosper, in "Incentive Systems that Support Sustainability: A First Nations Example," urges policy makers to consider the "potlatch system" of aboriginal peoples of the Pacific Northwest as a possible solution to the global ecology crisis. Unlike Western capitalism's emphasis on private property, the potlatch tradition supports the sharing of surpluses with the larger community. Trosper asks whether this approach could serve as a viable model for the global ecology of the twenty-first century. Looking to aboriginal models is not necessarily a derivative of some "New Agey" world-view; Trosper offers evidence about the economies of the potlatch societies that he believes are useful to our own societies.

I had hoped to include an essay by Grace Thorpe in this anthology; unfortunately, due to her brief illness, her article arrived too late for inclusion. Grace is the daughter of Jim Thorpe, the Native American athlete who was the hero of the 1912 Olympics and who is regarded in some circles as the "Athlete of the Century." In addition to keeping the memory of her father alive, Grace Thorpe is a tribal judge and health commissioner for the Sac and Fox Nation of Oklahoma. She also serves as president and director of the National Environmental Coalition of Native Americans, and is working with determination to prevent the dumping of radioactive wastes on Native American lands in the American West. The opening paragraph of her statement might serve as a fitting preface to this section on "Some Solutions to the Ecology Crisis" in that it reminds us that ecology is not an arcane subject for "experts." Indeed, every living creature is an expert to be honored and cared for, a concept that has its resonances in many cultures, religions, and societies. She writes: "The Great Spirit instructed us that, as Native people, we have a consecrated bond with our Mother Earth. We have a sacred obligation to our fellow creatures that live upon it." And she concludes: "As a mother and a grandmother, I am concerned about the survival of our people just as Mother Earth is concerned about the survival of her children . . . The Iroquois say that in making any decision one should consider the impact for seven generations to come. As Thom Fasset, who is Iroquois, reminds us, taking such a view on these issues often makes us feel we are alone, rolling a stone up a shill. It keeps rolling back down on us. That may be the only way, however, for us to live up to our sacred duty to the land and to all of creation."

From A Carbon Economy To A Mixed Economy: A Global Opportunity[1]

A curious feature of human economies is that they have always been based upon the same chemical element that is the foundation for life itself. Carbon is the common ingredient in the fuels we buy and burn, and also the fuel for photosynthesis and the raw material of which we are made.

Photosynthesis is critical for our lives and well-being, for despite all advances in modern technology, we still lean almost entirely upon that elemental process for both energy and food. Through photosynthesis, plants on land and in the oceans harness the power of sunlight to convert carbon dioxide, water, and minerals into organic (carbon) matter such as leaves and wood. In these materials, the captured energy is stored until they slowly decay or chance to burn.

The energy of carbon—most of it in coal and oil deposits from organisms that lived millions of years ago—is one of the major natural resources that we utilize today. Carbon powers factories, heats and lights homes and working places, and fuels transportation. It was carbon that made the Industrial Revolution possible, and it is the ever-increasing use of carbon fuels since that time that has so profoundly improved the quality of life for many of the Earth's peoples. But as is now well known, in pursuing these ends we have released enough carbon dioxide into the air to affect the course of climate, and potentially, the well-being of peoples and nations around the world, for centuries to come. And each day we add more.

This article is about the role of carbon in human life and actions that might reduce that role. It reviews how we came to be dependent upon stored carbon energy, including what happened in the transition from predominantly agricultural to more urban societies, as well as some of the environmental effects. Assuming that reducing our present carbon dependency is in the human interest, it presents a range of conceivable governmental policy options as well as actions that individuals and companies can take, quite on their own. Finally, it considers some of the complications involved in arriving at policies to deal with elevated levels of atmospheric carbon dioxide and other greenhouse gases.

---

1. Article by Richard C. Rockwell from *Consequences* vol. 4, no. 1. Reprinted with permission.

CARBON-BASED LIFE, CARBON-BASED ECONOMY

The three major kinds of life—producers, consumers, and decomposers—are all involved in the cycling of carbon through the Earth system, and each plays a different role.

Plants, the foundation of all life, are the primary producers. The organic compounds that they create through photosynthesis are consumed in a complex food chain, with humans (for now) at the top. Like many other animals, we consume either the plants themselves or the fats and proteins of food animals, which are produced from plants or animals that they themselves have eaten. A waste product of all these consumers is carbon dioxide.

Yeast and fungi and soil microbes are all examples of decomposers; their metabolism also releases carbon dioxide when they reduce complex organic molecules into simpler compounds.

The global carbon cycle relies heavily upon the work and interactions of these three kinds of life. This was as true in the days of the dinosaurs as it is today, for animals of all kinds have always exploited carbon energy.

With the advent of humans the role of carbon in the global environment took a qualitatively different turn.

The first steps

With the advent of humans the role of carbon in the global environment took a qualitatively different turn. Although their own impacts were immeasurably small, it was proto-humans of several million years ago who initiated the practice that has led, inexorably, to the difficult energy decisions that vex the leaders of the world today. When Neanderthals first learned how to control fire, they unlocked the stored energy of carbon in trees and thus began to tinker with the cycling of carbon through the Earth system.

Around the world, we have systematically cleared forests to make room for farms and pastures and settlements, and to utilize the wood that is cut for fuel and building material. The cutting and burning of forests worldwide is probably the most visible alteration that we have made to the face of the Earth. Rapid and nearly complete deforestation at the local level has followed human settlement on every continent that bears trees, since the time that humans adopted settled forms of agriculture.

The clearing and burning of forests is not peculiar to the modern age, or even to the millennium that is about to end: Plato noted that he could look out over hillsides that within living memory had borne forests but that now could barely sustain bees in their search for flowers. The island of Madeira, which means "wood," was densely covered by primeval forest when Henry the Navigator colonized it in the 15th century. Within a decade, massive fires had cleared the entire island for settlement and agriculture, producing soil that had been enriched by the ashes of trees. The European colonists of North America were amazed at the extent of the primeval forest, which stretched almost unbroken from the Atlantic to the Mississippi River. A squirrel, some said, could travel halfway across the continent without ever touching the ground. As one pioneer put it, the settlement of North America required a "war on the woods," and that war was fought and won in a remarkably short time.

Coal and oil

Carbon in a different form was in use as early as the 4th century B.C., when blacksmiths were already burning coal in their stalls. Today, our continued reliance on stores of naturally-sequestered carbon—largely, coal and oil and natural gas—adds billions of tons of carbon dioxide to the atmosphere each year, over and above that generated by decomposition, the respiration of animals, and other natural processes.

Our reliance on carbon-rich fossil fuels began—like most other dependencies—in a small way: a primitive steam engine, fueled by coal from Welsh and English mines, was developed by Savery in 1698. More than six centuries earlier, William the Conqueror had failed to recognize the immense value of the coal that lay beneath the land in the islands that he had taken. In directing his ministers to survey English landowners and all their property, to gather information for the Domesday Book, he included standing timber but neglected coal, even though Romans had burned it in Britain before 400 A.D. Until steam engines came along, coal was simply not a very important resource.

About 150 years ago, the available carbon energy sources were further expanded to include petroleum products, when techniques were devised, in 1854, to distill fractional products from crude oil. Before that time, crude oil had been used primarily for lubrication, road building, and the caulking of ships. Without question, the availability of distilled petroleum fuels vastly accelerated the global-scale environmental changes that concern us today, although the burning of coal, alone, would probably have led us to the same eventual problem.

ENVIRONMENTAL IMPACTS OF A CARBON-BASED ECONOMY

The burning of timber, peat, and particularly coal, oil, natural gas, and other fossil fuels has enormous impacts upon the environment. The effects appear in different forms at different scales, from the smoke of backyard charcoal grills, to smog in urban areas, to air pollution that crosses the boundaries of countries and continents, and ultimately, to the potential for climate change on a truly global scale. The last of these effects is quite different from the others, in that climate change takes far longer to develop, will last for decades to centuries, and is essentially irreversible within a human lifetime. Once released into the air, carbon dioxide and some of the other greenhouse gases can remain there from decades to a thousand years or more.

Soot and smog and toxic gases

Short-term air pollution—comprised of both invisible, noxious gases and minute but more apparent solid particles—is an almost unavoidable environmental consequence of a carbon economy. Carbon fuels differ greatly in what they release into the air, with natural gas ordinarily the least polluting. When petroleum products such as gasoline or diesel fuel or heating oil are burned, nitrogen oxides and hydrocarbon vapors (which lead to toxic ozone at ground level), solid particles of various sizes, and toxic carbon monoxide are all released into the air. This combination, when exposed to sunlight, is the classic recipe for photochemical smog, which can at times be deadly in some cities, particularly for residents with respiratory problems. Carbon fuels can also generate sulfurous smog when fossil fuels, especially coal, are burned. This different kind of smog, combined with other airborne particles, has produced high rates of lung disease in the cities of many developing nations.

With the stimulus of clean air and water laws, the developed world has reduced its emissions of pollutants such as sulfur dioxides, nitrogen oxides, and carbon monoxide. In many cities of Europe and North America, the air is becoming cleaner, although perversely, the catalytic converters installed in motor vehicles to reduce urban air pollution have now been found to produce a greenhouse gas, nitrous oxide.

The most severe air pollution can now be found in large cities of the developing world, and particularly in Asia, Africa, and Latin America. If the developing countries follow the carbon path of the industrialized nations, economic growth will add far more pollution: the improvement of living standards in the developing world is already putting more cars and trucks on the roads, increasing the demand for electricity, and adding more factories. In most countries, every one of these improvements now relies on fossil fuels.

Other improvements in living standards compound the problem. People in developing countries are systematically changing their diet, to eat more of their meals at the richer end of the food chain. The cattle and sheep that provide meat are often raised on pastures that were cut or burned out of forests that once stored carbon. Economic development, if it follows the well-worn path of fossil fuel dependence, inevitably tips the natural balance between carbon storage and carbon emissions. Population growth, which adds new consumers, can only push it farther.

The most obvious environmental consequence of conventional economic growth in the developing world will likely be even dirtier and less healthy air in cities that are often already terribly polluted. Ironically, it may be this more readily-sensed form of air pollution that will help slow the

The most obvious environmental consequence of conventional economic growth in the developing world will likely be even dirtier and less healthy air in cities that are often already terribly polluted.

global build-up of greenhouse gases. In the short-term interests of cleaner air, people in polluted cities and towns may come to resist the burning of coal and oil. Cleaner energy technologies lean less heavily on carbon or avoid it altogether, and reduce total carbon dioxide emissions.

CARBON DIOXIDE AND THE GREENHOUSE EFFECT

Federal clean air and water legislation did not include carbon dioxide as an air pollutant, for although a product of combustion, it poses no direct threat to human health. Indeed, with every breath we add some to the air, ourselves.

Although carbon dioxide makes up less than 0.04 percent of all the air around us, this minute and invisible fraction is a critical ingredient for sustaining the surface temperature, and hence the climate of the Earth. With the help of a handful of other greenhouse gases, it holds the heat of sunlight in, serving as a kind of blanket or natural thermostat to keep the temperature of the Earth in a habitable range. The most prevalent of these *radiatively-active* gases is water vapor, but the most important, in terms of both sensitivity and the impacts of our own activities, is carbon dioxide.

Effects of higher surface temperatures: the meaning of a few degrees

More than twenty years of ever-better models of the effects of increased CO_2 leave little doubt that the surface of the Earth will as a result warm, significantly. But the amount and timing of the temperature increase differs from model to model, depending on the assumptions and simplifications that they employ.

The most recent report of the Intergovernmental Panel on Climate Change, endorsed by hundreds of the most respected atmospheric scientists in the world, projects an increase of from 2 to 5° C (about 4 to 10° F) over the next 100 years.

An increase of a few degrees on any thermometric scale seems small and inconsequential, and far too small to justify mandated changes in the economies and way of life of both developed and developing countries. Indeed, a change of a few degrees is not much more than the difference in the average temperatures of Miami and Key West, and both are doing fine, thank you. What is more—as opponents of controls on fossil fuel emissions are quick to point out—warmer is better in some ways: what we should fear, they say, is not hotter temperatures, but colder ones.

In fact, a change in either direction of but one degree C in the mean temperature of the whole planet is a lot, and as much as modern man has ever seen. Far more is involved than slightly warmer days or nights. Most scientists agree that the most important of the climatic changes that will accompany the global warming of an enhanced greenhouse effect will be alterations in the timing and distribution of precipitation. Computer models demonstrate that such changes are a direct outcome of altering the balance of heat energy between the tropics and temperate zones.

Changes in precipitation

Much of the world's agriculture depends not only on how much rain or snow falls but also upon when it comes, and in what doses. Changes in the timing of precipitation have more serious effects on some crops than do changes in the total amount.

Some areas of the world barely sustain agriculture under today's precipitation patterns. While some of these marginal areas might receive more rain with global warming, a larger number may become ill-suited for even subsistence agriculture. Sadly, and as a result of who lives where today, almost all such areas are found in the poorer countries of the developing world. Countries that experience cyclical droughts, such as India or southern Africa, are likely to experience more sustained and perhaps more frequent dry periods.

Other effects

Growing seasons will also change in many latitudes. Associated changes in precipitation will mean that agricultural zones for some crops will shift to higher latitudes, with more of Canada and Siberia likely to become suitable—where soils allow—for cereal grains. Animals and many plants will also need to migrate. For many animals and some plants, migration will be made more difficult by the way we have altered and fragmented the land—and for some species the shift will be more dangerous because of new predators for which they are unprepared. Some of the organisms migrating into newly warmer, wetter, or drier territories could be bacteria, fungi, viruses, and other disease organisms new to the area.

With climatic change, the agricultural productivity of some nations could rise, and others fall. The agricultural sectors that will be hardest hit are now thought to be those in developing countries in ·tropical latitudes, and these are already disadvantaged. The economic development of these nations could be seriously curtailed were climatic change to compromise their ability to feed themselves. Adaptation to altered climate regimes is possible in agriculture as in other economic sectors, but most of the changes that are called for carry either an economic or cultural price: intensive irrigation may be too expensive for many small farmers, for example.

People are also affected by temperatures and precipitation. Extreme weather events, such as strings of very hot days, could cause deaths in both the developed and developing countries. Whether storms, including violent events such as tornadoes and hurricanes, would increase in a warmed world is not yet fully known.

It is likely that coastal regions, which are the most intensively used of all land, will face changes due to rising sea

While some of these marginal areas might receive more rain with global warming, a larger number may become ill-suited for even subsistence agriculture.

levels. The sea has been rising throughout this century, due to thermal expansion of the oceans and some melting of ice. Forested wetlands at low elevations are believed especially vulnerable to sea level rise, and coastal salt and freshwater marshes (such as are found on the coast of Florida) may be converted to open water. Groundwater in coastal zones may become saline, as is already happening on some Pacific islands.

There is also reason to speculate that this rise in sea level will exacerbate the damage caused by severe storms. Even if the ocean rises but a few centimeters, storm surges will be somewhat more destructive and will travel further inland. Low-lying islands, including much of insular Asia and Oceania, as well as low-lying continental areas, such as Bangladesh, could be at serious risk in this eventuality. Indonesia—now the world's fourth most populous country—is comprised of more than 4,000 islands, and the people that live on them cannot all cluster on the rocky sides of mountains when heavy storms occur. Nor can they continue to grow rice on lowland soil that has been made saline by the infiltration of sea water into aquifers.

The El Niño–Southern Oscillation (ENSO), the most significant cyclical weather phenomenon of the present era, could be geographically more widespread in a warmed world, and it could be somewhat more intense as well. The severity of the 1997–1998 El Niño, which brought some of the warmest months in more than 100 years of record, may or may not be ascribed to this century's warming trend. But its diverse impacts give examples of what can be expected in a world made warmer by CO_2. For example, the fires that began burning out of control in Indonesia in the autumn of 1997 and that made much of Malaysia and Thailand difficult places to live and breathe were almost certainly associated with the delayed onset of a rainy season. During the previous El Niño, fires burned throughout the western Pacific, including some that licked at the edges of cities in Australia. In the dry late spring of 1998, fires burning in Mexico caused air pollution in the southeastern U.S. and Texas, and similar conditions in the summer brought fire storms in Florida that raged for weeks.

THE CONTEXT OF A RESPONSE

The global warming that is now expected will follow on the heels of two dramatic changes in the history of the Earth: the enormous growth of the human population and the similarly enormous expansion in the economic productivity of much of the world. In about 170 years, from 1820 to 1992, the number of people on the planet increased five-fold, from about 1.1 billion to nearly 6 billion. In the same span of time, the economic productivity, per person, grew by about a factor of eight. The product of these two large rates of growth

The global warming that is now expected will follow on the heels of . . . the enormous growth of the human population and the similarly enormous expansion in the economic productivity of much of the world.

was a truly awesome increase in the global economy of about a factor of forty.

In the industrialized nations the principal driver of economic growth in this century has been rising productivity, while in the developing countries it is the increasing number of people. About 90 percent of the population growth of the next twenty-five years will occur in the developing world, with all but about 10 percent of it in urban areas. The result will be a world divided into developed nations of nearly stable populations and developing nations with growing populations, with enormous per capita differences in production and consumption of goods and services. Each person in the industrialized countries produces and consumes about fourteen times as much as do those in the poorest of the developing countries.

Each person in the industrialized countries produces and consumes about fourteen times as much as do those in the poorest of the developing countries.

It was carbon that made the economic growth of the industrialized countries possible, for fossil fuels provided about 75 percent of all the energy that they used. That energy was expended on transportation, heat and power for industrial production, and on mechanization, fertilization, and irrigation in agriculture, with each investment increasing the productivity of the average worker. Their evolution from countries that were primarily rural and agricultural in 1820 to predominantly urban nations today, sustained by a relatively tiny but extremely productive agricultural labor force, was the result of agricultural investments in energy.

The more than 120 developing countries of the world are now making similar investments of energy and human capital, reaching for economic security, if not yet for prosperity. If they should all achieve the economic level of industrialized nations of today, their combined economy would be about five times larger than that of the entire globe today. And if those economies rested on the burning of carbon fuels, the result would be massive increases in CO_2 emissions.

The responsibility for transforming economies from those based on carbon to more diverse, or "mixed" economies, falls first on the developed nations. It is they who have contributed by far the greatest share of carbon to the atmosphere—and they will continue to do so, on a per capita basis, for many years to come. But responsibility also falls upon the countries of the developing world.

This article maintains that the path of these nations to a mixed energy economy does not lead through the technologies that are now predominant in the industrialized nations, but rather through dramatic improvements in energy efficiency and renewable energy technologies, which work in their best interests. These improvements are becoming available for both the developed and the developing countries, and some of them are ready to be deployed, today.

CURES FOR THE CARBON DEPENDENT AND CO-DEPENDENT

Today, with so much else perturbing the global environment, it may seem strange that political attention and debate is focused so intently on but one element of one problem: the reduction of a portion of those emissions of carbon dioxide that stem from human actions. But few if any major problems can be tackled all at once. Moreover, long-standing addictions, particularly, are probably best addressed in small steps, one day at a time.

Costs and benefits of quitting

When faced with the need to find replacements, carbon—for many applications—can be a hard act to follow. Fossil fuels are a proven and relatively cheap source of energy, and for developing countries, one which can be quickly and easily employed to reach their economic goals. Many nations have readily-available reserves of carbon energy, including the vast coal reserves in China and abundant wood in tropical forests. Some other energy technologies—such as nuclear power—as yet still require higher levels of investment and greater levels of skill to maintain them. Moreover, developing nations rightfully note that every one of the developed nations became that way, in part at least, by burning carbon fuels.

It might thus seem that a shift to non-carbon energy sources would impose a much greater burden on developing countries than on richer ones. That perception—coupled with the tacit acknowledgment that the highly disproportionate per capita consumption of fossil fuels in richer nations is the root cause of today's carbon problem—was no doubt behind the initial stance taken by most of the developed nations at the 1997 Kyoto conference on climate change: namely, that the less developed countries could and should be exempted, altogether, from carbon controls.

In fact, if the more efficient and cleaner alternative technologies become available at a low enough price, it may prove far *easier* for developing nations to switch quickly to other fuels.

The Energy Foundation is a San Francisco–based, grant-making organization funded by the MacArthur Foundation, the Rockefeller Foundation, the Pew Charitable Trust, and the Joyce Mertz–Gilmore Foundation to aid in the transition to a sustainable energy future. It has pointed out that less developed nations have much less invested in carbon dependency, and can start *now* with the more advanced energy infrastructure, and "leapfrog" today's industrialized countries into a new age of more efficient and cleaner energy. In meeting global standards for reduced carbon emissions, they will avoid many of the costs of long-term environmental degradation and clean-up that are associated with fossil fuels, and reduce the pollution that now plagues many cities in the developing world. The choice before the developing countries is between mimicking the resource-intensive development path taken by today's industrialized nations or taking the higher road of modern, more efficient technologies.

The hurdle that looms so high for developed nations is the enormous cost of replacing most of their existing energy infrastructure and associated technologies, in a span of time that is far shorter than prudent investment would normally dictate. The ordinary life span of a coal-fired power plant is at least fifty years. If it is replaced earlier, only a portion of its economic value will have been realized. That calculation will undoubtedly affect and may retard developed nations in taking the steps that are needed to reduce their emissions. But the calculation just stated was not complete: we should also include the costs to health and the environment of not replacing dirty technologies that are heavy emitters of CO_2.

The hurdle that looms so high for developed nations is the enormous cost of replacing most of their existing energy infrastructure and associated technologies.

What the other sources of energy are

The range of possible alternate energy sources is large: hydrogen (as in fuel cells), solar, geothermal, tidal, hydropower, wind, renewable biomass, and nuclear options are all available and should all be explored. One oil company has predicted a near future in which one-half to two-thirds of the energy now derived from fossil fuels comes instead from renewable energy sources. Economies with mixed energy dependencies will eventually replace carbon economies through the use of such alternative fuels, most of which are becoming better and cheaper each year.

We need to look anew, as objectively as we can, at the nuclear option, for times have changed. The strong public reaction to first, the Three Mile Island accident in 1979, and then the 1986 Chernobyl disaster, has had the effect of eliminating from consideration one of the several available energy options that contributes almost no carbon dioxide. To be sure, with fission reactors of the type now employed, there is a serious problem of nuclear waste disposal. But the threat of catastrophic failure, as at Chernobyl, no longer need apply, because fission reactors can now be designed to be inherently safe. Still, despite the apparent environmental advantages of a new generation of nuclear technology, it will take political courage for this option to be seriously explored, even within the developed world.

Nuclear power should also be considered by at least some developing countries. It is obviously in the world's interest that all countries which take the nuclear path have the capacity to operate reactors safely, and commit, somehow, to use their nuclear capability only for peaceful ends. This means more than having qualified technicians and allowing regular inspections by United Nations teams. It may well imply that nuclear reactors should primarily be restricted to countries with stable and democratically-elected governments.

Meeting the carbon dioxide challenge could also open tremendous business opportunities for industries of the developed world, both within and outside their borders. In spite of the recent downturn in parts of Asia, the economies of some developing nations are among the fastest-growing in the world. New energy technology—or products related to it—that can be purchased and maintained at a reasonable price is likely to appeal throughout the world to both governments and industries. This would seem particularly the case for technologies that could offer greater efficiency and less pollution at about the same cost as those built around carbon.

The "Clean Development Mechanism" of the Kyoto Protocol provides a structure in which incentives for such development could exist. However, technology transfer continues to be politically controversial. Stringent governmental controls on the export of sophisticated computers to manage windmill farms, for example, could block the needed transfer of technology.

A WIDE RANGE OF POLICY RESPONSES AND ACTIONS

Two policies that have been considered to facilitate a switch from carbon fuels include (i) a global carbon tax and (ii) regulatory changes designed to reduce emissions through improved energy efficiency. The tax on how much carbon a fuel contains would induce industries and consumers to consider technologies that are more energy efficient or to switch fuels. The regulatory changes would be designed to ensure that those technologies are available. As a package, these policies might be extremely effective in reducing emissions.

Still, there are difficulties with both proposals. Were the carbon tax a heavy one, it could depress economic performance enough to limit the ability of an economy to switch to more efficient technologies. In any event, the carbon tax is probably politically impossible to enact in this country at this time. Similarly, the intended benefits of regulations could be accompanied by perverse effects, particularly if they dictated the use of specified technologies. This has often been the case when government-dictated policies act against the forces of the prevailing market.

Another policy, favored by the present U.S. Administration, would make it internationally legitimate for industries in certain countries to trade the right to emit greenhouse gases. This proposal blends regulation with market forces, in creating a legal right to trade a product—CO_2 emissions—that has no intrinsic value. The value of the trade resides, of course, in the avoidance or mitigation of climate change.

Some other options

Both before and after the Kyoto conference, the public focus regarding CO_2 emissions was on policies and regulations. That is because Kyoto was an intergovernmental event, and governments think in terms of taxes, emissions trading rights, and energy regulations. Meanwhile, others were acting: automobile companies were developing fuel cells and better batteries, engineers were improving solar panels and electric motors, and architects were designing more compact cities. In fact, there is a wide range of options for reducing carbon dioxide emissions, and only some of them can be directly controlled by the government.

The possibilities for emissions reductions include the alternative energy sources cited above but are not limited to them.

The possibilities for emissions reductions include the alternative energy sources cited above but are not limited to them. Energy conservation in all forms—including better insulation or more efficient electric motors—merits renewed attention. Much was achieved in the U.S. to conserve energy during the oil crises of the 1970s, but far more could be done today. Improved energy efficiencies, in the home, the personal automobile, the office building, and the factory, are all attainable and within the reach of each citizen and each company.

Greater attention to conventional and unconventional methods for sequestering excess carbon is also merited, even though these methods are likely to buy us no more than a limited period of grace, since the carbon stored in biomass, for example, eventually returns to the atmosphere as CO_2. A conventional example that relies on the natural storage of carbon through photosynthesis is reforestation, which is prominent in both the Kyoto Protocol and the Clinton Administration's plans for meeting its Kyoto obligations. Another is the more effective use of biomass as an energy source, with its continuous cycling of carbon between plants and the atmosphere. It has also been suggested that purposive alterations to the earth system, such as altering parts of the oceans to make them more acidic, could augment carbon storage unconventionally, although the ecological consequences of deliberately perturbing so vast a natural system remain to be explored.

Homes and working places could be more closely clustered to minimize commuting and to reduce pressures on natural ecosystems. In fact, America's "urban sprawl" is both a significant contributor to its level of CO_2 emissions and a noticeable force in reducing the amount of carbon that is sequestered in trees. Telecommuting might eventually reduce energy use, but at least initially it seems to lead to more, rather than less, travel.

The hidden costs of what we do

While we have control over the use of the fuels that we purchase ourselves, we are limited in what we can do, as individuals, to reduce the amount of carbon dioxide that each of us indirectly contributes to the atmosphere. Most of the carbon dioxide for which humans are responsible is emitted by activities that are at least one step removed from the consumer's direct control. Personal transportation, sometimes thought to be the predominant source of emissions, accounts for roughly 20 percent of all the CO_2 that we add to the air, but not for the majority. Industrial steam power, motors, and appliances account for about the same percentage of emissions. In general, about 1/3 of the added CO_2 comes from all forms of transportation, 1/3 from industrial uses, and 1/3 from building uses such as space heating.

Recognizing that consumers do not have direct control over the emissions from some of the activities from which they benefit, the Detroit Edison Power Company has offered to sell electricity that was produced with cleaner energy technologies, at a higher price per kilowatt hour. This gives customers an opportunity that is not otherwise available to determine their own contributions to CO_2 emissions. The pricing, however, is obviously perverse, since the immediate economic incentive for the buyer is to take the cheaper option, even though in releasing more carbon to the air, it imposes a greater cost on society. The case illustrates a general problem: the ultimate costs of much of what we buy or use are not included in the price that we are charged, be it the generation of electricity, the burning of gasoline, or the destruction of a rain forest.

In this country, for example, each time any of us buys a ton of Portland cement (for example, to add a sidewalk or pave a driveway), we have indirectly introduced about a ton of carbon dioxide into the atmosphere, since that much was emitted in producing what we purchased. We are also responsible, though one more step removed, when we support, through taxes, a highway improvement, or when we rent or purchase an apartment or home, since the same ton-for-ton ratio applies to the cement used in constructing each of these. And although its label says nothing about carbon dioxide, a garment purchased in a Fifth Avenue shop, for example, may have been produced in a factory that derived its power from the burning of soft coal.

What governments can do

The fact that the problem is so often beyond the reach of the individual is one of the reasons why governments must be involved in reducing greenhouse gas emissions. Through force of habit, they will most likely try to act through either fiscal or regulatory means.

Around the world, however, there have been all too many examples of the limitations of either of these blunt tools when used to force intended social or economic goals. In situations as complex and personal and fundamental as the production and use of energy, they could prove particularly inappropriate. In addition, many governments are relatively weak, and lack the policy instruments that are available to more affluent and industrialized nations.

What governments can do best is to facilitate innovation. In some cases, all that is needed is to remove archaic regulations and subsidies. If building codes would permit, Portland cement can be replaced with stronger and better construction adhesives and cements that are associated with far lower carbon emissions. Governments can also provide leadership that encourages business and industry to make the changes in the design of engines, or plants, or jobs, that only they can make. They can fund technological research to develop alternative energy sources and ways to reduce energy consumption or, perhaps better, provide tax credits to industry for undertaking these needed steps. Perhaps most importantly, governments are the principal sponsors of the research that clarifies the ways in which humans are significantly affecting the global environment, and in specifying possible ways to cope with these perturbations.

SOME THOUGHTS ABOUT PITFALLS AND OPPORTUNITIES

We have much to learn, as governments, companies, and individuals make decisions about policies and programs to reduce and control CO_2 emissions. It may help to keep in mind some of the pitfalls and difficulties that have come to light in the past when science and policy intersect. A few of these are given below.

- Dialogues are more efficient and productive than monologues: governments should speak with, not to, industry. And the developed world should speak with, not to, the developing countries.
- The essential openness of science regarding margins of error or remaining uncertainties in any finding can weaken what it has to say. It is also all too easily exploited by any who have reason to filibuster or delay.
- The often called for "balanced viewpoint," to be of any worth, need recognize which and what fraction of the more knowledgeable hold divergent views. It is not hard to round up lone dissent on almost any question in science, if one wants to find it. But these voices from the fringes of opinion need to be weighed in the same balance by which responsible consensus is defined.
- The fact that something is "only a theory" does not in itself argue against its validity. Many if not most responsible health or environmental warnings, from contaminated food to floods and tornadoes and global greenhouse warming, call for prudent action well before every conceivable doubt has been removed, which often comes only with the threat itself.
- Concepts that are central to the formulation of policy, as is the concept of "sustainable development" in the Framework Convention on Climate Change, must be

defined very carefully and explicitly, to avoid almost certain confusion and conflict.

- The actors in changes as far reaching as the global transformation of a carbon economy into a mixed economy will not only be governments. They will also be supra-national, intergovernmental, and non-governmental organizations, and multinational corporations. These organizations and companies may ultimately play more important roles in reducing emissions than national governments.

- As new measurements and findings come to light, what we know about climate change and global greenhouse warming is improved and refined, in ways that can impact adaptation and mitigation strategies. Policies that address these issues obviously need to be framed in the light of the best and most recent knowledge. For example, a recent finding that a forest in Manitoba was a net source of CO_2 in the years when the spring season arrived earlier, raises questions as to whether some of the forests identified in the Kyoto Protocol as sinks for excess carbon might only add more CO_2.

- Technology is also changing rapidly, and regulations that specify the use of particular technologies may soon prove ineffective or obsolescent. It is far more effective to specify goals, and allow industry to find the optimum ways of obtaining them.

Regulations that specify the use of particular technologies may soon prove ineffective or obsolescent.

- Limited steps, such as those that are mandated in the Kyoto Protocol, are seen by some environmentalists as too small to be of use, but they are often more achievable than more sudden, sweeping changes. We will probably have to settle for a basket of small steps, none of which is itself a cure, rather than seek a single, perfect policy.

- Some of the steps that will help in small ways to decrease CO_2 emissions will bring added and immediate environmental benefits. One of these is the more efficient burning of coal, for it will also reduce air pollution and consequently, lung disease. Steps of this nature should be taken as soon as they are recognized to be feasible.

- Large steps, such as reducing the rate of population growth in countries where it is still high, cannot be ignored just because they are difficult and will take many years to achieve.

- Wasteful manufacturing processes cause environmental damage and ultimately cost the manufacturer money, if only in environmental clean-up. Reducing waste, as through programs that are intended to reduce the industrial consumption of resources, could significantly reduce emissions of all sorts.

- Long-term planning horizons—reaching well beyond next year's budget or the next election—must somehow be made more realizable. Lessons may be learned from the planning of the New York City water system, with its roots in the 19th century, and that city's water-tunnel building program, still underway, that will not be completed until well into the 21st. In an uninterrupted effort for the public good, the vision and the efforts to accomplish it have been kept alive and handed on from generation to generation of city planners.

- Needed environmental policies, such as those to reduce CO_2 emissions, can be made more realizable if we put the correct price—including the ultimate costs to society—on what we consume. Pricing can be a powerful lever for effecting social change, for the choices that we make each day are influenced very strongly by the costs that are involved. Yet in a year when much of the world's attention was fixed on carbon dioxide emissions, in the U.S. a gallon of gasoline was priced less than a gallon of spring water.

- The world's cultures seem to be evolving away from a focus on economic security toward one on non-material "goods"—such as the quality and protection of the environment—although indeed more slowly in the developing world. Democracy, unlike authoritarian societies, offers a way to express these values at the ballot box.

A PERSONAL CONCLUSION

Hundreds of years from now, long after we have moved on from a carbon economy to one mixed with other energy sources, scientists and citizens may look back in wonderment upon the time when people and nations finally accepted the serious nature of the enhanced greenhouse effect, and took the first hesitant steps to mitigate or adapt to its impacts.

From that distance, and with the wisdom of hindsight, they will surely find much for which to blame us. They cannot fault us for the CO_2 that was added to the air before the likely effect was known, just as we do not blame our great-grandparents for taking the energy path that made us one of the world's richest societies. Nor can they fault us for not knowing everything, and they may indeed reflect, as did Tennyson long before, that "science moves but slowly, slowly; creeping on from point to point."

But they will charge us, surely, with a fundamental failing: the long time it took science to make itself heard, and the ensuing decades of delay in acting on a solid theory that was supported by mounting empirical evidence. They will mostly wonder how we could not see that adding more and more greenhouse gases could only warm the Earth. And they will question why we did not move faster to employ technologies that were more energy-efficient, and alternative fuels that were cleaner, once we knew that they were available.

Five Hundred Year Plan[2]

A SIX FOLD SYSTEMIC APPROACH ADDRESSING:
* Global Forest Protection
* Certified Logging
* Fiber Supply
* Demand-Side Management
* Transformation of Government & Corporation Policy
* Sustainable Economic Development

BASIC PREMISE

The world's deforestation to date and its rate of increase have given rise to a state of global emergency. Yet an effective response to this problem could, more than anything else, help us build a sustainable society in our lifetime. The 500 year sixfold approach is offered as a framework to halt deforestation and its consequences.

BACKGROUND AND CONTEXT

Wild naturally evolving forests are an essential component of the biosphere's life support system. Aside from providing innumerable services to humanity, forests fulfill the vital functions of preserving wildlife habitat, stabilizing the Earth's climate, protecting watersheds, and maintaining soil productivity. They are home to most of the world's vast array of life forms. Natural forests need to be viewed as dynamic, diverse, and integrated systems as articulated in the emerging science of conservation biology and ecology. Their whole systems character must be both protected and restored.

If local community rights to utilize and control the local commons had been clearly established, and an understanding of the ecological and social costs had been reflected in price mechanisms and cutting practices over the last 500 years, the actions below would not be necessary. Such rights and internalizing of external costs have not been and are still not in place. Tragically, subsidized destruction is practiced instead. Market models that do not value whole forest systems or biological diversity cannot be depended on to protect them. The desperate situation requires a surgical cut away from industrial society's increasing dependence on wood fiber from natural forests. Until such time as community rights, local control, and a deeply-held ecological ethic are in place, the positions outlined below are suggested as a framework of sufficient strength to reverse the tragic tide of logging caused deforestation and its consequences. What remains is to make these positions politically feasible while assuring that they are economically and socially just.

Natural forests need to be viewed as dynamic, diverse, and integrated systems as articulated in the emerging science of conservation biology and ecology.

2. Article by Randy Hayes from Rainforest Action Network Web site. Copyright © Rainforest Action Network. Reprinted with permission.

No set of universal principles can adequately address the political and economic reality of every local community. Local communities–informed of all potential ecological and social costs - should have an increasing level of power to decide such issues. Exceptions to the outlined approach will need to be made on a case by case basis. However, adherence to this six point framework will orchestrate an environmental "U-turn", stabilize existing primary and secondary forests, and provide for society's needs. Over time this approach will increase the quantity and quality of forest ecosystems and the vital services they provide for all inhabitants of the Earth.

THE PLAN

In order to better ensure a world of forests, Rainforest Action Network believes that society in general, but in particular governments and corporations should:

A. Take an official position that the world's deforestation to date and its rate of increase have given rise to a state of global emergency and that an effective response to this problem will help us build a sustainable society.

B. Clarify the underlying key ecological and human values or goals. An initial list includes:

- a functioning biosphere (or healthy planet) maintaining ecological services and evolutionary processes such as hydrologic and nutrient cycles
- a large network of reserves representing each type of wild, intact, natural ecological systems with migratory corridors and buffer zones
- an increase in primary forest cover throughout the world helping foster viable populations of native species in natural patterns of abundance and distribution
- prosperous communities, rooted in place, with meaningful work
- social equity between people and groups, now and in the future
- democratic self-governance with accountability: transparency, access to information, and effective public participation in decision making
- sustainable economic models or systems that incorporate social and ecological costs into the price one pays for goods or services.

C. Implement an independently verifiable cap on investments (trapped capital) in ecologically harmful activities (such as logging in primary old growth forests or chlorine bleach pulp mills). Input on the types of investments that need to be capped should be sought from diverse interests including ecologists and citizen activists. All employees from entry level positions to the Board of Directors should be schooled systematically in the basic principles of ecology.

This will help people identify problem areas and opportunities.

D. Take a six fold systemic approach to global forest protection, certified logging, fiber supply, and demand-side reduction as a framework to halt deforestation and its consequences. This plan would encompass the following points:

1. Primary Forests

Low impact traditional local wood use can and should continue. However, a moratorium should be instituted (with compensation where appropriate) on all commercial export logging in remaining primary forests worldwide. This should be on public and private land. Domestic use bans should follow shortly thereafter. [Communities that protect natural forest systems are rendering an essential service to the rest of the world.]

a) Provide incentives for individuals, companies, local communities, or governments controlling primary forest that agree to protect the remaining primary forests from logging and other forms of deforestation.

b) Parties should be recognized and honored for protecting these forests by all of us who ultimately benefit from their protection.

c) In part, massive deforestation and the timber trade have contributed financial benefits and hence lifestyle improvements, as well as political and economic leverage over less deforested countries. Those who have previously benefited should provide the compensation for primary forest protection as a way to help offset the loss of ecosystem services deforested countries no longer provide to the biosphere.

d) A global compensation fund should be established and governed by an authorized international body, which includes citizen groups (or NGOs).

e) Compensation should be paid on a periodic basis upon verification by an independent international body of successful protection of primary forests.

Using the principles of conservation biology, efforts must be made towards restoring primary forest functions and values.

Charting the Increase of Primary Forests While Supplying the Human Needs Now Met by Wood Fiber Products

2. Secondary Forests

Secondary forests should be encouraged to mature. Using the principles of conservation biology, efforts must be made towards restoring primary forest functions and values. Local people and current land owners should be trained and employed in this process.

Natural selection eco-forestry practices should be used whenever commercial logging is carried on in secondary forests. Independent certification should be mandatory using the Forest Stewardship Council model.

3. Commercial Restoration Zones (CRZ)

Utilizing a transparent, public participation process, revert degraded land or existing plantations toward mixed native species (trees and other flora) mimicking native conditions while maintaining commercial extraction viability. Local community values, rights of approval, and local employment must be incorporated into this process.

- Society should look to CRZs for the main wood product supplies for the next 20 - 200 years.
- Independent certification for CRZs should be mandatory using the Forest Stewardship Council model.
- In about 100 years, start a 300 - 400 year process to manage an appropriate percentage of commercially logged secondary forests and CRZs for a return to late successional primary forest values. This should be done in areas adjacent to primary forests' core areas to create buffer zones and provide corridors for wildlife.

4. Tree Farms/Plantations

Tree farms are not forests and do not foster or protect as broad an array of biological diversity as a natural forest. However, where it is socially, ecologically, and economically-acceptable, utilize existing plantations or convert marginal or unused agricultural land to mixed species plantations.

- This will help build needed carbon sinks.
- Societies should plan to convert tree farms or plantations to CRZs over the next 200 years and then to managed secondary forests and eventually to primary forests.

5. Alternative Fibers

The use of alternative fibers such as Kenaf, hemp, and agricultural waste will allow us to shift demand away from virgin wood fiber and reduce pressure on the world's remaining primary forests. Alternative fibers can be used in virtually all papers and many building materials.

6. Additional Demand-Side Management

Alternative fibers (as described in point five) are a form of demand-side management that can help alleviate pressure on forests to supply wood fiber. Using a holistic or systemic approach to the supply of wood products opens up additional opportunities. For example, we can meet the lumber needs of home building by utilizing earth architecture techniques.

Demand-side management promotes the most ecologically, economically, and culturally sustainable ways to meet the human needs now met by forest products. An aggressive search for options will be necessary for the environmental U-turn and allow for the realization of a goal such as the one stated below.

Demand-side management promotes the most ecologically, economically, and culturally sustainable ways to meet the human needs now met by forest products.

Institute the gradual reduction of wood and wood paper use of 7.5% yearly for the next 10 years (totaling 75%). Analogous goals have been set in the Netherlands. This should be done while supporting additional and appropriate economic activities at 8 + %. This process alone will create an increase in sustainable economic activity while generating more meaningful jobs developing alternatives.

The general sectors of industrial wood use are:
- Paper and packaging
- Construction
- Pallets and other shipping uses
- Finished wood products such as furniture

Categories of demand-side activity to reduce wood use (in the above general sectors) are:
- Decreased per capita consumption—reduce
- Increased reuse—re-use
- Increased recycling—recycle
- Increased use of alternative materials—replace
- Increased efficiency in processing—redesign
- Product durability, design improvements—redesign

Using a holistic demand-side approach opens up many solutions. Communication systems can shift to electronic mail and reduce wood use. An example would be accessing telephone directories via computers. Reusing copy paper by vacuuming toner off of the paper might be another solution. Salvaged wood from renovations, demolition, and natural disasters would be a way to increase reuse and recycling. Likewise, building techniques might replace wood with other natural materials such as earth or straw. Redesigned building codes can result in safe, strong wood-frame houses that use 30% less wood.

E. Commit to a timetable and submit a transition plan for implementation and independent verification. Ensure that all related government agencies, companies, operations, or divisions integrate this systemic approach into their business in order to become ecologically sustainable.

F. Avoid working with other corporations or governments which do not adhere to the above systemic approach and standards of ecological sustainability.

CONCLUSION:

Along with our practical day to day work, those in the timber trade, finance community, ecology movement, and general public need first and foremost to speak the truth about what must be done. Additionally, we need to orchestrate ecological policy shifts and real world practices in a manner that achieves social equity (within and between nations). Nature - with her ecological systems and myriad life forms - cannot speak for herself in our government chambers, and corporate or environmental board rooms. It is our responsibility to speak on her behalf as best we can. We cannot ask for too much, and we had better not ask for too little. Everyone must aggressively do their part. If we do not, history will be justifiably unkind to us. While fostering (in our lifetime) a sustainable society, we must demand what is needed to support all life on Earth.

Definitions & Comments

Alternative Fibers: In this paper alternative fibers refers to non-wood fibers. Examples include: Kenaf, hemp, and agricultural waste. They will allow us to shift demand away from virgin wood fiber and reduce pressure on the world's remaining primary forests. Alternative fibers can be used in virtually all papers and many building materials.

Commercial Restoration Zones (CRZ): Utilizing a transparent, public participation process, revert degraded land or existing plantations toward mixed native species (trees and other flora) mimicking native conditions while maintaining commercial extraction viability.

Demand-side Management: Anything that changes consumption patterns. In the context of forest protection, it means redesigning the way we use timber products and wood-based papers, in order to reduce pressure on the world's remaining primary forests.

Natural Forest: Primary and secondary forests. Tree farms or plantations are not forests.

Tree Farms/Plantation: Tree farms or plantations are not forests. They do not foster or protect as broad an array of biological diversity as a natural forest.

Incentive Systems That Support Sustainability: A First Nations Example [3]

ABSTRACT

Prior to contact with European settlers, the incentive and governance systems used by First Nations peoples of the Northwest coast of North America provided more sustainable use of the fisheries and other resources of that region than did subsequent systems. This paper explores the major reason for that success: the requirements of the potlatch system that chiefs share their income with each other. Because chiefs controlled well-defined territories and subjected each other to review, the potlatch governance system embodied the characteristics of negative feedback, coordination, resiliency, and robustness that political scientist John Dryzek identifies as means to support ecological rationality in the management of ecosystems. This ecological rationality occurs because the sharing of income made chiefs aware of the effects that their actions had on the income of other chiefs. In addition, public discussions that occurred at feasts would allow chiefs to coordinate their actions as needed. The paper concludes with proposals for application of the potlatch system to modern circumstances. Such application means changing the rules for the distribution of income from using ecosystem resources so that all entities share their surplus income with each other. The potlatch system can be applied to modern organizations by noting that chief executive officers are like chiefs, that profit is like surplus income, and that corporations can be viewed as similar to the houses of the traditional Northwest systems. One major change is that profit is no longer privately owned, and must be shared with other organizations that use an ecosystem. Although controls on behavior mandated by state power would be reduced, a modernized potlatch system would still need to operate within a context provided by governments and international agreements.

INTRODUCTION

As ecological systems and the social systems that depend on them face crises, investigators have become interested in

---

human-ecosystem interactions that preserve the ability of ecological systems to provide goods and services in perpetuity. Some of the aboriginal peoples in North America, First Nations peoples in Canada and American Indians in the United States, appeared to have had such relationships at contact. This paper uses one of the examples, the residents of the Northwest Coast. In addition, when metal tools became available and population levels recovered from the epidemics, many First Nations peoples continued to use their ecosystems sustainably. For instance, the Menominee Tribe, Taos Pueblo, and Hopi Tribe in the United States, and many Cree First Nations using the boreal forest, have done so. What were the incentive and governance systems that caused members of those societies to make economic decisions that preserved the ability of their ecosystems to continually support people? Might it be that these societies, those that survive, are refugia for ideas that may be useful today?

Not everyone agrees that aboriginal peoples in North America used ecosystems in a sustainable manner.

Not everyone agrees that aboriginal peoples in North America used ecosystems in a sustainable manner. Some cite the purported fact that human immigrants caused Pleistocene extinctions of large mammals. Even if this is true, the extinction process came to an end; few were recorded between 10,000 and 400 years ago. As Callicott (1989a) suggests, perhaps a lesson was learned. Others have argued that pre-contact native population sizes and primitive technology would have prevented challenging ecosystem capabilities. Although this may have been true in some locations, recent evidence shows that estimated aboriginal populations and average harvests give total harvests that could have been near river capacity on the Columbia and Fraser Rivers (see Smith 1979, Glavin 1996). In her history of the Canadian coast fisheries, Diane Newell (1993) writes in her summary of the aboriginal system:

> Aboriginal groups developed highly successful fishing and fish-preservation technologies and regionally based systems of resource management and distribution. There is no reason to believe that Indians on the Pacific Coast were perfect conservationists. And because of the tremendous amount of salmon caught for subsistence, trade, and ceremony before contact with Europeans, we can safely assume that the aboriginal salmon fishery, with its highly productive technology, was so large that it may have significantly taxed the resource. But . . . the salmon fishery of aboriginal British Columbia sustained yields for several thousand years. What is striking is the net effect of this system. It assured everyone adequate stocks of fish over the long term. The same cannot be said for the state-regulated industrial fishery that replaced it in the late nineteenth century.

Newell is referring to population numbers that were high prior to the effect of disease. Aboriginal peoples had excellent fishing technology. One should not assert that all aboriginal peoples were good caretakers; counter-examples surely exist. This paper analyzes one region for which the evidence is strong that good caretaking did exist.

If the aboriginal system on the Northwest Coast assured adequate stocks, what incentives caused this to occur? This question does not direct attention to the usual topic: values (Hughes 1983, Callicott 1989a,b). If we are interested in modern applications of ideas provided by First Nations, adoption of their value systems as a policy recommendation has some merit. A major characteristic of the modern era is individualization, which includes personal choice of belief systems (Giddens 1990, 1991, Beck 1992, Beck et al. 1994). Thus, implementation of the policy recommendation requires persuasion; a literature of such persuasion has developed (e.g., Suzuki and Knudtson 1992). Suppose that the persuasive project succeeds: two problems (at least) would remain (1) The group of people who respect nature will need to coordinate their actions. (2) They will also have to control or counteract the actions of those who have not been persuaded. If an effective majority is persuaded that sustainability is needed, then people should act to change incentive systems. What incentive systems should be adopted to accompany the change in values?

Among the candidates are those used by First Nations peoples to organize their use of ecosystems. Many neoclassical and other current economic models presume a private property system, with the courts of a modern state enforcing ownership rules. The state provides other policies that mitigate the effects of decisions within the private property system. External effects are to be controlled with taxes, subsidies, and quantitative controls. The modern state has considerable difficulty in using these tools for controlling external effects. Among the problems are those of information, bureaucratic incentives, log-rolling in legislatures, and enforcement costs. Because First Nations peoples did not utilize modern states, we should not be surprised to discover that their incentive systems did not require state authority.

Their incentive and governance systems did, however, require that groups of people sanction those who did not obey the rules. The rules in the Pacific Northwest had three main characteristics: control of territory was clearly defined, the chiefs ruled as a polyarchy, and the whole society had an elaborate system of exchanging wealth, known as the "potlatch." The requirement to share wealth is a fundamentally important idea for managing ecosystems. When combined with the checks and balances of a polyarchy, sharing income focuses human attention on the interconnections of the ecosystem.

The requirement to share wealth is a fundamentally important idea for managing ecosystems.

This paper begins with a framework for evaluating incentive systems for their ecological rationality, drawing on work by Dryzek (1987). It next sketches a Northwest Coast incentive and governance model, and asserts that this "potlatch model" addresses ecological rationality. The paper closes with suggestions about how a modernized version of the potlatch model could be constructed through modification of contemporary organizations.

ECOLOGICAL RATIONALITY

Based upon a careful reading of the literature on how ecosystems function, political scientist John Dryzek (1987) has distilled five principles as a way to judge the ability of a human institution or collection of institutions to respond to the needs of good ecosystem management: negative feedback, coordination, robustness, flexibility, and resilience. He has also applied these categories to modern institutions such as the capitalist market and modern bureaucracies (which are found to have low scores). He did not analyze traditional institutions along with modern ones, although he briefly discusses the political organization of hunter-gatherers.

Negative feedback

If the ecosystem is departing from its best method of operation, how are signals about the negative trends processed by the human institutions? Do the negative signals lead to changes in behavior that restore ecosystem functioning to the range desired?

Coordination

Ecosystems have connections, and human institutions need to coordinate decisions to take the connections into account. Coordination within choices occurs if fishery managers avoid the tragedy of the commons. Coordination across choices occurs if waste disposal levels from one ecosystem component do not disrupt or eliminate the function of another part of an ecosystem. Does a particular human institution provide coordination across and within choices, so that ecosystem structure and function are preserved?

Robustness or flexibility

Although coordination and allocation address the issue of selection of an ecosystem state, the idea of robustness addresses the local stability of the state. Conditions in which management of an ecosystem occurs may vary from external effects. Response to the variation can be either robust (in which case the ecosystem management system can handle variation without much modification), or it can be flexible (in which case the management system makes changes to deal with the changed conditions). Response to variation can be fragile, in which case a deviation from one state may not lead to a return to that state, but rather to continued deterioration in ecosystem productivity.

Dryzek argues that robustness and flexibility are substitutes for one another, and that either, in combination with negative feedback and coordination, is a sufficient condition for ecological rationality when systems are behaving normally.

Resilience

If ecosystem functioning has degraded so much that its operation is far out of the normal range in which the above characteristics operate, can the management system implement procedures to restore normal functioning? Dryzek's idea of resilience can be distinguished from that of robustness in this manner: robustness applies to maintenance of ecosystems that are assumed to have a global equilibrium. Resilience applies when an ecosystem is in danger of flipping to a different equilibrium altogether, as during a period of reorganization (Holling et. al. 1995). Dryzek uses resilience to describe such extreme circumstances: what Holling labels ecological resilience. Many ecologists use resilience to refer to a combination of robustness and flexibility: what Holling labels engineering resilience.

A MODEL OF NORTHWEST COAST ECOSYSTEM–COMMUNITY INTERACTION

A model of the Northwest Coast system of managing both fisheries and hunting grounds illustrates the ways in which a native system of resource management can address Dryzek's ecological rationality. The model is based on the literature describing the Kwakiutl, Gitksan, and Wit'suwit'en. The Kwakiutl sources are Walens (1981), Johnsen (1986), and Weinstein (1994); these sources differ from earlier interpretations by Franz Boas. For the Gitksan, this description is based upon Adams (1973), Cove (1982), Copes and Reid (1995), Pinkerton and Weinstein (1995), and Pinkerton (1998). The Wit'suwit'en are described by Mills (1994). Skoda (1987) provides useful maps of the Gitksan and Wit'suwit'en lands. Because each tribe implemented its approach differently, this synthesis distorts each to an extent, but their example provides some principles that can be useful today.

Geography

The tribe's land area consists of a watershed with a river leading to the sea. Near the ocean, the river flows through a succession of narrow canyons; each of the canyons contains fishing sites that can be used for different salmon runs.

If ecosystem functioning has degraded so much that its operation is far out of the normal range in which the above characteristics operate, can the management system implement procedures to restore normal functioning?

Although the river is too strong in the canyons for a weir to span it, the speed of the river leads many salmon to go upstream along the banks, using eddies for rest. Consequently, fishermen with dip nets can catch many fish. Fish swimming away from the bank or below the nets pass by. The tributaries to the river, however, can be completely barricaded by weirs and traps, allowing precise control of escapement as well as harvest of the entire run. At times, the river is a mixed-stock fishery; the tributaries are always single-stock fisheries.

Hunting and gathering grounds upstream are sources of food and materials. The pattern of the year is for the people to harvest salmon in the summer, at summer villages along the river and its tributaries. Berries are also harvested in the summer. In the winter, people move inland to winter villages, living on dried salmon and berries and upon the results of winter hunts. The forest provides firewood in the winter, as well as wood for houses and canoes.

Property rights and chiefs

The land is divided into territories owned by houses. Villages consist of groups of houses, with a duality principle defining village structure: each village has two sides, and each side has two groupings of houses. A village, therefore, always has an even number of houses. For example, a village of 12 houses would have six on a side, and each side would have a grouping of two houses. Although each side of the village is equal to the other, there is a ranking within the sides, meaning that the higher ranking group provides the chief for the entire side, with the chief of the second group being "second-in-command." In the case of the 12-member village, then, each of the three-house groups has a "head chief" of the group, with two subchiefs. Each chief, whether high or low in rank, has complete authority within the lands of his house. The following rule enforces house ownership: "Any person who harvests from a house's land without the chief's permission can be killed." Even such a justified murder, however, would mobilize the dispute resolution machinery of a tribe (Mills 1994:146). Members of the house have a right to receive permission to hunt. All hunters have to follow rules specified by the relevant chief.

The hunting lands of the village are contiguous. Each house also owns fishing sites that are also controlled by the chief. Some of these sites are not within the hunting lands of the house because they are along the main stem of the river, practically within the lands of other houses.

Feasts: public decision-making, enforcement of decisions, and dispute resolution

A portion of the year (usually the winter) is designated for feasts, which can occur for many reasons, usually having to do with birth, marriage, and death. Although many different things happen at feasts, my interest is in the giving away of property, speeches, and group decisions.

One common event is that a new chief of a house holds a funeral feast for his predecessor. His side of the village hosts the feast, and his house pays the primary expenses of the feast: food for everyone, and gifts for the other side of the village. The higher the rank of the house hosting the feast, the greater the amount of gifts that are expected by the guests, and the more villages that are invited. Several years after the funeral, the new chief will hold another feast, to raise a totem pole in his predecessor's honor. Both the funeral and pole-raising feasts require saving up wealth for several years; the wealth comes from the lands of the house through the labor of members of the house, who live from food taken from the lands and the fishing sites. The chief shows his worthiness by generating the surplus required for the feast, and the guests acknowledge his position when they accept the gifts.

A belief in reincarnation can support sustainable use by increasing the weight given to future income.

During the feast, guests are invited to speak, and any public business that needs attention can be placed before the assembly. Sides take turn speaking, there is no limit placed on the time for any speaker, and any decision is reached by consensus of the chiefs present. If no consensus is reached, the matter will be postponed to another feast. If other villages need to be involved, a feast will be scheduled to invite them to discuss the matter. The feasts are a system of peer monitoring (Arnott and Stiglitz 1991).

Intertemporal considerations: reincarnation

Houses are assumed to last forever, with people occupying leadership positions in the houses during their lifetimes. Most of the tribes believe in reincarnation. The belief is so specific among the Wit'suwit'en that elders determine which children are reincarnated previous chiefs. A chief, therefore, may know who he or she was in a prior life, and may expect to be reincarnated into a position in the tribe, if not in the very house in which the person now resides (Mills 1994:118-119). Other Northwest Coast tribes were also specific in their knowledge of the identities of reincarnated souls (Mills and Slobodin 1994).

A belief in reincarnation can support sustainable use by increasing the weight given to future income. Even in the presence of a belief in reincarnation, chiefs could give lower weight to their own future income, based on uncertainty about the future. One might expect believers in reincarnation, however, to give greater weight to the future than would nonbelievers.

Production equilibrium for a common-pool resource: the fishery

Because each house owns fishing sites along the river, each controls a portion of each run's catch. Each has control of some spawning locations. The runs of salmon that pass one house's fishing sites go to spawning grounds on other houses' territories. Because the harvest from the upstream weirs affects subsequent run sizes, much interdependence exists in salmon production. If the first house is downstream and the second is upstream, near the spawning grounds, then the harvest of the first house in one season affects the harvest of the second house in that season. However, the harvest of the upstream house affects that of the downstream house only in a later year, when the next generation of the particular run returns. Such interdependence in fisheries is often modeled by use of the prisoner's dilemma game.

Production equilibrium for a watershed ecosystem hierarchy: forests, game and fish

Interdependence also exists for hunting, because many animals such as deer, moose, and bear have wide ranges.

Interdependence also exists for hunting, because many animals such as deer, moose, and bear have wide ranges. . . . The model assumes that the cost functions of firms each depend upon the quantities produced by other firms, and shows that a symmetric generosity rule causes firms to select production quantities that achieve a social optimum. When cost functions are separable, the firms can reach a mutually acceptable solution by independent action. Each can determine the right level of harvest without previously knowing that of the other firms.

In the more realistic case of nonseparable costs, the model becomes more complicated; individual firms cannot determine their private optima without knowing what the other firms intend to do. To reach a global optimum, some degree of common discussion and agreement is needed. This discussion can happen in the feast hall.

Because the models . . . are abstract, in the tradition of economic analysis of externalities, the results are quite general. The quantity of production by one firm raises the costs of production for other firms. Examples from the Northwest Coast could be as follows. Bears depend on berries and fish, among other sources of food; harvest of the bears' food by man could reduce bear populations and increase labor effort in harvesting. Had there been technology for extensive timber cutting, the harvest of trees would have, as it has in modern times, reduced fish populations through effects on rivers and stream habitat. For migratory animals such as moose, harvests on one house's lands would affect total population levels, in a manner similar to the problem with fisheries.

Once the problem of harvest level has been determined, the problem of cheating remains. When each house keeps its own profits, there is a strong incentive to cheat at the social optimum. When each house has to share its profits uniformly with others, . . . the incentive to cheat is removed.

Let modernity bring a wood fiber market

The pre-contact trade among tribes on the Northwest Coast primarily involved trade in fish and animal products. In the modern era, a market has developed for wood fiber. Excessive or incorrect harvest of trees can damage spawning and rearing portions of streams, lakes, and rivers. This is a one-way interaction, in that there is not a strong feedback: excessive harvest of salmon does not reduce tree production, although the salmon carcasses do contribute nutrients. As long as houses remain interdependent through feasts, the introduction of a market for wood fiber will not necessarily lead to excessive negative effects on salmon production. Houses that cut trees would have to share their wealth with other houses. If the timber harvest were to reduce salmon harvests, it would affect the house on its own fishing sites and would affect the ability of other houses to generate wealth for distribution at feasts.

THE ECOLOGICAL RATIONALITY TEST

If sustainability can be implemented with Dryzek's ecological rationality, a method of managing an ecosystem in a sustainable manner has to provide Dryzek's characteristics.

Negative feedback

The potlatch system provides negative feedback through the signal that a house chief gives to other chiefs with the quantity of goods given away at potlatches. A chief who is unable to maintain adequate gift-giving is subject to scrutiny by the other chiefs. Because these chiefs are themselves experts in fishery management, they can provide good review. (Because a poor harvest may be due to random environmental variation rather than management, expertise may be needed to distinguish the cause.) If a chief is not performing, his right to hold office is in jeopardy. Members of houses also have a way to signal to a chief that his management is not good: they can move to other houses (Weinstein 1994). In many of the house systems, any one individual can select among his or her kinship connections in associating with one or another house. There are two ways, therefore, for a chief who is not managing the resource well to be notified of his difficulties by other people. His direct monitoring of the resource provides a third source of information.

However, income can be generated by unsustainable activities. If a chief, in his desire to have many workers and show his ability, harvests above a sustainable rate, other chiefs have a way to deal with the problem: insisting on a greater distribution of goods at feasts. Penance for excessive harvest is sharing the output, which is the way in which a feast system solves the prisoner's dilemma in fishery management.

Coordination

. . . The sharing of surpluses among the houses addresses the effects of externalities directly. Each chief will be aware of activities by his house that reduce the income of other houses. The other chiefs will inform him of the problem in the feast hall, and he will also have a reduction of potlatch gifts received from other houses.

Robustness or flexibility

A potlatch system has some robustness for a fishery because it reduces competition and encourages restrictions on capacity (as a determinant of fishing effort). This consequence follows from the solution provided to the prisoner's dilemma. . . . Social robustness exists because the sharing of land rent among the entities means that a crisis in the productivity of what is owned by one house can be weathered by reliance on the production from other houses. If the rules for the distribution of surplus are flexible, the system as a whole may be flexible.

Resilience (far from equilibrium)

If a stock or run falls to extremely low levels, harvest must be suspended in order to save the resource. In a potlatch system, an owner can call upon the gift-giving capacity of neighbors within a scheme in which those neighbors can be assured of return to them when needed. This social insurance aspect of such reciprocity systems is well-recognized; by providing some social resilience, pressure upon a stressed resource stock can be reduced. Arthur Ray (1991) reports on a time when a failure of their salmon runs caused one village to spend an entire winter with another. Within the potlatch system, such generosity by the hosting village created obligations for the other community.

Dryzek (1987:122) argues that "polyarchy" is not good at addressing generalized interest, and among these is long-term resilience of the ecosystem. However, when there is generalized sharing of this type, attention of each of the polyarchs can be focused on the general interest in sustainable use of harvestable resources.

A MODERN IMPLEMENTATION OF THE POTLATCH SYSTEM

How might a potlatch system be implemented today? Although certain characteristics, such as capital punishment for trespass, would not be acceptable, other features might be quite reasonable. This section provides a translation from the language of houses, chiefs, and feasts to modern terms such as CEO, corporation, and profit distribution plans. One would not need to discard all characteristics of modern organizations; a reorganization of relationships might be enough.

In a modern potlatch system, let the major type of organization be a "trust," which is run by a caretaker and which hires employees. A "trust" is a general name for organizations, which can be like modern organizations such as firms, corporations, and nonprofit corporations. They correspond to what in the traditional Northwest Coast systems were called "houses."

The "caretaker" is the chief operating officer of a trust. Such a person might be called a boss, chief executive officer, executive director, chief, or trustee.

The "ecosystem review board" consists of all of the caretakers of the trusts with ownership of components of the ecosystem. The ecosystem review board has the role of a board of directors. In this case, however, the board is not representative of shareholders, because shareholders do not exist in this system. In native systems, this would be the "council of chiefs," and would consist of the governing body for the tribe as a whole.

The trusts each generate a "surplus" after all wages and costs of purchased inputs are deducted from the value of products produced by the trust. This surplus is a combination of what is called profit and rent. Each trust does not fully own its surplus, but it owns a right to a share of other trusts' surplus.

Outside persons and entities. The rights of people in the ecosystem and the rules of ownership and control apply to the ecosystem residents, the trusts, and the employees and their families. Duties to outside governments are to pay taxes to contribute to the overall enforcement and defense system of the government. Other outside entities do not have rights not granted to them by residents of the ecosystem. For instance, the right to purchase land from a house caretaker by an outsider would be subject to compliance with the rules governing the authority of trust caretakers. The caretaker, as manager of a trust, has "control ownership" of the land; he or she does not have "income ownership" (Christman 1994). This lack of income ownership means that sales of land would need the approval of all the other trusts that share in the surplus.

Rules. The right to be the "caretaker" of a "trust" would depend upon completion of an apprenticeship. A caretaker would have to demonstrate knowledge of how to manage the land, reach of river, or run of fish, or else he would lose his position. The caretaker also would have to demonstrate understanding of the rules of ownership and citizenship in this system of governance. Each caretaker, when he or she first obtained control of a "trust," would be subject to a probation period of significant length: more than a year, but possibly less than five years. The rules for removal of the

The potlatch model, in its modern form, should be applicable to boreal forests as well as to other ecosystems, because all ecosystems have common-pool resources, externalities, and problems of information among participants.

caretaker during this period would need to be specified, and they would be less stringent than the rules for removing the powers of a caretaker who has passed the probationary period. A major part of judging the quality of a caretaker would be her or his ability to provide a generous share of the surplus from her or his trust. Yet, the generation of surplus would have to be done in a manner meeting the approval of the other caretakers, who would act in their capacity as an ecosystem review board. After completion of the probationary period, certification of full caretaking powers would be given by other caretakers in the ecosystem.

Maintenance of caretaking responsibilities would depend upon annual performance. Some performance measures might be: (1) annual reporting of management outcomes and income earned to all other caretakers; (2) annual submission of investment plans for general caretaker approval; and (3) periodic distribution of a share of the value of products sold or harvested to other caretakers in the system. If the distribution is scheduled to happen annually, then each caretaker would, after receiving the distribution of surplus from the other trusts, make a plan of distribution for the surplus that his or her trust would end up holding. Some of the surplus would be distributed as "bonuses" to the employees of the trust, some would be set aside for investment, some would go to children of employees, and some would augment the retirement income of those employees who have retired. Some would also have to be paid as taxes to the governments with jurisdiction. If the trusts were providing local public services, possibly through the actions of the ecosystem review board, a portion of the surplus would also have to be paid for that. In effect, the surpluses of all of the trust organizations would be pooled and redistributed according to agreed-upon rules and commitments.

The rights of "noncaretakers," the employees of the trusts and their families would also need to be spelled out in a complete specification of this system. There would have to be employment rules, rules for hiring, rules for retirement, and so forth. None of these would necessarily be all that different from current practice, except that a plan to distribute the shared surplus to employees as well as to the trusts themselves might assist in making everyone aware of the ecosystem connections.

Application to boreal forests

The potlatch model, in its modern form, should be applicable to boreal forests as well as to other ecosystems, because all ecosystems have common-pool resources, externalities, and problems of information among participants. A potlatch system addresses common pools by solving the prisoner's dilemma. It addresses externalities by creating shared surpluses. It addresses information problems by introducing peer monitoring.

Although boreal forests are quite different from coastal river systems, specific externalities can be identified. One major source is the role of fire. Lewis (1982) investigated the use of fire by aboriginal peoples of the boreal forests. The models of this paper describe the management of populations of mammals and fish that are important food sources, and the main tool for management is harvest rate. Fire, however, is an ecological process, not a harvest rate. As applied in small-scale cases, such as a beaver trapline, fire improved the character of harvested resources, probably without externalities. However, the landscape implications of many small fires in spring do address two externalities: the maintenance of meadows and the incidence of catastrophic fire. Meadows had to be burned to prevent encroachment by woody species, for the benefit of wildlife. Areas of the forest with high fuel accumulation had to be burned in the spring to prevent hot summer fires. Both activities were viewed as community activities by the people Lewis interviewed.

To re-institute systems of sharing in boreal forests in Canada, a number of policy changes would be needed. First, the rights of First Nations peoples to territorial control would have to be recognized. Open access to non-native hunters, as documented in Brody (1988), would have to be removed. When modern technologies are applied, such as the construction of hydroelectric dams, the sharing of surplus with natives would also be needed, with a reciprocal sharing by natives of the product of the natural ecosystem with the hydroelectric authorities. Joint governance of the system might be "co-management," but the potlatch model places much control with local leadership and very little with state bureaucracies.

Joint governance of the system might be "co-management," but the potlatch model places much control with local leadership and very little with state bureaucracies.

Conclusion

This short paper cannot provide a full discussion of the many complexities of transition from the current system of private property, open access, and bureaucratic control to a system of closed territories managed by trusts under the direction of caretakers who have to share their surplus. The purpose is to show that alternative institutions make some sense, have been used in the past, and may contribute to improved resource management. Whether they are, in fact, adopted in modern circumstances depends on many issues, among which is the intensity of the crises resulting from unsustainable management of ecological and social systems in coming years. Thorough changes such as those suggested here would need a strong impetus; people deciding to change their property and distribution institutions would need to discuss the reasons and come to some mutual agreement about the wisdom of making changes. In addition, such changes would need to be nested in some manner within existing governments and international agreements.

Bibliography

Books and Pamphlets

Bookchin, Murray. *Urbanization Without Cities: The Rise and Decline of Citizenship.* Black Rose Books, 1992.

Crosby, Alfred. *Ecological Imperialism: The Biological Expansion of Europe.* Cambridge University Press, 1986, 1993.

Damkoehler, Dianna and Helen Gehrenbeck. *This Planet Is Mine.* Scholastic, 1995.

Ehrlich, Paul and Anne. *Betrayal of Science and Reason: How Anti-Environmental Rhetoric Threatens Our Future.* Island Press, 1996.

------------------. *The Stork and the Plow: The Equity Answer to the Human Dilemma,* Putnam, 1995.

Elias, Norbert. *The Civilizing Process.* Blackwell, 1939.

Gadgil, Madhar and Ramachandra Guha. *This Fissured Land: An Ecological History of India.* University of California Press, 1993.

Clotfelty, Cheryll and Harold Fromm, eds. *The Ecocriticism Reader: Landmarks in Literary Ecology.* University of Georgia Press, 1996.

Gore, Albert. *Earth in the Balance: Ecology and the Human Spirit.* Penguin, 1993.

Griffiths, Tom and Libby Robin, eds. *Ecology and Empire: Environmental History of Settler Societies.* University of Washington Press, 1997.

Griffiths, Tom. *Hunters and Collectors: The Antiquarian Imagination in Australia.* Cambridge University Press, 1996.

Grove, Richard. *Green Imperialism: Colonial Expansion, Tropical Island Edens, and the Origins of Environmentalism, 1600-1860.* Cambridge University Press, 1995.

Hammond, Allen. *Which World? Scenarios for the 21st Century.* Island Press, 1998.

Headrick, Daniel. *The Tentacles of Progress: Technology Transfer in the Age of Imperialism, 1850-1940.* Oxford University Press, 1998.

--------------------. *The Invisible Weapon: Telecommunications and International Politics.* Oxford University Press, 1991.

Kjekshus, Helge. *Ecology Control and Economic Development in East African History: The Case of Tanganyika 1850-1950.* J. Currey-Ohio University Press, 1996.

Leslie, John. *The End of the World: The Science and Ethics of Human Extinction.* Routledge, 1998.

Lines, William. *Taming the Great South Land: A History of the Conquest of Nature in Australia.* University of California Press, 1991.

Mackenzie, John M. *The Empire of Nature: Hunting, Conservation, and British Imperialism.* Manchester University Press, 1988.

May, Rollo. *Politics and Innocence: A Humanistic Debate.* Saybrook, 1986.

Metzger, Mary and Cinthya Whittaker. *This Planet Is Mine: Teaching Environmental Awareness and Appreciation to Children.* Simon and Schuster, 1991.

Mitchell, George. *World on Fire: Saving an Endangered Earth.* Scribner, 1991.

Montez, Michelle (illust.) *50 Simple Things Kids Can Do to Recycle.* Earthworks Press, 1994.

Ponting, Clive. *Green History of the World: The Environment and the Collapse of Great Civilizations.* Penguin, 1993.

Renner, Michael. *Fighting for Survival: Environmental Decline, Social Conflict, and the New Age of Insecurity.* W. W. Norton, 1996.

Robin, Vicki and Joseph Dominguez. *Your Money Or Your Life: Transforming Your Relationship with Money and Achieving Financial Independence.* Penguin, 1993.

Schama, Simon. *Landscape and Memory.* Vintage, 1996.

Schneider, Stephen. *Laboratory Earth: The Planetary Gamble We Can't Afford to Lose.* Basic Books, 1997.

Simon, Julian L. *Scarcity or Abundance? A Debate on the Environment.* W. W. Norton, 1994.

The Ultimate Resource 2. Princeton University Press, 1996.

Tickell, Crispin. *Climatic Change and World Affairs.* Harvard University Center for International Affairs, 1986.

Warren, Karen J., ed. *Ecofeminism: Women, Culture, Nature.* University of Indiana Press, 1997.

Additional Periodical Articles with Abstracts

Readers interested in learning more about global ecology may refer to the articles listed below. Please note that some of the articles listed reflect issues not addressed in this book, and are intended to help readers broaden their knowledge of contemporary issues associated with global ecology.

Current Challenges on the Orinoco. Malatesta, Parisina; Morales, Ruth, tr. *Americas*. v. 50 no6 p6-13 N/D '98

Both private and government organizations are involved in the attempt to preserve biodiversity along the shores of Venezuela's Orinoco River. The river, which is the ninth largest in the world, is threatened by deforestation, contamination, overexploitation of systems, expansion of the farm frontier, the increase of urbanization, illegal mine operations, and poaching. Among the vulnerable species dependent on the river are the West Indian manatee, the Orinoco crocodile, and the arrau river turtle. Organizations such as the Foundation for the Development of Physical, Mathematical, and Natural Sciences (FUDECI) have established nurseries for endangered species in an effort to conserve them. In addition, private landowners across Venezuela's central plains have established refuges for a variety of jungle animals.

The Era of the E-topia: The Right Reactions to the Digital Revolution Can Produce Lean and Green Cities. Mitchell, William J. *Architectural Record*. v. 187 no3 p 35-6 Mar. '99

To create sustainable cities, architects must be more radical and create "e-topias": lean, environmentally friendly, electronically serviced, globally linked cities that work more smartly rather than harder. Current cheap and ubiquitous digital telecommunication and computation systems offer the key, and if they are used cleverly, they will help architects do much more with far less. The writer presents a list of five starting points for cyber-sustainable architecture: dematerialization, demobilization, mass customization, intelligent operation, and soft transformation.

National Audubon Society's Living Oceans Program. Flicker, John. *Audubon*. v. 101 no3 p.8 My/Je 1999

The National Audubon Society's Living Oceans Program, which frequently works with the United Nations on important marine issues, is expanding its work in five major areas. These areas focus on rebuilding endangered fish and seabird populations, offering information to seafood consumers, establishing marine reserves, and introducing global standards for aquaculture.

Where the Tide Pools. Harlin, John. *Backpacker*. v. 27 no3 p33-5 Ap '99

Tidal pools are wild aquariums with a rich ecology. The diversity of marine life in a tidal pool flourishes when the tide is at its lowest, and can include sea anemone, California stichopus, rock crabs, and snubnose sculpins. When observing tidal pools, it is acceptable for observers to pick up and examine many of the pool's creatures. Guidelines for observing tidal pool ecology are presented.

Marine Ecosystem Sensitivity to Climate Change: Western Antarctic Peninsula.
Smith, Raymond Calvin; Ainley, David G.; Baker, K. S. *BioScience*. v. 49 no5
p393-404 My '99

Long-term research in the western Antarctic Peninsula (WAP) region reveal how
changes in the physical environment are linked to changes in the marine ecosystem. Analyses of paleoclimate records have indicated that the WAP region has
changed from a relatively cold regime between about 2,700 years before present
(BP) and 100 BP to a relatively warm regime during the 20th century. Moreover,
polar ecosystem research and paleoecological records have detected ecological
transitions that have occurred due to this change, including a shift in the population size and distribution of penguin species. The writer discusses such topics as
the four climate indicators examined in the WAP, conceptual models used to link
climatic processes and ecosystem responses, and the mechanisms of climate
change.

Who's Where in North America? Ricketts, Taylor H.; Dinerstein, Eric; Olson,
David M. *BioScience*. v. 49 no5 p369-81 My '99

Conservationists have proposed various criteria to identify areas of highest conservation priority, but species richness is usually the principle parameter. The prominence afforded to species richness arises because of the significance of so-called
biodiversity hotspots, given that preventing species extinction is the main aim of
conservation. The problem with overall species richness as a standard, however, is
that inadequate range data have been obtained so certain indicator taxa must be
used to infer results about the distribution of other taxa. Moreover, the three most
widely known choices for indicator taxa worldwide are not the most informative
and accurate, whether they are used alone or in combination. Instead, species richness data should be combined with other indicators, including species endemism,
levels of threat, and ecosystem service value.

Microclimate in Forest Ecosystem and Landscape Ecology. Chen, Jiquan; Saunders, Sari C.; Crow, Thomas R. *BioScience*. v. 49 no4 p288-97 Ap '99

The importance of microclimate—the suite of climatic conditions measured in
localized areas near the earth's surface—in influencing ecological processes has
become an essential component of current ecological research. Human activities,
such as agriculture and forestry, and natural disturbances, such as outbreaks of
insects and diseases, can modify the physical environment of an ecosystem by
altering structural features. Typically, forest structure is described at the stand and
landscape levels. Landscape structure can be defined by the spatial arrangement of
elements of topography, vegetation, soil, or the physical environment itself. The
writer discusses the microclimatic environment at the landscape scale.

Globalization and the Sustainability of Human Health. McMichael, Anthony J.;
Bolin, Bert; Costanza, Robert. *BioScience*. v. 49 no3 p205-10 Mr '99

During this decade, the threat posed to human health by unprecedented large-scale
environmental changes has been largely recognized. The problem is no longer one
of localized environmental pollution and its immediate toxicological dangers;
instead, it refers to the altered life-supporting functions of entire biophysical systems at global and regional levels and within a longer time frame. Topics discussed
include ethical and technical challenges and strategies for matching the scales of
problem and response.

Biodiversity and Ecosystem Functioning. Wall, Diana H. *BioScience*. v. 49 no2 p107-8 Fe '99

A special section on the biodiversity of soils and freshwater and marine sediments. Only a small fraction of the subsurface environment has been investigated, and for the majority of organisms that live in those environments, knowledge is lacking to identify geographical patterns of diversity, to list the endemic species, or to identify species that may control key ecosystem processes. New techniques now available, however, are making it easier to explore life in soils and sediments. Articles discuss the role of species diversity in ecosystem functioning in soils, the state of research on the biology of freshwater benthic invertebrates, the levels and patterns of biodiversity in marine benthic systems, comparisons of important biota and processes across all domains, and the use of Internet-based systems in biodiversity research.

One hundred Years of Forest Modeling: Research by Harry Valentine. Schoen, Deborah. *BioScience*. v. 48 p 7 Ja '98

Part of a special section on the research discussed at the annual meeting of the American Institute of Biological Sciences, which was held in Montreal, Quebec, Canada. A new quantitative forest model has been developed. Harry Valentine of the USDA Forest Service in Durham, New Hampshire, and his colleagues have devised a model that combines a carbon-allocation model with a canopy level model. Known as Pipestem, the model contains the structural detail needed to estimate adequately how production of dry material or respiration will change over time.

Ecosystem Consequences of Changing Biodiversity. Chapin, F. Stuart; Sala, Osvaldo E.; Burke, Ingrid C. *BioScience* v. 48 p 45-52 Ja '98.

Evidence about the ecosystem consequences of changes in species diversity is summarized, and a research agenda to address these consequences is presented. The planet is presently in the midst of the sixth major extinction event in the history of life. The event is biotically driven, specifically by human impact on land use, species invasions, and atmospheric and climatic changes. Indeed, current extinction rates are 100-1,000 times higher than prehuman levels. Moreover, changes in human activity change the types as well as the numbers of species, with fast-growing, nutrient-demanding plant species increasing in abundance in highly populated countries. The evidence presented suggests that it would be wise to conserve the present levels of diversity as insurance against an uncertain future.

Coral Reefs in Crisis. Hinrichsen, Don. *BioScience*. v. 47 p554-8 O '97.

Coral reefs are in danger of disappearing. Reefs around the globe are facing increasing threats from land based pollution and booming coastal development. Already, 10 percent of all reefs are degraded beyond recognition, and 30 percent of the remainder are in critical condition. Coral reef expert Clive Wilkinson of the Australian Institute of Marine Science has estimated that, if nothing is done to conserve and manage coral reefs, then 70 percent of them worldwide may disappear within 40 years. These vanishing ecosystems are reviewed, together with the problems that plague them and the strategies for saving them.

Toward a Health Community: An Interview with Wendell Berry. *The Christian Century*. v. 114 p912-13 + O 15 '97.

Wendell Berry, author of over 30 books of fiction, poetry, and essays, has a passionate love for the land and a concern that people live in responsible relationship with it and each other. In his essays, Berry connects a biting criticism of the much-touted "global economy" with a call to rejuvenate and sustain local communities. He calls on his readers to think about how their choices and lives affect the community's land, local economy, and future. In an interview, among the topics discussed by Berry are the elements required for a healthy community, people's responsibilities with regard to agricultural production, and the link between his fiction and poetry and the public themes of his essays.

Malthus vs. Faustus: Discussion of November 1998 Article, Reverend Malthus, meet Doctor Faustus. Huber, Peter W. *Commentary.* v. 107 no2 p`3-7 Fe '99

Jonathan H. Adler, Max Singer, J. R. Dunn, Peter Korman, and Ted Baker respond to Peter W. Huber's article "Reverand Malthus Meet Doctor Faustus," which appeared in the November 1998 issue and questioned the benefits of increases in wealth and technology and discussed the effects of market-driven advances in efficiency and technology on the environment. Huber replies.

Species Lost. Pistorius, Alan. *Country Journal.* v. 24 p 36-9 Jy/Ag '97.

Part of a special section on birds. The writer examines how certain species of birds have become extinct and suggests ways in which man can work to preserve endangered species.

News About Old-Growth Forests. Morrissey, Laurie D. *Country Journal.* v. 24 p12-13 N/D '97.

Old-growth forests are disappearing because of development, logging, mining, and other activities. There are estimated to be anything between 1 million and 5 million acres of old-growth, or ancient, forests in the United States. Although they are concentrated in Oregon, Washington, Alaska, the Upper Midwest, and the Adirondacks of New York, patches of old-growth forest can be found all over North America. They are being lost because not all of them fit the "forest primeval" image and therefore often go unrecognized for what they are. However, when they vanish, unique ecosystems and irreplaceable benchmarks for evaluating past and future land-use practices are also lost. Ecologists are attempting to find remaining areas of old-growth forest and, whenever possible, save them from diminishing further. The protection of old-growth forests is discussed.

Nasty, Brutish, and Dirty: research by David Pimentel. *Discover.* v. 20 no2 p30 Fe '99

Ecologist David Pimentel and his graduate students at Cornell University assembled statistics from the WHO in Geneva, Switzerland, the Centers for Disease Control and Prevention in Atlanta, Georgia, and other sources to analyze the effects of population growth and environmental degradation on human disease. Six of their findings are presented.

The Value of the Free Lunch Value of Ecosystem Services Measured by Robert Costanza. Zimmer, Carl. *Discover* v. 19 p104-5 Ja '98.

Part of a special issue on scientific discoveries in 1997. Robert Costanza, an ecological economist from the University of Maryland, is part of an expanding movement of researchers that is attempting to gauge the value of ecosystems. The researchers try to measure the value not merely of the ecosystems' commercial products, such as forest timber, but also the less obvious ways in which they make the planet habitable: Forests stop soil erosion and mud slides that would be costly to stop artifi-cially, and coral reefs both act as nurseries for young fish and help protect the shoreline. Costanza and colleagues estimated that the total value of the globe's ecosystems is roughly $33 trillion a year.

Damning Dams. Robbins, Elaine. *E/the Environmental Magazine*. v. 10 no1 p14-15 Ja./F '99

New scientific evidence suggests that the benefits of constructing large dams do not outweigh the human or environmental costs. Dams have brought wonderful benefits to society, including rural electricity supply and irrigation of arid areas, but they have a huge impact on their surrounding ecosystems, fragmenting river habitat and disrupting migratory fish patterns and spawning habits. Moreover, mil-lions of people have been displaced by large dams, and many archaeological trea-sures have been lost. A range of environmental groups is calling for the dismantling of some dams in a bid to restore the ecology of the areas surrounding them, and environmentalists and river advocacy groups contend that more effi-cient energy use and water distribution can do much toward making new dam projects unnecessary.

Biomass Energy Versus Carbon Sinks: Trees and the Kyoto Protocol. Hall, David O. *Environment* v. 41 no1 p5+ Ja/Fe '99

It has been accepted for a decade that using biomass as a substitute for fossil fuels as a source of energy is better than using it purely to create carbon sinks. The point for policymakers is that although trees and other forms of biomass can be used to sequester carbon, they must eventually be used as a source of fuel. If not, years of use as carbon sinks will be wasted as the trees rot or burn naturally. Although bio-mass has great potential for an environmentally friendly future, trees must be used for purposes other than carbon storage to reap maximum benefit.

Sixteen Impacts of Population Growth. Brown, Lester Russell; Gardner, Gary; Halweil, Brian. *Futurist*. v. 33 no2 p36-41 Fe '99

The continuing growth of the global population may be the most pressing issue of today. The doubling of the world's population within the last 50 years combined with rising individual consumption is stretching the planet's resources beyond its natural limits. The writers examine 16 effects of population growth in order to establish how future population trends may affect human prospects.

Galapagos: Paradise in Peril: Benchley, Peter. *National Geographic*. v. 195 no4 p 2-31 Ap '99

The Galapagos Islands, a Unesco World Heritage Site, are a precious natural trea-sure in jeopardy. Plagued by a combination of politics, overcrowding, economics, and the disastrous weather provided by El Nino of 1997-98, the islands are close to becoming recognized as officially endangered. The ecology and wildlife of the islands are some of the most important on Earth, yet the detritus of human devel-opment and immigration, driven by tourism and the fishing industry, threatens many of the Galapagos Island's 1,900 endemic species. The writer describes his recent visits to the islands.

Parks Are for the Birds. Wauer, Roland H. *National Parks*. v. 73 no3-4 p. 26-9 M/ Ap '99

National parks protect the ecosystems and habitats that are necessary for the survival of many species of birds. The areas the parks encompass are free from agriculture and grazing, major developments, and biocides, all of which helps them protect native species and provide stopover and staging areas for migrating waterfowl and other winter birds. The writer discusses the national parks that are best for observing birds.

Apocalypse Gore: Views in *Earth in the Balance*. Wolfson, Adam. *National Review.* v51 no4 p37-40 Mr 8 '99

In his 1992 book *Earth in the Balance,* Vice President Al Gore discusses his views on environmental issues in addition to providing insights into his political and moral beliefs. The book has an academic tone but is also is a very personal work by the Democratic presidential candidate in the 2000 elections. Reviewers have tended to concentrate on the book as mainly a policy statement on the environment, overlooking the fact that it also describes Gore's personal philosophy. Gore's views on the environment and on Western political and economic systems are discussed.

Water over the Dam: Sierra Club Proposal to Drain Lake Powell. Zengerle, Jason. *The New Republic.* v. 217 p20-2 N 24 '97.

The Sierra Club is attempting to reinvent itself, and it is making a strange bid to drain a lake a key issue. To many in the arid Southwest, Lake Powell and the Glen Canyon Dam, both created in 1963, are testaments to man's ability to harness nature's strength and put it to productive use. Radical environmentalists have long dreamed of draining the lake, but few serious-minded people paid much attention until late last year, when the Sierra Club, one of America's oldest, biggest, and most respected environmental organizations, came up with its own proposal to keep the dam but empty the lake. The group is attempting to stave off complacency by reverting from a watchdog role to a crusading approach, and it is pinning its hopes on its twenty-something president, Adam Werbach. In trying to find such a crusade, however, the Sierra Club may be just restoring itself to special interest status, and its drainage plan does not even make much sense in environmental terms.

Great Lake Effect: Pollution, Greenhouse Effect and Urban Sprawl Threaten the Great Lakes. Annin, Peter; Begley, Sharon. *Newsweek* v. 134 no1 p52-4 Jy 5 '99

The Great Lakes face a number of problems. First, the rising water temperatures may encourage alien species to colonize Lake Superior and may greatly reduce the numbers of cold-water plankton that the creatures who live there rely on for food. Second, the lakes are being polluted by poisonous chemicals that are carried through the air from far-off countries. Third, urban sprawl may irreparably change the lakes' ecosystem. The good health of the Great Lakes, which, in one of the most dramatic triumphs of environmentalism, has been saved over the last 30 years, will not continue unless somebody determines how this new generation of threats can be countered.

Failing our Farmers. Berry, Wendell. *New York Times.* pA17 Jy 6 '99.

The U.S. farm policy is destroying farmers and farmland. A primary goal in this country should be to come up with a policy that is healthful, dependable, and ecologically sound.

White House to Present $7.8 billion Plan for Everglades. Wald, Matthew L. *New York Times*. pA14 Jy 1 '99.

In a move that has bipartisan backing, the Clinton Administration will formally present a plan today that calls for spending $7.8 billion over 20 years to re-channel billions of gallons of water a day into the Everglades in what supporters are calling the largest effort at environmental restoration in history. The plan seeks to undo the vast network of canals and levees constructed in the Everglades between the late 1940's and the early 1970's and that critics say has cut the population of wading birds by more than 90 percent, damaged marine fisheries and coral reefs, and threatened what is left of the Everglades' unique ecosystem. Half of the money to fund the plan will come from Florida and the other half from the Federal Government.

Forests the Way They Used to Be. Foster, David R. *New York Times* pA p13 Je 26 '99

The writer is the director of the Harvard Forest at Harvard University. Forests have returned to the Northeast as the 19th-century agrarian landscape continues to disappear, but that doesn't mean that the original nature the Pilgrims saw is being replicated. There have been many shortsighted attempts to manage and conserve the forest landscape, the result of a failure to consider history.

Fiddling while Antarctica Burns. Helvarg, David. *New York Times*. Mr 7 '99 p15 Sec 4

Antarctica is a wildlife-rich peninsula that is in the midst of a dangerously quick climatic change. Scientists for 30 years have predicted that global warming would occur most rapidly at the poles, and while global temperatures have on average warmed by 1 degree Fahrenheit over the past 100 years, they have increased by more than 5 degrees in just 50 years in the Antarctic Peninsula, threatening wildlife and melting the ice shelf. Both situations have major implications for the rest of the world.

Everglades Restoration Plan Does Too Little, Experts Say. Stevens, William K. *New York Times* Ap1 + F 22 '99

According to experts, an ambitious $8 billion plan to restore the Florida Everglades to health ecologically is not enough. The critics contend that the main reason that the plan will do little in the way of restoration is that it does not go far enough in re-establishing the natural flow of shallow water that once moved unbroken down the South Florida peninsula, creating a home for one of the world's largest assemblages of marsh wildlife.

Deep in Siberia's Forest, Finding Clues to the 'Missing Sink': Theory that Forests Can Absorb Excess Carbon. Shapley, Deborah. *New York Times* Fp3 D 1 '97.

Part of a special section that previews the conference on climate change in Kyoto, Japan, and discusses global warming in general. One of climatology's most pressing mysteries is the whereabouts of the almost two billion tons of carbon dioxide that disappear annually into something other than thin air. Now, it appears that a vast army of larch trees in the Siberian tundra and other forests in the Northern Hemisphere could be the "missing sinks"—carbon sink being the term used by climate scientists for anything that absorbs and retains carbon dioxide. While the Russian larches are viewed by many climate scientists as a symbol of hope, of the chance that some unpredictable natural mechanism will moderate an otherwise inexorable trend toward a warmer world, they are quick to note that the Russian forest, which makes up one-fifth of the world's trees, could just as easily symbolize something else: the many uncertainties in the face of a young science being asked to forecast a system that is as complex as the earth itself.

A Retrospective: Paul Shepard's Brave and Lonely Work. Rawlins, C. L. *Orion*. v. 16 p89-90 Summer '97

Nature writer Paul Shepard argued that Man's propensity for environmental damage is due to the progressive failure of his customs and institutions to allow his necessary growing up. The writer reflects on the influence of Shepard's nature literature on his own work and presents a list of books by or about Shepard.

Regulation of Keystone Predation by Small Changes in Ocean Temperature: Sanford, Eric. *Science*. v. 283 no5410 p. 2095-7 Mr 26 '99

Key species interactions that are sensitive to temperature may act as leverage points through which small changes in climate could generate large changes in natural communities. Field and laboratory experiments showed that a slight decrease in water temperature dramatically reduced the effects of a keystone predator, the sea star Pisaster ochraceus, on its principal prey. Ongoing changes in patterns of cold water upwelling, associated with El Nino events and longer term geophysical changes, may thus have far-reaching impacts on the composition and diversity of these rocky intertidal communities. Copyright 1999 by the AAAS.

Warm, Warm on the Range: Interrelation of Global Climate Change and Earth's Ecosystems. Melillo, Jerry M. *Science*. v. 283 no5399 p183-4 Ja 8 '99

In this issue, Alward and colleagues report on the different sensitivities of rangeland plants to minimum temperature increases. Using a decade of measurements at the National Science Foundation's Long-Term Ecological Research site in the short-grass steppe in northeastern Colorado, the researchers conclude that increased spring minimum temperatures correlates with a reduction in the abundance of buffalo grass and an increase in native and exotic forbs.

Long-term Agroecosystem Experiments: Assessing Agricultural Sustainability and Global Change. Rasmussen, Paul E.; Goulding, Keith W. T; Brown, J. R. *Science*. v. 282 no5390 p893-6 O 30 '98.

Long-term agroecosystem experiments can be defined as large-scale field experiments more than 20 years old that study crop production, nutrient cycling, and environmental impacts of agriculture. They provide a resource for evaluating biological, biogeochemical, and environmental dimensions of agricultural sustainability; for predicting future global changes; and for validating model competence and performance. A systematic assessment is needed to determine the merits of all known experiments and to identify any that may exist in tropical and subtropical environments. The establishment of an international network to coordinate data collection and link sites would facilitate more precise prediction of agroecosystem sustainability and future global change. Copyright 1998 by the AAAS.

Biomass Collapse in Amazonian Forest Fragments. Laurance, William F; Laurance, Susan G; Ferreira, Leandro V. *Science* v. 278 p1117-18 N 7 '97.

Rain forest fragments in central Amazonia were found to experience a dramatic loss of above-ground tree biomass that is not offset by recruitment of new trees.

These losses were largest within 100 meters of fragment edges, where tree mortality is sharp increased by microclimatic changes and elevated wind turbulence. Permanent study plots within 100 meters of edges lost up to 36 percent of their biomass in the first 10 to 17 years after fragmentation. Lianas (climbing woody vines) increased near edges but usually compensated for only a small fraction of the biomass lost as a result of increase tree mortality. Copyright 1997 by the AAAS.

Rain Forest Fragments Fare Poorly: Study by William Laurance. Williams, Nigel. *Science* v. 278 p1016 N 7 '97.

The fragments of rain forest left when expanses of such forest are cut down seem to be making their own, unanticipated contribution to the carbon dioxide equation. In this issue, William Laurance of Brazil's National Institute for Research in the Amazon in Manaus reports on a 17-year study indicating that, once isolated from the bulk of the rain forest, fragments below a particular size are unable to maintain the structure of the original forest. They lose sizable levels of biomass as big trees, exposed to wind and weather extremes, are killed or damaged, decreasing the amount of biological material in the forest fragment that can absorb carbon dioxide during growth.

Restoring Ecosystems. Richter, Wayne; Aronson, James; Hobbs, R. J. *Science.* v. 278 p997-1001 N 7 '97.

Three letters discuss an article by Andy P. Dobson, A. D. Bradshaw, and A. J. M. Baker, which appeared in the July 25 issue and optimistically reported on the potential for ecological restoration of ecosystems damaged by conversion to human use. The writer of the first letter criticizes the failure of the article to address sources of human damage other than direct conversion, and the writers of the second letter claim that Dobson and colleagues were overly simplistic in their analysis. The writer of the third letter maintains that the article does not consider the serious philosophical case against the idea, if not necessarily the practice, of restoration ecology. A reply is included.

Biodiversity and Ecosystem Function: The Debate Deepens. Grime, J. Philip. *Science.* v. 277 p1260-1 Ag 29 '97.

In this issue, three groups contribute to the debate over whether biodiversity leads to superior ecosystem function. One group reports on results from synthesized plant assemblages in the Cedar Creek Reserve in Minnesota, and the others report on biodiversity-ecosystem studies carried out on natural systems in Mediterranean grassland in California and northern forest in Sweden. In each study, variation in ecosystem properties is found to be linked to differences in the functional characteristics, in particular resource capture and utilization, of the dominant plants. No convincing evidence was found to suggest that ecosystem processes are essentially dependent on higher levels of biodiversity.

Patchy Forests and Greenhouse Gases: Research by William J. Laurance. Mlot, Christine. *Science News.* v. 152 p347 N 29 '97.

In the November 7 *Science*, William F. Laurance of the National Institute for Research in the Amazon in Manaus, Thomas E. Lovejoy of the Smithsonian Institution in Washington, D.C., and their colleagues report that a cut-up piece of tropical rain forest north of Manaus, Brazil, has lost a considerable amount of its plant matter, or biomass, over the past 10 to 17 years. After repeatedly measuring the diameter of some 56,000 trees, the team discovered that biomass had fallen by as much as 36 percent in some plots. Other studies revealed that without the surrounding forest to act as a buffer and support, many large trees at the edges of plots are blown down. As large areas of forest are cleared each year, the fallen trees' decay could be contributing substantial amounts of carbon dioxide to the atmosphere, biomass loss therefore possibly representing an unknown contribution to atmospheric greenhouse gases.

New Light on Diversity: Study of Panamanian Rain Forest. Wiley, John P., Jr. *Smithsonian* v. 30 no2 p 20+ My '99

Researchers have discovered that diversity in tropical forests is not as clear-cut as previously assumed. Until now, most tropical biologists believed that forest disturbances, such as gaps made by fallen trees, spark a sequence of growth in species diversity in which successional tree species replace one another in the regrowing site. Stephen Hubbell of Princeton University, who has been working on this theory for almost 20 years on Barro Colorado Island in the Panama Canal–the main research site of the Smithsonian Tropical Research Institute–and seven of his colleagues now report in Science that species diversity in gaps is no higher than in the surrounding forest. The team explains the anomaly through recruitment limitation: When a gap forms, trees that do not disperse well or seeds that simply fail to germinate may not be in the immediate vicinity and may miss their opportunity to grow.

The Stuff of Life: Do You Own It, or Does It Own You? Sanders, Scott R. *Utne Reader.* no90 p 46-51 N/D '98

A special section on consumerism and simple lifestyles. In an article excerpted from the July/August 1998 issue of Audubon the writer describes how a jarring return to life after a peaceful Rocky Mountain idyll drove him to reflect on why people are so driven to accumulate things and what would occur if they could only stop. Articles discuss topics that include the myths behind such issues as recycling and advertising, the plastic-dominated decor of a Brooklyn apartment, and the campaign started by a United Methodist Church to spend no more than $100 at Christmas.

Index